Awkward Reverence

AWKWARD REVERENCE

Reading the New Testament Today

Paul Q. Beeching

SCM PRESS LTD

0 334 02687 3

First published in Britain 1997
by SCM Press Ltd
9-17 St Albans Place, London N1 0NX
by arrangement with The Continuum Publishing
Company, New York
Typeset and printed in the United States of America

Grateful acknowledgment is made to the publisher
for permission to reproduce the following material:
"Last Days of Alice" from *Collected Poems 1919–1976*
by Allen Tate. Copyright © 1977 by Allen Tate.
Reprinted by permission of Farrar, Straus & Giroux.

Contents

v

Introduction

E very other spring for the last dozen years I have taught an undergraduate course in the New Testament, a habit that has now followed me into
retirement. Over these semesters I have discovered that in our time the best
thing that could happen to the New Testament *has* happened to it. Within
the university, at least, it has become just a book. Though the Gospels may
have suffered a loss in religious status, they no longer have to carry the
immense load of belief and commitment and guilt with which they once
were burdened. Having been raised a Christian, and a Catholic, I consider
this a kind of liberation. I no longer have to search the Gospels for scenes in
which Jesus creates the papacy or "institutes" the sacraments—holy matri-
mony, for instance, by his appearance at the wedding in Cana.

During this same period, however, my students have more and more
exhibited a different sort of change. When I began teaching the New Testament, Protestants came to class with a good grasp of the Gospel narrative
and almost all of the Old Testament stories it assumes; they recognized
many allusions and quotations. The Catholic students were less informed,
but could be counted on for the passages generally read at mass. All that has
changed. Today, only the fundamentalists are familiar with *anything* in the
Bible, the children of parents who are not only Christians, but Christians
who have deliberately resisted the influence of modern culture and science.
These students have a built-in resistance to any historical inquiry into what
they take to be an inerrant, timeless text. Indeed, they honestly cannot
engage in such study. On dropping my course, one said to me,

"Mr. Beeching, I just can't stand listening to you."

"That's odd, " I joked. "Mrs. Beeching has that same problem."

But, of course, that wasn't what he meant. He meant that he could not stand to hear these documents discussed as actual pieces of writing, the products of fallible human beings, regardless of inspiration. He could not bear my treating the New Testament as just a book.

Yet in these last dozen years, another, wholly new kind of student has begun to appear, youngsters innocent of religion itself, and particularly innocent of Christianity. It is why they take the course; they have "always heard of it." After a lecture recently, one of these young men asked me, "Who is this fellow Paul? Some kind of preacher?"

A few academics consider this last development a kind of blessing: "students don't have to unlearn all that stuff any more." But the number of professors who share that opinion has shrunk dramatically as the barbarity of American life, off and on campus, has dramatically increased. I don't mean only our moral barbarism; I am speaking also of our cultural level. The Bible is simply one of the many books our students haven't read; and therefore it functions as an alarming index to the general ignorance of our high school graduates.

Paradoxically, for any teacher who remembers the old days, these secular youngsters are often preferable to their believing predecessors. For one thing, they are actually interested in the course. For another, it is undeniably refreshing to teach them the ancient texts unencumbered with all the baggage they used to carry. One's feelings of elation are often tempered, however, by trying to convince these secular youngsters of the importance of the issues dealt with—the importance to me, of course, and other old fuddy-duddies like me. Indeed, I have often found myself rearguing some point that nearly caused a riot in the college classrooms of my youth, only to lower my eyes from the ceiling to the puzzled faces of the blue-jeaned pagans in front of me who are trying to look politely concerned. This is a particular source of dismay for professors of my age, who have always underestimated their dependence on the shock of disillusionment. Without that emotional jolt, much of undergraduate education is quite dull and uninteresting, for as Bernard Shaw says somewhere, when you first learn something you feel as if you have lost something.

These secular students are the products of dynamics within and without Christianity whose course is difficult to predict. What will classes in the New Testament be like in the next millennium? I cannot think that the defensive posture of the far right has much to offer; indeed, their more serious representatives are already writing about the emptiness of fundamentalist theology. On the other hand, secularism is a dry, gray, unsatisfactory religion, so emotionally unsatisfactory that it triggers all sorts of odd, comforting beliefs: theosophy, crystal gazing, Ouija boards, even a reverence for Big Foot.

It is in this changing contemporary religious atmosphere that I have tried to put together what I believe I have learned about the New Testament, not excluding what I have stopped believing and what I have *felt* in the process. I hope to read the book sensibly, neglecting neither scientific nor emotional data; for I also am trying to come to terms with this text which was so central to my childhood. The scholarship is, of course, not mine; I came much too late to this study for such pretensions. New Testament scholars should begin at age thirteen or thereabouts. What I am going to report are the common findings of those who study this matter scientifically; and my indebtedness to them is wide and deep. Where I am dealing with the views peculiar to a given scholar, I will try to name that person in the text. For these citations and for generally accepted positions and information, I have supplied a list of works at the end of the book.

What I hope to describe is how an educated person necessarily reads this text in the light of biblical scholarship—for that is what *sensibly* means today. Such a reading will not result in an "authoritative" understanding of the text. Scholarship is always a matter of the state of the art; it is always ready to be undone or redone. I can try to tell you only what I know of what is known or guessed at today; and you must always remember that even as you read, someone digging in the sands south of Cairo may be approaching an ancient brown bit of papyrus that will blow us all out of our opinions, if not our minds. Yet I would like to convince you that such a reading does not make the old religious questions go away or seem trivial—quite the reverse. Indeed, the fear of reading the New Testament in the light of scholarship is not that you may lose your faith but that you may wish to gain it back; for a "sensible" reading makes it a better book than it ever was before.

I myself have often felt the desire for Christian faith. Not long ago I thought I might just pick out one of the most ridiculous of our old Roman Catholic notions and begin believing it again: the throat blessing of St. Blase, say, or the Nine First Fridays, or Pius XII's Assumption of Mary. But it occurred to me that I would only make myself look foolish, maybe more than foolish. Besides, I can no longer believe on command; perhaps I lack the guts for such existential, "absurd" commitment. Yet this very inborn inability has sometimes struck me as sinful. In what would posthumously become *Waiting for God,* Simone Weil wrote, "I never read the story of the fig tree without trembling. I think that it is a portrait of me. In it also, nature was powerless, and yet it was not excused. Christ cursed it." Though an extreme emotion, as befits a saint, the feeling is apparently not unusual. On the other hand, there is a corresponding joy in intellectual honesty. Though it is impossible to read this Hellenistic anthology free of its long and checkered doctrinal history and therefore without guilt, it is equally impossible not to rejoice in the scholarship that has made that "free reading" possible. In any case we have little choice. Today, we *must* read the New Testament rationally.

Perhaps the healthiest attitude is contained in Paul's remark that he wasn't "ashamed of the gospel" or in Philip Larkin's "Church Going."

> Once I am sure there's nothing going on
> I step inside, letting the door thud shut.
> Another church: matting, seats, and stone,
> And little books; sprawlings of flowers cut
> For Sunday, brownish now; some brass and stuff
> Up at the holy end; the small neat organ;
> And a tense, musty unignorable silence,
> Brewed God knows how long. Hatless, I take off
> My cycle-clips in awkward reverence. . . .

Let me begin by saying that, whatever else it may have been or is, the New Testament is a very good book, an excruciatingly interesting anthology of Hellenistic religious writing. The copy I use is the third edition (1975) of the Greek text designed for translators and first published in 1965 by the United Bible Societies. This edition was edited by an international committee whose British member is Matthew Black of St. Andrews and whose American members are Professor Bruce Metzger of Princeton and Allen Wikgren of Chicago. A fourth revised edition has already appeared. In fact, so much does the interpretation and evaluation of the manuscript evidence progress that a new New Testament will be issued every ten or twenty years for the foreseeable future. Each successive edition is an attempt to reconstruct the "original" Greek text more accurately.

That the New Testament is a Greek book often startles people who have learned that Jesus and the people he converses with in the Gospels spoke Aramaic, a western Semitic language related to Hebrew. But with the exception of a very few words and phrases, all of the New Testament books were composed in *koinē,* or "popular" Greek, the language spoken throughout the eastern Roman Empire in the first century. These books vary widely in so-called educational level. The Letter to the Hebrews is the most learned and rhetorically correct; the Gospel of Mark (and Revelation), the least.

Though there is no evidence that any of these works were translated directly from written sources (no Aramaic originals), some passages contain Aramaisms, that is, Greek words or phrases used in a sense that would be more natural to Aramaic. Helmut Koester points to Mark 4, for instance (devoted to the parables of Jesus), the miracle stories in John (passages long recognized as some of the earliest in the New Testament), and liturgical materials like the two versions of the Lord's Prayer (*Introduction to the New Testament*, 1:110–13).

These two facts may come as a shock: that the New Testament text is fluid and changes from time to time as new manuscript evidence is discovered or rethought, and that it is (and always was) Greek. Yet a glance at the prefatory matter to any good Bible—or a brief study of its footnotes—should convince you of the general truth of what I say. It follows that no Greek edition, let alone any translation, is ever presented with complete confidence. At any one time so many passages are seen to be the result of fallible and changing decisions that the international committee has adopted a system of ratings to tell the reader how close to being "certain" a printed passage is. One of the first things I do in a course in the New Testament is read aloud the following from the United Bible Societies' "Introduction." It is often a sobering moment.

> By means of the letters A, B, C, and D, enclosed within "braces" { } at the beginning of each set of textual variants, the committee has sought to indicate the relative degree of certainty, arrived at on the basis of internal considerations as well as of external evidence, for the reading adopted as the text. The letter A signifies that the text is virtually certain, while B indicates that there is some degree of doubt. The letter C means that there is a considerable degree of doubt whether the text or the apparatus contains the superior reading, while D shows that there is a very high degree of doubt concerning the reading selected for the text.

Contrary to the impression many preachers leave with their hearers, this New Testament was a product of the church, rather than the reverse. Its twenty-seven documents were composed by early Christian writers from the 50s to about the 140s of the Common Era, but the precise table of contents we have today is not recorded before 367 C.E. when our particular "table of contents" appears in a letter written by Bishop Athanasius. For the nearly four hundred years of the formative period of Christianity, therefore, there *was* no New Testament. In fact, Papias, an early father of the church, liked it that way, preferring the oral tradition. But from at least the 90s, a collection of Pauline letters circulated, perhaps with Ephesians as a kind of cover letter; and sometime in the second century the four Gospels were added, along with the book of Acts. Other works, both canonical and non-canonical were often also included: the *Wisdom of Solomon*, the *Apocalypse of Peter*, the *Shepherd of Hermas*, and others. Moreover, the contents of the New Testament continued to vary from place to place long after that list of Athanasius.

Apparently it was St. Jerome's translation of our twenty-seven documents into authoritative Latin that finally settled the matter, though as late as Luther's day people disagreed on which books were "fully" canonical. People still do, though they generally don't make their selectivity explicit, even to themselves. The Third Letter of John (3 John), for instance, and Revelation and the Second Letter of Peter (2 Peter) have all seemed unnecessary or offensive to some; and people attracted to Paul's theology have reservations about the Letter of James. But in a larger sense, Christians have always drawn differing theologies from the New Testament simply by emphasis, while insisting, of course, that the whole canon was the word of God. A peculiarly modern development of this sort is a scholarly lack of reverence for the canon and a renewed interest in those documents once considered "apocryphal," particularly the *Gospel of Thomas* and the *Gospel of Peter.*

As might be expected, written documents gathered together in the hit-or-miss fashion that created the New Testament (humanly speaking, of course) also represent a whole range of literary forms. As we go along we will be reading letters and tracts disguised as letters; apocalypses and gospels that contain apocalypses; songs; creedal poems; and hymns. We will begin with the so-called Synoptic tradition, the Gospels of Mark, Matthew, and Luke. These three are by no means the earliest Christian writings in the New Testament—that honor goes to Paul's authentic letters—but the Synoptic Gospels will be discussed first because they afford the most immediate way into the fundamental Jesus story. These Gospels are called *Synoptic* because when placed side by side and "viewed together" they tell roughly the same story; indeed, large sections are nearly or actually verbatim. Because each of these narratives provides a similar account of the life and death of Jesus of Nazareth, scholars have understood from the earliest days that they made up a unit, though the relations of the texts within that unit long remained unclear. Today we know that Mark's Gospel was composed first and that the Gospels of Matthew and Luke are rewritings of it. In fact, each document came to be called a "gospel" or "good news" (as if that were the name of a literary form) because of the use of this word at the beginning of Mark. It is the literary conventions of a "gospel," a literary form invented by the early Christians, that we must understand before we can read these works sensibly.

Gospels are not historical accounts, either in the sense of history understood by, say, Xenophon or even Herodotus, or in the modern sense of history as a documented account of the past. Gospels are primarily preaching devices intended to preserve and strengthen the reader's faith; and in recent years great progress has been made in our understanding of how these "devices" came about. Today, students of Christian origins even attempt to go behind the texts to isolate their earliest layers, not so much to understand the New Testament but to illuminate the historical figure Jesus of Nazareth. A major effort in this direction is the ongoing research of a nonsectarian group of scholars known as the Jesus Seminar. In 1993, after some six years of study, the seminar published a volume called *The Five Gospels*: a new translation of the four canonical Gospels and the *Gospel of Thomas*. By color coding, the editors indicate those sayings which they believe to be nearly verbatim remarks of Jesus and those that have been edited by, or wholly invented by, the early church.

Obviously such a work is controversial—and is meant to be—but it should come as no surprise. For a century or so, most students have recognized that the first Gospel, Mark, was composed outside of Palestine some forty years after the crucifixion. Clearly it was a Gentile re-creation in Greek of remembered or invented moments in the life of the Lord. This has meant, of course, that its passages of dialogue must be read as reconstructions of the kinds of things Jesus *might* have said, not as magically preserved transcriptions of actual speech. The only thing surprising about the work of the Jesus Seminar, therefore, is the scholarly neatness and perhaps unwarranted confidence with which it has conveyed its thinking.

Though I recommend the publications of the Jesus Seminar and the lively new translation they use, I must warn the reader that my own goal here is entirely different. In what follows, my purpose is to understand the text of the New Testament *as it stands;* only secondarily will I focus on its origins. This is to say that, for historical reasons if for none other, my aim is to read the New Testament intelligently, irrespective of the fragments that can be recognized beneath or beyond it. It is this text, not its component or underlying parts, that finally came to represent the Christian religion; any understanding of that religion must come to terms with *this* book, not its sources. To put this another way, I am concerned to understand the various portraits of Jesus presented by the evangelists, rather than any "historical" Jesus that may underlie or even contradict them. That such a "split" in scholarship is an ideal which I must occasionally fall short of perhaps goes without saying.

Where the mosaic, pieced-together nature of a given Gospel or epistle *must* be considered in the reading, I will do so.

Before we begin our reading let me emphasize one final point, something I have already mentioned in passing. Though we talk glibly of the writings of Matthew, Mark, Luke, and John, or even Jude or James, these names are wholly a matter of custom. Of the twenty-seven documents in the New Testament, only a few epistles and Revelation make reference to their authors' names. (The Beloved Disciple who is said to be the authority for the Gospel of John is unnamed.) All the other documents were originally anonymous (the familiar evangelical names were applied to them only later) or were intentionally pseudonymous from the beginning. In particular, the four Gospels initially circulated without authors' names; as late as the middle of the second century Christian writers speak of them without any authorial attribution. Only later did someone write "according to Mark" or Matthew or Luke or John on the manuscripts. There is nothing really very astounding about this; most of the other Christian material written at this time is also anonymous or pseudonymous—as are the books of the Old Testament. But since most modern readers have heard the names of the evangelists since their youth, it is difficult to keep in mind that—apart from legend—these names function only as a means of reference. As we take up each document, therefore, I will briefly advert to this problem; but for the rest of the time, please remember that though I use the traditional names to refer to the various writers, I do so only for convenience. Generally, I will quote the text as it appears in the New English Bible. But where inclusive language is appropriate I will use the New Revised Standard Version.

Our first task before addressing Mark itself is to consider the notion of "literary conventions," those unstated agreements between author and reader which make all writing and reading possible. Similar to the transparent conventions of language itself—those silent rules that tell us to proceed from left to right or vice versa or that a little squiggle *s* represents a certain sibilant sound—these literary conventions are taken for granted by people who are used to them, but they are puzzling to strangers. In narratives like those of the Gospels, one of the most important of these conventions is *point-of-view*. In its widest sense this hyphenated term refers to the "stance" from which an author sees a story. Does the author speak as if the events were immediately unfolding before him or is he looking backward at them in time? Is he primarily concerned with one main character or is he presenting a panorama of people all of whom have a kind of equality of interest? More specifically, *point-of-view* refers to the grammatical "person" with which the author writes. Does he address us in his own right as a real or imaginary eyewitness, "I then heard Jesus say . . ." or does he speak in the third person, "Then Jesus said . . . ?" Though it is possible that some of these documents were written by women, there is no direct evidence for this; and the masculine pronoun is traditional.

It is the third person point-of-view that is used everywhere in the Synoptics, except for the first sentence of Luke's Gospel, and even there the writer does not identify himself. And though you may not have thought about it, the third person point-of-view has certain complexities. It is one thing to write, "Then Jesus said . . ." when Jesus is talking to others in an observable situation. It is quite another to write "Jesus said" when he is explicitly described as being alone. Who heard him? The difference is even more marked if one writes, "Then Jesus thought . . . ." To whom did he subsequently report his thoughts?

Having chosen to write in the third person, therefore, an author must further decide whether he will limit himself to describing observed (or observable) speeches and events or adopt the so-called *omniscient point-of-view.* This term means exactly what it says: the author knows everything pertaining to his tale, with no constraints regarding the observable or unobservable, time or space. He can give the reader the speech of his characters even when they are soliloquizing; he can enter into their minds to describe their motives and feelings; he can even editorialize by judging these thoughts as good or evil or extending them through interpretation. Modern historical writing quite rightly prohibits the use of such omniscience, though you may have occasionally run into a writer of juvenile works or of historical fiction who is capable of saying, "Feeling a sudden sense of determination, Lincoln thought, 'I must free the slaves.'" But the Synoptic Gospels revel in omniscience. When a woman who wishes to be cured touches Jesus' garment, Mark tells us, "Jesus, aware that power had gone out of him, turned round in the crowd and asked, 'Who touched my clothes?'" (5:30). In Matthew, the narrator reports to us a conversation between Jesus and the devil, both supposedly isolated on a "very high mountain." In all three Synoptics we overhear what are apparently Jesus' exact words as he prays *alone* in the Garden of Gethsemane—"Jesus said." Moreover, our omniscient authors feel free to *interpret* the words of the Lord. After Jesus has said that "nothing that goes from outside into a man can defile him," Mark adds in his own right, "Thus he declared all foods clean" (7:19–20). One can argue, of course, that divine inspiration dictated all this material, but then one is left with the problem of why divine inspiration dictated these matters in various and sometimes contradictory ways in different Greek styles written by the three Synoptic writers. Sensibly, today's reader must conclude that the authors are individually using literary conventions that are nowadays limited to fiction.

Quite apart from the specifics of point-of view, there is a general problem concerning speech and dialogue in ancient writings. Classical and Hellenistic authors, including the evangelists, had no access to stenographers or tape recorders; with few exceptions they made up the speeches they reported even when these had been delivered publicly. Thucydides, who was a contemporary of the characters he wrote about, mentions the problem in a famous passage of his *History of the Peloponnesian War* :

> ... some speeches I heard myself, others I got from various quarters; it was in all cases difficult to carry them word for word in one's memory, so my habit has been to make the speakers say what was in my opinion demanded of them by the various occasions, of course adhering as closely as possible to the general sense of what they really said. (1:22)

Other literary conventions occur simply because we are reading a book. In the opening pages of Mark, for instance, Jesus appears at the Jordan as a common woodworker from the obscure village of Nazareth. But clearly we—and the first readers in 70 C.E.—*already* know who he is and that his coming is good for us; otherwise, why are we reading this document? In other words, from the first line the narrative depends on our knowing that Jesus is a superior being. Yet on the odd chance that we are pagans who have picked up a Gideon Bible in a motel somewhere, the first line of this Gospel as we now have it tells us that this is the "good news of Jesus Christ the Son of God." There is a fifty-fifty chance that the words "Son of God" are not original but have been added by a later copyist for the very purpose I have mentioned. (In a modern work this same information would be given on the cover or in the blurb on the dust jacket.)

As did the Greek dramatists, the evangelists also made use of the fact that the reader knows how their plot "comes out." Readers quite naturally suppress this knowledge even while encouraging the emotions that go along with it; if they didn't, the Gospel would be without suspense. From the very beginning, therefore, though we know what is going to happen to Jesus, we pretend we don't; so too did the first readers, who, after all, were Christians. We do the same thing at a production of *Hamlet*. When Bernardo and Francisco first step onto the stage, we already know about the ghost and Hamlet's destiny; we even know who will lie dead at the end of the show. When Oedipus steps on stage in the opening of *his* play and tells the people of Thebes that he is committed to finding the murderer—"I mean to leave nothing untried. With god's help, our health shall be secured, or our ruin"— everyone in the theater knows *which* he shall secure. Shakespeare and Sophocles—and Mark—clearly craft their speeches to take advantage of this prior knowledge.

Oddly enough, because they have read the other canonical Gospels, modern readers actually know more than each evangelist "knows" and must make a serious effort to repress this additional or contradictory information. Such knowledge can be a very real problem, as we will discover. As we go along in Mark we will have to suppress whatever we may think we know about the birth and childhood of Jesus—Mark knows nothing of this. When we read Matthew's infancy story, moreover, we will have to suppress Luke's contradictory version. And vice versa. We will even have to do the same thing in reading two versions of the Lord's Prayer! A comparable situation arises when a member of the audience knows variant lines or passages from the uncut *Hamlet* or, while watching Shakespeare's *Lear,* is aware of the "happy ending" given this play throughout the eighteenth century.

It should be noted that the characters *within* each of these narratives—including the character "Jesus"—do *not* possess such superior knowledge. Only the writer and the readers. You may recall that when Jesus was about to cure the bleeding woman, he first turned to the crowd and asked, "Who touched my clothes?" Jesus doesn't know; but, through the courtesy of the omniscient author, the *readers* do. If they didn't, the little scene would fall completely flat. This "ignorance" of Jesus can be very important. Without it he could not sincerely pray in the Garden of Gethsemane that the cup of suffering pass from him. Conversely, the readers *cannot* be in ignorance. The readers must know that the cup will not pass from Jesus, for the pathos of the whole scene depends on it. In the same way, the first scene of *Oedipus Rex* depends on the audience's knowledge that Oedipus himself is the murderer.

Though narration in the Synoptic Gospels is therefore wholly different from what one might today call "real reporting," it does not follow that the scene in Gethsemane, or any other New Testament event, is imaginary or untrue. What it does mean is that the scenes of the story are presented to us through the techniques of fiction. Asking, therefore, "To *whom* did Jesus report his thoughts and prayers so that they became available to the evangelists?"—a question Celsus asked about 170 C.E.—may make a certain scholarly sense for those interested in Christian origins. But such questions are inappropriate for a reading of the Gospel as a whole; *that* depends on an acceptance of the literary convention of the omniscient point-of-view.

The concept of point-of-view also extends to the author's world of ideas. In these New Testament stories we will find a series of beliefs completely foreign to us, beliefs that are held to be untrue everywhere else nowadays except in this particular book. Collectively we might call these the "world-view" of the New Testament. Just as we must agree to accept the point-of-view used in the Gospels, we must also accept this bundle of odd ideas. Our acceptance is, of course, only for the sake of the tale and ends when we stop reading. It would be disastrous if, having closed the New Testament, we were to continue holding some of these notions—as the history of Christian sects dramatically makes clear. At Jesus' baptism, for instance, the heavens "break open." This cannot have happened; the writer says it happened because he believes that the sky is still that same old blue, solid-wall "firmament" it was in Adam's day—with windows in it for the rain. Similarly, he believes that demons cause disease, light goes out from the eye to capture the objects of sight, dead people (or their "shades") can appear as Jesus' conversationalists, dreams foretell the future, and so on.

Perhaps most wrenching in all this is the matter of the demons. All the characters in these stories assume that evil spirits and demons are fairly common in Palestine in the first century. *Were* they common? One would hardly think so from reading Josephus or Plutarch or any other educated Hellenistic writer. But then how common were ghosts on the south bank of the Thames in 1600? What I am suggesting is that the question is beside the point. Mark's characters, like Shakespeare's, *think* there are demons. Indeed, they think demons are so common and behave so predictably that there is a regular way of exorcising them. If the demons know your name, they will almost always refer to it, since this gives them power over you. To get rid of them, you in turn must mention the name of some *greater* spiritual power. You don't have to be on intimate terms with this higher power—but you do need to know its name. Some unknown fellow apparently once used *Jesus'* name in an exorcism (see Mark 9:38–39)! In any case, the whole process is called "rebuking" the demon, and it is responsible for one of the few deliberately humorous passages in the New Testament. In Acts 19:13–16, the seven sons of Sceva, a Jewish high priest, attempt to exorcise a demon with the formula: "I adjure you by Jesus whom Paul proclaims." The demon replies: "Jesus I acknowledge and I know about Paul, but *who* are *you*?" He then beats up all seven plagiarists.

Even within a general belief in demons, *Synoptic* demons are rather peculiar. They cause certain illnesses but not others. Sometimes they seem Gentile rather than Jewish (in Mark 6 they willingly enter a herd of swine).

Some are more difficult to deal with than others and require prayer and fasting; others are oddly stronger in certain localities, weaker elsewhere. Despite their malignity, people don't seem very perturbed by these spirits, perhaps because they are not very powerful. Typically, the demons quail before Jesus and flee at his word. In fact, Jesus handles the evil spirits with such superb ease that they lose most of their dramatic value.

All of these matters concerning the worldview of the New Testament are difficult, and when added to sudden cures of the lame and the deaf and blind, and the multiplication of foodstuffs, and walking on water and the raising of people from the dead, they make the Gospel story very hard to read *sensibly*. Yet the evangelists, like other writers of popular literature in the Hellenistic period clearly delight in such "powerful acts," as the Synoptics call these wonders. Josephus says that he himself witnessed a certain Eleazar casting out demons by a method of exorcism (slightly different from that used by Jesus) which had been given to Solomon by God himself—while Vespasian watched! He also tells the story of a rainmaker Onias. The Talmud has a wonder-worker named Hanina ben Dosa, who performed a miracle at a distance—as Jesus does regarding the servant of the centurion (Matt. 8:13) Both Onias (Honi) and Hanina were Galileans. In popular Greek writing, there are the same sorts of figures—as indeed there are on our own newsstands. Empedocles cured people and Apollonius of Tyana made a whole career of wonder working, especially exorcisms.

Some people still wish to think that, at least in the New Testament, such mysterious acts actually occurred, that they were *miracles*; that is, packages of odd events not explicable by natural causes. Unfortunately, an argument formulated by David Hume in the eighteenth century prevents this. Suppose I stand in front of you and perform one of these odd deeds: fly about the room, let us say, without any obvious means of support. Inevitably you will ask, "How did he do that?" and begin to look for Peter Pan wires behind my chair or movie projectors with mirrors and so on. In so doing you will be searching for what you think of as the "natural causes" of what occurred. You do this because having been born after, say 1740, you consider it more probable that you are deceived by me than that the regularity of nature has been interrupted.

Now, asks Hume, when can you logically quit looking for those secret devices of mine? Or "at what point does one stop his inquiry and assign a supernatural cause?" The answer to this question is *never*. It is *always* more probable that an event has occurred as the result of identifiable causes rather than theoretically unidentifiable or supernatural ones. In fact, that is actually what we moderns *mean* by truth as far as occurrences in space and time are concerned. We hold that a true explanation of what happens is one that, on the basis of past experience, is the most probable. By the very same logic, a miracle or act contrary to the regularity of nature is precisely what is improbable and *un*true; and we can never sensibly assert its truth.

Let me quickly point out the peculiarity of Hume's argument. It does not prove that miracles don't occur; it proves a much more deadly thing: *as a modern human being you can never believe in a miracle.* I may have actually flown about you in the room, but—as a rational person—you can never assert that this happened. And if you should *say* you are asserting that, you are actually saying something else—something about your own emotional state or something of the form, "I am a member of a church that makes a practice of asserting these words."

It might be useful to pause for a moment to contemplate this rather involved and wholly modern argument. It implies that the world we live in may in fact be a very spooky place, full of mysterious unknown forces, but that the only way *we* have to deal with it is by probability. What is important here, however, is not whether Hume and the logical positivists and Wittgenstein are correct about all this. What is important is that though there may have been a few people in the actual world of the first century who were capable of framing such an argument, none of them wrote Gospels. Though often concealed from us by familiarity, the Gospel world is a kind of dream landscape in which anything can happen—anything, that is, which fits the ideological scheme of its author. For though all the evangelists tell the same story, each tells it differently and according to his own predilections.

A crucial matter, as we shall see, is the way the authors tell us of Jesus' death. Each New Testament writer apparently faced the question: Why was Jesus' death necessary? and then reported the death in a way that answered that question. Paul, the earliest, considered the crucifixion of Jesus some sort of sacrifice which would rescue him (us) from sin. To Paul, the death of the Lord was a cause for celebration, the center of the new religion: "I resolved that while I was with you I would think of nothing but Jesus Christ—Christ nailed to the cross" (1 Cor. 2:2). Mark, though he knew of this idea of a sacrificial death, seems to think that Jesus died in order to bring about an imminent new cosmological order, which did not in fact occur. Matthew and Luke, writing later, see Jesus' death in relation to the founding of the new world-wide religion they profess.

One final troubling assumption made by all the Synoptic writers concerns sacred texts. Along with the Jewish teachers of their day, the evangelists feel free to wrench any passage they wish from the Hebrew or the Septuagint Greek scripture and to use it as a prophecy fulfilled in their narrative. In fact they will go further and misquote scripture or distort it to make their point. If college students were to do what the evangelists do, we would fail them. But if you wish to read early Christian documents sensibly, you have to understand this ancient habit and accept it for the duration of the tale. Unfortunately, this can get complicated. For Mark's Gospel to work, you must believe that Isaiah correctly predicted that this stranger, John, would come out of the desert to "prepare the way" for Jesus. It will then come as something of a surprise to learn in Luke that John is a near relative, well known to Jesus' family.

Some readers, even when they recognize the fictionlike literary conventions and the exotic worldview of the Gospels, persist in ignoring the conclusion that follows from them: that these are not reports of historical events or accurate transcripts of ancient speech—though historical events and actual speeches may be mentioned—and that any truth that may arise from this "good news" concerning Jesus, Son of God, will be a general moral truth and will arise from the narrative's overall design rather than from any "factual" detail. The truth of the Gospels, if they contain any, will necessarily be what philosophers call "truth of meaning" rather than "truth of reference"—a "theme." To ask about the truth of Mark is akin to asking about the truth of *Hamlet.*

Again I do not mean to deny that something *like* the events of this Synoptic story actually happened. Indeed, Jesus' last year may have corresponded almost point for point to what is said in *Mark. But the narrative conventions of the Gospel prohibit using the Gospel itself as a historical record of that year.* It is quite legitimate for a person to ask, Did Jesus really exist? Was he a divine being? Did he found a religion? But such questions cannot be answered or *even profitably asked* of narratives in which the author tells us what is in peoples' heads or brings folk back from death—Moses and Elijah—or generalizes his geography into "a desert place" or "high mountain" or reports the private remarks of God.

I realize that this idea, a commonplace of modern scholarship, still seems difficult and disturbing and, yes, even blasphemous to some. If that describes your situation, I ask you to hold your feelings in brackets while you and I read at least this "first" Gospel together—*sensibly*—trying to proceed as late-twentieth-century men and women, cognizant of scholarship, without prejudgment, shucking off for the moment whatever we have learned about the story of Jesus from later materials in the New Testament and from the religious instruction of our childhood. This attempt will not be without danger, of course, and it may prove impossible, a Victorian endeavor wholly inappropriate to our age. That contemporary readers should be able to remove themselves from the prejudices of their upbringing and enter into those of an ancient culture is perhaps a last-century fantasy: Alice's croquet game or the voyage of the Owl and the Pussycat. Nevertheless let us try.

CHAPTER 1

The Sadness of Mark

Does the sadness I feel in reading the Gospel of Mark come from the text or from me? I don't mean from me personally, though that is the way I put it. I mean from me as a member of a generation of educated, apostate Catholics, a brood of vipers born nearly eighty generations after the events Mark tells us about. Can the story be as melancholy and despairing as it seems to me? To us? Or do I see it that way because of a guilty sense of having lost its ancient tradition?

If you have not read Mark recently, or if you have not read it "sensibly," as I have been calling it, you may find my feeling odd. But bear with me as we go along, checking your own feelings about this narrative. We begin with Mark because it is the earliest Gospel. No one knows who the author was—the text never mentions its author—and the attribution *KATA MARKON* (according to Mark) seems to have been affixed to it late in the second century. But whoever "Mark" was, it is clear that he was hazy about Palestinian geography and Jewish customs, that his Greek was unlearned and unpolished, that his notion of the miraculous was primitive, and that he wrote shortly before or after the destruction of Jerusalem in 70 C.E. Some scholars think that he wrote in the aftermath of Nero's persecution of 64 or 65 C.E.—which is also what the early fathers thought.

Scholarship in this century has shown that, whoever he was, Mark assembled what were originally independent anecdotes about Jesus—his parables and miracles and teaching—and put them together into an imagined year of his life (John has three years), ending in his death in Jerusalem. In so doing Mark shaped these stories to fit his own view of the Lord—as would Matthew and Luke when they came to rewrite this material. Detailed comparisons show that all three writers felt free from any historical chronology or any need to transmit material with verbal accuracy. Their Gospels are in fact exercises in theology.

Peculiarly, though Paul's letters had been written nearly twenty years earlier, Mark seems unaware of Pauline theology. Nevertheless, he shares with Paul some of what had by his time become a Christian tradition, in particular the communion service. On the other hand, Mark's brief Gospel lacks some of the most familiar parts of the later Synoptic tradition. It contains no infancy story, for example; it has no Sermon on the Mount, no beatitudes, no Lord's Prayer. Most importantly, it has no postresurrection narrative; for in its most authoritative and oldest version, this narrative ends abruptly at 16:8—an empty tomb, the women running away and *telling no one*.

For whom was this Gospel written? I once devoted a whole day to an author who by suppertime had convinced me that southern Syria or northern Galilee was unquestionably its setting and that Mark was writing for the Syro-Phoenician Christians who lived there. On the following day I spent about the same amount of time with another fellow who demonstrated that the Greek-speaking Christian community of Rome—newly set off from its synagogue parent and persecuted by Nero—was the only place where this Gospel could have been written. This author held that the "abomination of desolation," a predicted catastrophe in Mark's "little apocalypse," referred to rumors that the emperor Nero was alive and about to return. On the third day I made up my own theory: Mark was a Greek-speaking Syrian-Christian who *moved* to Rome and wrote a Gospel for the Christian community there. I suspect this burlesque scholarship of mine was as "true" as the stuff I had been reading. The Syrian origin fits not only Mark's Gentile theology but also his inaccurate Palestinian geography and his erroneous explanations of Jewish customs. The move to Rome explains the church's long belief in the Gospel's Roman origin and Mark's translation of the Palestinian-Greek coin *lepta* to the Roman *quadrans*. I am not, of course, offering my theory seriously. I wish only to demonstrate the problematical nature of a good deal of what passes for New Testament learning. In what follows, therefore, please keep in mind what I have earlier said about the "state of the art."

The Preaching Mission
(Mark 1:1—8:26)

As we read through the first few chapters of Mark's Gospel we should note how literary conventions and the assumptions of the Hellenistic world about nature and the supernatural interpenetrate to make our reading diffi-cult. You may recall that the first sentence, "Here begins the gospel of Jesus Christ [the Son of God]," seems to have defined the literary form *gospel* (*euaggelion*) as the "good news" about Jesus: a narrative summary of his preaching followed by an account of his passion, death, and burial. In the next sentence, we learn that Jesus had a herald, John, a stranger to Jesus, a holy man who has come out of the desert and across the Jordan River to preach repentance. John is dressed like Elijah, whom kings called that "trou-bler of Israel." God had promised to send him back to earth before the final "Day of the Lord"—on the very last prophetic page of Malachi, the "last" book of what was then recognized as Hebrew scripture. Jesus' herald thus serves to link not only the old religion and the new but also the old religious *scripture* and the new. To make sure we understand this, Mark describes John with a pastiche of quotations which evoke the angel of Exodus 23:20 and the heavenly voice heard in Deutero-Isaiah. He assumes, that is, that we readers are the sort of people who will pick up such literary allusions and will understand that they can be used with that odd freedom discussed in the introduction. This in turn means that, even though the author and his readers were not minutely informed about Jerusalem and its religious cus-toms, they *were* acquainted with at least the Greek translation of the Torah and the peculiar literary conventions involved in its citation.

When John—both the historical *and* the symbolic figure—baptizes Jesus in the river, Jesus sees the heavens break open; and "the spirit" in the form of a dove comes down upon him. He also hears a voice from above (pre-sumably God's) telling him "Thou art my son, my Beloved; on thee my favor rests" (Mark 1:11). Notice that the omniscient author hears and sees what, according to his narrative, only Jesus hears and sees. We should note that in telling about this event, the author also assumes that his readers understand the rite of baptism, though in fact no one today *does* understand precisely what it meant or how it was performed. Mark clearly associated this "dip-ping" in water with repentance for sin—but *why* remains mysterious.

Immediately afterward, Jesus is "removed" into "the wilderness" for forty days. This is the sort of generalized diction we shall meet with again and again in the Gospels, which often describe events as taking place in a kind of dream landscape. It is in this sort of locale that Jesus lives among wild beasts, is tested by Satan, and is ministered to by angels—though the "tempting dialogue" with Satan familiar to you from Matthew and Luke is missing. Returning from this vague wilderness, Jesus is found strolling along the shore of the Sea of Galilee, where he stops to call Simon and Andrew his brother as they fish just off shore. "And at once they left their nets and followed him" (1:18). The same thing then happens with another pair of fishermen, James and John, the sons of Zebedee; they also come along without a word, leaving their father with only hired men to work the ship.

Here we can see the further use of the literary convention embedded in that opening remark about the "Son of God." It explains the peculiar behavior of these men. Ordinarily we would ask *why* two sets of middle-class fishermen leave their father in the boat with the employees and suddenly walk off from their occupations and property? You may never have thought of this question. You already know that Jesus is the Son of God (a fact confirmed to Jesus himself by the voice from above) and that he has some sort of divine calling. It does not occur to you, therefore, that these fishermen are doing something quite implausible. Within just these first few sentences, then, you find yourself reading this complicated text as you would if you were caught up in a piece of fiction, exercising knowledge prohibited the characters in the story and hearing things no witness ever could hear. When you read further that the taciturn little party goes into Capernaum, where Jesus has a home, you therefore accept the fact that he not only stands up in a Sabbath synagogue to preach, but then *exorcises a demon*. It may still come as a surprise, however, that the congregation seems more amazed at Jesus' authoritative manner than at the appearance of the evil spirit. In fact the insouciance of the Galileans at having a demoniac in their congregation—let alone having his devil exorcised before their eyes—may still puzzle some readers, for it will be a while before all are *completely* attuned to the worldview of this author and the people he writes for.

In Capernaum itself, Jesus cleanses a leper, releases a man from paralysis, and on a Sabbath and in a synagogue cures another man with a withered hand. Later, having crossed back to Galilee from Gerasa in the Decapolis, he will cure a woman with a hemorrhage and raise a young girl from death, or near death. Some scholars distinguish these "ordinary" acts of healing not only from exorcisms but from "nature miracles" like walking on water and multiplying loaves and fishes, as if to rank Jesus' wonders in plausibility. But surely Mark's first readers would not feel the force of such categorization. As Raymond Brown puts it, Jesus came as Lord of "man and nature" (*New Testament Essays*, 179)—although, as we shall see, that Lordship is oddly limited.

What we twentieth-century readers must get used to here is the kind of Hellenistic "Nature" that is assumed by the Gospel writers and characters in their story. For them, the natural world knows no regularity or law; it is a place where anything can happen. Though not an everyday occurrence, miracles are frequent enough here so that their occurrence is never questioned, only their propriety or the nature of the power by which they are performed. Nevertheless, descriptions of the same miracle differ markedly from Gospel to Gospel: those in Mark often seem quite primitive when compared to their retelling in Matthew or Luke.

An example of how literary point-of-view can intertwine with a primitive worldview is Mark's story (5:25–34) about the woman with the twelve-year "issue of blood." She stands in the crowd along the lakeside saying to herself (by way of the omniscient author), "If I touch even his clothes, I shall be cured." She *does* touch them; and Jesus is straightaway aware that "a power had gone out of him." Turning around he asks, "Who touched my clothes?"

On the one hand, Mark has reported to us what the woman *thought*; on the other hand, he makes it clear that Jesus' knowledge is limited. We readers know who touched him, but Jesus doesn't. Looking at the passage as a narrative, we might say that Mark gets into the woman's head to set up the tale dramatically; he has Jesus ignorant of her touch for the sake of suspense—will she come forward? But embedded in it is that fact that Jesus' power to work miracles acts independently of his will, as if it were a kind of electricity. Like the presence of the demons, this is not simply a literary convention but an ancient worldview. Mark or his unknown source *thinks* of miraculous power as a kind of stored up energy that can be tapped through Jesus' clothing. The idea occurs elsewhere; in Acts (19:11–12), Luke reports that Paul's handkerchiefs were thought to have the same property.

Such notions bring us face to face with a foreign element in the Gospel. We are not used to such a "power." Nor are we used to thinking of Jesus as having limitations in his miracle working. The whole matter is deeply puzzling. We might ask, for instance, If the Lord can cure this fellow's leprosy, why not *leprosy*? Or, if he can banish this kid's demon, why not *demons*? But in the dream world of the Gospels, these questions never arise.

On this first preaching excursion, Jesus also selects his closest helpers. We have seen that the Galilean fishermen Andrew and Simon (Peter) first joined Jesus; they were followed by James and John, the sons of Zebedee—also fishermen. Then near the "lakeside" Jesus finds "Levi, son of Alphaeus, at his seat in the customhouse" and tells him to follow also. Finally, "up in the hill country" according to Mark, Jesus "called the men he wanted." These are the "Twelve" of later Christian history and legend, and a certain amount of mystery is associated with them. For one thing the term *apostle*, that is, someone who is "sent out," seems more appropriate in the mouth of later Christians who had a memory of their "missions," than in Mark, who uses it only once. There are also puzzles about their names. In addition to those already mentioned, these are: Philip, Bartholomew, Matthew,

Thomas, James the son of Alphaeus, Thaddeus, Simon the Zealot, and Judas Iscariot. You will note that this makes thirteen "apostles" rather than twelve; the problem is apparently the tax collector Levi, who is either not a disciple or is to be identified as "James the son of Alphaeus." Further confusion over the Twelve will persist in the subsequent Gospels; no list will be identical with any other, and descriptive epithets like "Boanerges" and "Iscariot" are still not fully understood. Further difficulties abound in both our restored Greek text and in the manuscripts behind it over the plurality of Jameses and the overlappings involving Matthew, Levi, and Thaddeus. But perhaps most remarkable is the inconsequence of all these people. Folklore apart, only Peter and Judas are of any later significance—all the rest are merely names. Even the idea that the Beloved Disciple of the Fourth Gospel is to be identified with John son of Zebedee is a mere assumption.

As this small, ambiguous band goes about Galilee, Jesus continues to work wonders and exorcisms and cures. In addition, however, Mark narrates a number of what are called "controversy" or "pronouncement" stories, conversations in which Jesus develops his own teaching over against the "scribes, doctors of the law, and Pharisees," by telling a brief anecdote ending in a punch-line pronouncement. Such stories were called *chreiai* by the Greeks (useful stories) and were used by biographers to illustrate the character of the teller—a philosopher, for instance—as much as to make the point involved. On a Sabbath, Jesus is said to be walking through a field of grain from which his disciples are picking kernels. When certain observers object to this desecration—of the holy day, not the field—Jesus reminds them that when David and *his* men were hungry and on the run from Saul, they went so far as to eat the sacred showbread. The story concludes with the line: "Therefore the Son of Man is sovereign even over the Sabbath" (Mark 2:23–26).

Reading this today, we often fail to realize that the punch line has lost its point. Like a dozen or so others in Mark, this tale is concerned with very contemporary issues—liberalizing the first-century holiness code so emphasized by late Judaism: Sabbath rest, dietary rules, ritual cleanliness, and so on. Jesus recommends, for instance, that people pay their taxes to Rome. At one point he denounces the Pharisaic fast; at another he limits the importance of prohibited foods and implies that eating with low-life people is no longer ritually defiling. No longer concerned with such matters, we read these stories as simply honorific of Jesus or, translating "sabbath," a bit of practical wisdom regarding required church attendance or "Sunday keeping." Jesus seems to be saying that necessity (in the other Synoptics the disciples are hungry) takes precedence over the Sabbath law.

Indeed, one wonders whether Mark himself was all that interested in revamping Jewish customs. I doubt it. I think he tells these inherited stories simply to illustrate Jesus' authority—his equality with King David, for instance. In any case, these useful sayings are hardly applicable to present-day life, even present-day *Jewish* life. Yet some readers always maintain that such anecdotes make up a New Testament ethic vital to their moral outlook. This notion is difficult to maintain, for only once does Mark's Jesus speak of a general code of conduct. In 7:20–23 Jesus disapproves of "evil thoughts, acts of fornication, of theft, of murder, of adultery, of greed, of evil; fraud, indecency, *the evil eye*, blasphemy, arrogance, *foolishness*." I print here my own translation because most Bibles fudge the "evil eye," which along with "foolishness" must strike every modern reader as a very odd sin indeed. Other moral peculiarities occur elsewhere in the text. Indeed, if contemporary Christians or Jews actually took Mark seriously they would be strangely burdened: not permitted to divorce for any reason, for instance, and enjoined to despise money as extremely dangerous. Moreover, they would be committed to accept freely the abominable suffering entailed in "following the Lord." Finally, should modern readers attain the afterlife, they would find it an interminable oriental banquet, the kind a starving person might long for in the midst of a desert, but no one else.

The absence of a "usable" code of behavior and belief—more obvious in Mark than the other Synoptics—has understandably prompted Christians to "read in" to this Gospel meanings more appropriate to their circumstances. In fact this phenomenon can be observed in the Gospel itself. The cluster of parables in Mark 4 contains the well-known anecdote of a man sowing his field by hand. As the sower sows, some seed falls on the path, on the rocks, and among weeds and never germinates. Other seed falls on good soil and is wonderfully productive. As Jesus first tells it, the parable is without interpretation: we don't know *what* the seed represents; and this is also the way it appears in the early *Gospel of Thomas*. Presumably, the story may originally have circulated in this form. Jesus seems often to have told stories which demanded that the hearers themselves produce the meaning, even as the anecdotes of Zen masters.

But this rather oblique manner of teaching must not have been acceptable to some early Christians, for whom Mark supplied an additional, allegorical explanation (4:14–20). In *this* understanding, the seed is equated with the word of God and the varying ground represents the various kinds of people who did and *did not* accept. it. The seed that falls on the path represents those whose faith is stolen away by Satan, for instance; that which falls on poor soil represents those people who have faith but "it strikes no root"; and the seed that falls on good ground represents true believers. The assumption underlying this allegory is that each of these categories accounts for a good bit of seed. This meaning of the parable is flattering to those who believe in the word, and presumably Mark's community found it encouraging; but it ignores the fact that when one broadcasts seed *most* of it falls on prepared soil—or it had better. The allegory makes a madman of the poor sower, who must fling his seed everywhere, like the wind—soil, footpath, rocks, indiscriminately—and therefore makes hash of the analogy.

Taken all in all, it is difficult to say precisely what Jesus preaches in Mark, except that most of his talk has to do with the coming of the "kingdom." Yet, as Paul Achtemeier has shown, Jesus is in general quite reluctant to give us any very clear idea of *that* (*Mark*, 57).

> The only explicit statement Mark makes about the kingdom in that vein is— the kingdom is a mystery! That statement itself is so "mysterious" that both Matthew and Luke thought they had to clear it up, so both changed Mark 4:11 to read "to you (i.e. disciples) it has been given to know the mysteries of the kingdom of God" (Matt. 13:11; Luke 8:10).

Even this information Jesus imparts to his immediate followers is part of a *deliberate secret* to be kept from "those outside." Indeed, from the very beginning Mark's Jesus has not wished to make his doctrine public. He has a penchant for secrecy that was noticed even by Celsus, the celebrated anti-Christian writer of the second century. Nor does Jesus want to draw attention to his authority or undergird his preaching with signs and wonders. This trait is evident as early as Mark 1:34, where he does not allow the demons to speak—specifically "because they knew who he was." A little later, having cured a leper, he tells him emphatically, "Watch that you say nothing to any one." Even when Peter finally names him the Christ, or Messiah, Mark tells us he ordered the disciples "to speak to no one concerning him."

Since about 1900, the conventional scholarly view of this matter has been that all such expressions were invented by the early church. The argument is that by 60 or 70 C.E. some Gentile Christians, though they still believed their Lord was truly the Messiah, the Son of God, the Son of Man, and so on, were disturbed that his full identity was not made clearer in the stories they had inherited about him. Consider that remark Jesus made about the Son of Man being lord of the Sabbath, for instance. Is he talking about himself or need we look for some other "Son of Man"? Moreover, if Jesus *was* the Son of Man and Messiah, why was he killed? Why didn't the people of Judea recognize their king when he arrived? The solution Mark found (according to these scholars) was to write a narrative in which Jesus keeps his kingship secret and is therefore killed by people who are *ignorant* of who he really is.

Though this theory of a "Messianic Secret" has influenced all subsequent thinking about Mark, it has its difficulties. If this was Mark's intention, why is he so inconsistent in applying it: his Jesus sometimes seems completely unconcerned about secrecy, and the crowds hail him with messianic cries. What is undeniable is the secrecy itself. Whatever its true meaning, it creates a puzzling, esoteric Jesus who brings into the world a special, restricted knowledge. In Mark, truth is for the few rather than the many. Mark's Jesus deliberately speaks to the crowds in riddles (parables) in order that they may *not* understand.

> When he was alone, the Twelve and others who were round him questioned him about the parables. He replied, "To you the secret of the kingdom of God has been given; but to those who are outside everything comes by the way of parables, so that (as Scripture says) they may hear and hear, but understand nothing; otherwise they might turn to God and be forgiven." (Mark 4:10–12; the allusion is to Isaiah)

What is worse, when Jesus takes "the Twelve and others who were round him" aside to explain matters to them, *they* fail to understand. The American critic Stevan Davies points out that most modern readers assume that the disciples' inability to understand Jesus' preaching is only temporary. "Maybe so," says Davies, "but that is not Mark's idea" (p. 97).

You may then well ask, Who *does* understand? Who are the few? The readers? Readers then or now? Is it us, Lord?

It is possible that that is *exactly* Mark's point. He may believe that the earliest Christians did *not* understand "The Way," at least not before Christ had risen, but that his own spirit-filled readers of 70 C.E. *do* understand it. From this point-of-view, Mark deliberately treated the apostles negatively, including their lack of understanding and their flight from the cross, out of animosity toward the Jewish-oriented Jerusalem church which these "apostles" eventually administered.

Why? Well, the argument goes like this. Mark is writing for a largely Gentile community that has already diverged from the ways of Judea. His readers believe that people in Jerusalem persist in thinking—thirty years after the crucifixion—that the new religion is still a branch of Judaism. And lately they have begun to put their trust in false prophets and a pseudo-Christ. Elaine Pagels makes the point that Mark and his readers may have thought of the destruction of Jerusalem in 70 C.E. as a kind of retribution for this error. In any case, Mark's readers are convinced that they themselves know the true meaning of the risen Christ, including the rejection of Judaism and the elimination of what they consider to be an outmoded Jewish holiness code.

We don't know if this was the case, of course. We don't even know whether a Jerusalem church still existed at the time Mark wrote. It might already have disappeared under the pressure of the Roman siege. But animosity between early Christian groups certainly occurred. We encounter a similar negative feeling toward these very same men in Paul's sardonic description of James (the brother of the Lord) and Peter as those who "seem to be pillars" of the church (Gal. 2:9); and in Paul's case these men were still alive and in power.

What we *do* know is that in Mark's Gospel everything goes wrong. Jesus' preaching is a failure; his family think he's mad (3:21); and even his most trusted friends fail to understand him. This debacle is concealed from most readers by the generally upbeat tone of the whole New Testament anthology, especially the Fourth Gospel, and, of course, by the philosophic optimism of the religion itself. In fact, quite early on, Mark was given a false ending to try to bring him in line with the optimism of the other later Gospels.

After this initial tour, Jesus returns to Nazareth, where, Mark tells us, "he could work no miracle, except a few cures." The difficulty seems to be that the people in his home area do not "trust" him—in contradistinction to those whom he has cured, whose "trust" has saved them. The necessity for faith or trust in the working of a curing miracle is a subtheme in Mark, which sharply contrasts with his idea of Jesus' power as a mechanical sort of energy. The former view will be emphasized by later Christian thinkers struggling to make whatever is miraculous also moral.

In any case, Jesus now summons "the Twelve" for missionary work. The rules he gives them for their oddly brief journey loom large in New Testament scholarship because they seem to offer a window through which to observe the practices of the earliest Christians, perhaps of Jesus himself—at least as each Gospel writer imagined him. Mark's version is radical: no food, no knapsack, no money, no extra clothes, only a staff and sandals—the kind of thing that will impress St. Francis. Having fortified them with these instructions, he sends them out two by two with authority over the demons (Mark 6:7–13). While they are away, as it were, Mark tells the dramatic story of the death of John the Baptist.

When the disciples return—a few verses later and rather too quickly for verisimilitude—Mark tells two sets of parallel stories or, more likely, tells the same set of stories twice. Scholars differ as to the contents of the two sets. One view is that each consists of a feeding miracle (6:30–44; 8:1–9), a "sea" anecdote (6:45–52; 8:10), and some healing stories. The two groups occupy Mark 4:35–8:26. Not all the parallels are terribly clear-cut, but the two feeding stories vary only in number: five thousand persons, five loaves, two fishes, twelve baskets of leftovers; as against four thousand persons, seven loaves, a few fishes and seven baskets of leftovers.

But what is most important and enigmatic—besides the sheer repetition of these anecdotes—occurs after the last feeding episode. When the entire party is sailing off across the lake, Jesus hears his men deploring their failure to bring bread along; and he suddenly reproaches them.

> Why do you talk of having no bread? Have you no inkling yet? Do you still not understand? Are your minds closed? You have eyes: can you not see? You have ears: can you not hear? Have you forgotten? When I broke the five loaves among five thousand, how many basketfuls of scraps did you pick up?" "Twelve," they said. "And how many when I broke the seven loaves among four thousand?" They answered "Seven." He said, "Do you still not understand?" (Mark 8:17–21)

To my mind, no passage in Mark is so illuminative of the "creativity" of his writing and the opacity of his theology. On the first let me turn to Paul Achtemeier's comment:

> ... the material in 8:19–21, where Jesus questions the disciples about the wondrous feeding of the multitudes, supposes not only that the two feedings already narrated in Mark have occurred (6:35–44; 8:1–10), but also presupposes the actual Greek form of those narratives. The two narratives of the feedings use different words for "basket"; that difference is accurately reflected in Jesus questions where the Greek word for basket in 8:19 [*kophinos*] corresponds to the word in 6:43, and another Greek word for basket, used in 8:20 [*spyris*] corresponds to the word in in 8:8. That summary, therefore presupposes not only the present order of events in Mark, but also *the present form of the Greek prose*. (*Mark*, 29–30; emphasis mine)

It is clear, therefore, that Mark or his editor deliberately put together these two versions of the same story—a story that closely parallels the miraculous feeding in 2 Kings 4:42–44—and then referred to the combination in a later passage. Why? We don't know. As for the difficulty of theology, what is one to make of the tone of this passage and of its apparent use of mystical, or at least mysterious, numbers? Here we encounter an element in the Gospel world that, try as we may, we cannot understand. It is not that we would reject some symbolism concerning food and number. The problem is *what* symbols? This opacity is the more unfortunate because these passages are so clearly important to the early church. Both series of stories are repeated in Matthew; the feeding of the five thousand occurs in Luke; and both the feeding *and* the walking on the water appear in John, where they are elaborated on and given clear symbolic values—the bread as the Eucharist, and the walking on water as a triumph over chaos. But what do they mean in Mark?

The next stop on the preaching tour is Bethsaida on the eastern shore of the lake, where Jesus cures a blind man in an oddly primitive way—he spits in the man's eyes and then touches them. This miracle is odd for another reason also; it occurs in stages. Jesus says, "Do you see anything?" And the man replies, "I see men; but they look like trees, walking." So Jesus touches the man's eyes again and they are completely restored. After this the group passes through the villages to Caesarea Philippi, where the matter of the Messianic Secret returns very forcefully. You may recall that it is here that Jesus asks, "Who do people say I am?" And for the first time in the gospel we hear from Peter, "You are the Messiah." Mark adds, "Then he gave them strict orders not to tell anyone about him."

Albert Schweitzer believed that Mark was *obliged* to add such a demand for secrecy,

> because he was conscious that Jesus was not recognized and acknowledged as Messiah by the people, nor even by his immediate followers, in the unhesitating fashion in which those of later times imagined him to have been recognized. Mark's conception and representation of the matter carried back into the past the later developments by which there finally arose a Christian community for which Jesus had become the Messiah. (*Quest of the Historical Jesus,* chapter 11)

This view, which amounts to the solution of the Messianic Secret problem, has—like the problem it addresses—influenced all subsequent scholarship. It holds that Mark was asserting that it is his own readers, rather than the people down in Jerusalem, who possess the risen Christ and truly understand the "Way."

Mark 8:27–13:36

For most readers, however, what is most memorable here is the dramatic shift in mood that comes over the narrative. When the party turns south, Mark tells us that Jesus began for the first time to try "to teach them that the Son of Man had to undergo great sufferings, and to be rejected by the elders, chief priests, and doctors of the law; to be put to death, and to rise again three days afterwards." Mark adds, "He spoke about it plainly." Readers have always found this opening of the second part of Mark's Gospel very moving; even after so many centuries, even through all its familiarity, this is a frightening moment. Some critics would go further to insist that these verses describe the "defining moment" of Mark's Gospel, the moment in which we understand that Jesus *has* to die. Why? So that as the risen Christ he can descend in the spirit upon us as, for Mark, he *already has*. Though the logic of this necessity seems opaque, the nature of "useful suffering" is potent in all religions; and it allows Mark's Jesus to tell the first readers (and us) what the great Lutheran martyr Dietrich Bonhoeffer, called "the cost of discipleship." Anyone who wishes to follow him, Jesus says, must take up his own cross—and soon.

The phrase "take up your cross" may be an indication that this speech was not spoken by Jesus, but was created by someone in the early church, since obviously the cross had not yet become a theological symbol. To Jesus' contemporaries, crucifixion was only a particularly shameful Roman method of execution. (This is the sort of observation the Jesus Seminar considers in attempting to find the authentic words of the Lord.) Contrast it with this statement just a few verses later on: "I tell you this: there are some of those standing here who will not taste death before they have seen the kingdom of God already in power." Such a remark, or something close to it, was almost certainly spoken by Jesus himself. The proof? Even in Mark's day this remark would have been received with incredulity and very soon would have been seen as simply untrue. Every copyist has had ample reason to change or eliminate this saying—and none has. Paradoxically then, the fact that Jesus' prediction failed to come true has guaranteed its authenticity. Or at least that is what scholars used to think. More and more, however, people who study such questions believe—contrary to Schweitzer—that despite this reasoning the apocalyptic passages in this Gospel belong to Mark rather than Jesus. For a brief moment around the year 70 this author and his community waited in confidence for the end; but not thereafter. Matthew and Luke both soften this view, and a full consideration of these versions well illustrates the work of students of Christian origins (see Mark 8:27–9:1).

Following this complex and important introduction to the second part of the Gospel is the enigmatic "Transfiguration," a *tableau vivant* God provides on one of those vague, synoptic "high mountains." Jesus' garments shine as he converses with two other figures, who are identified (as if they had subtitles under them) as "Moses" and "Elijah." Then presumably the same voice that spoke at the Jordan is heard again: "This is my son, my beloved; listen to him" (9:8). Even though this vision falls within those worldview conventions that have also provided heavens that open up and an offstage desert testing by demons, it remains wild and strange. Why don't these figures speak? What sort of beings are these phantasms of Moses and Elijah? Are they what Homer thought of as "shades"? Possibly. Many Greeks still believed that ghosts or mirror images or shadows of the dead persisted in the underworld. These creatures were not actually alive but given the right magic one could talk to them. In Homer, you'll recall, Odysseus visits with the shade of Achilles. Is that what Mark has in mind? We don't know. The whole occurrence is so odd that Peter's reaction seems true of the reader also: "He did not know what to say."

Traveling southward, Jesus a second time predicts his betrayal and murder (9:31). But again the disciples fail to understand, with Mark weakly explaining their inadequacy: "they were afraid to ask." As the journey proceeds, Jesus utters a whole series of aphorisms (9:33–50). He who wants to be first, shall be last; whoever accepts my representative accepts me; whoever is not against us is for us; all acts of charity are "counted." More importantly, perhaps, he also delivers some hyperbolic, perfectionist "hard sayings"—moral admonitions fit only for angels and saints. If your hand or your foot or eye offends, get rid of it. He forbids all divorce (implying a Roman form of marriage in which wives can also initiate separation), and he insists that one must enter "the kingdom" as a child would—whatever that may imply. He even rejects the honorific address "Good teacher," saying, "No one is good except God"—a difficulty for those later Christians who conclude that *he* is God. Finally, he all but destroys a rich young man who wants to reach perfection; Jesus advises him to sell all he has and give the money to the poor—it is in this speech that we find the well-known image of the camel and the needle's eye.

Sayings of this extreme sort occur now and again throughout the Gospels, and they obviously pose a problem. A few in each century will take them literally and castrate themselves or join the Jesuits. Most will consider them simply "Middle Eastern hyperbole," as I once heard a New Hampshire preacher say. Perhaps, as others would have it, they were meant as corporate metaphors; for it is just possible that these terrible pronouncements originally referred to group solidarity. Verbs like "plucking out" or "cutting off" meant in effect to "excommunicate." In any case, the motive for all this strict behavior is said to be the avoidance of "Gehenna," which Mark describes with a quotation from Isaiah as a place, "where the worm never dies and the fire never goes out." Gehenna was actually the city dump of Jerusalem, but apparently because it was always afire it functioned as a metaphor for hell.

Now Jesus makes a third prediction of his passion (10:33–34) in a speech almost certainly composed after the crucifixion and set back in time. This is the most circumstantial forecast yet, full of "prophetic detail" drawn from Deutero-Isaiah. The "chief priests and the doctors of the law" will condemn the "Son of Man" to death and hand him over to the foreign power; he will be mocked and spat upon, flogged and finally killed, but after three days he will rise again. Reaching Jericho, Jesus cures a blind beggar and then, climbing toward Jerusalem, stops in Bethphage and Bethany "at the Mount of Olives." From there he sends his disciples into "the village opposite" for a colt to ride on during his "entrance." If one reads this section as historical, or nearly so, Jesus must already have been known in Judea; for people not only allow his men to take their animals, they strew his route with brush (the "palms" are in John). In fact, the people of Jerusalem shout, "Blessings on the coming kingdom of our father David! Hosanna in the heavens!" (11:10). Unfortunately, this glad reception runs counter to Mark's secrecy motif. Mark seems to want the Messiah to be both secret and famous.

Jesus now visits the Temple. Then "as it was now late" they all return to Bethany. This is a pattern Jesus will maintain throughout the last days of his life. For whatever reason, he does not wish to spend the night in the city. On the following morning, as he goes into Jerusalem to preach, Jesus is said to feel hungry, and finding no figs on a tree "for it was not the season for figs," he curses it with the words, "May no one ever again eat fruit from you." The tree subsequently withers (11:4, 20). The author's unsentimental intention may have been to demonstrate Jesus' power—fig trees do not have feelings, or ears for that matter. Furthermore, since in a typical Markan way, this anecdote is set within the longer story concerning Jesus and the Temple, it may be Mark's intention to allow the fig tree to stand for the Temple Judaism he considers outmoded—"it was not the time for figs." More prosaically, it may simply be that the second part of a fig tree story, which is given in Luke 13:6–9, has slipped from the text and found its home here. Yet Christians are so used to reading the whole Gospel as somehow pertinent to their daily life, that this little incident has always been troubling. I have already mentioned Simone Weil's understanding of it: that a tree or man—or a whole religious tradition—can be worthless and unprofitable even without conscious sin or free will. I have heard many others.

While in the Temple, Jesus is said to drive out the buyers and sellers, a notion difficult to accept in light of the size of the Herodian Temple and its hundreds of employees. Moreover the buyers and sellers and money changers were absolutely necessary; they provided animals for sacrifice; and they changed foreign currency offerings, which were considered ritually unclean. Yet all the evangelists tell this story—though John locates it at the beginning of Jesus' ministry rather than the end—and Jesus' act of civil disobedience has become famous. But its exact nature and intention remain unknown. Some readers have supposed that the various "legal" trials Jesus undergoes, the details of which similarly make little sense, were occasioned by this action. Others think that he drove out the money changers as a symbol of the "coming" demise of Temple functions. In either case, this story clearly stands in opposition to the Jewish establishment and its official religion.

The critic Werner Kelber develops the point at some length: Jesus's whole life, he says, "culminated in a sharp disagreement with the temple authorities, the disqualification of the temple, and the prediction of its destruction. His own death, resulting from his denunciation of the temple and initiated by the temple authorities, in turn anticipates the death of the temple. At the moment of his death the temple curtain is torn asunder" (*Mark's Story of Jesus*, 92).

Nevertheless, Mark's Jesus remains in the Temple and its environs while preaching in the city. And it is in the Temple precincts that Jesus tells the fearful tale of the man who leased out his vineyard and sent for his rents. Time and again the workers kill his messengers—even murdering his only son, "the apple of his eye." Finally the owner returns in person, slaughters the guilty workers and gives the vineyard to others. Whatever this story originally meant (there is a shorter, perhaps earlier form in the *Gospel of Thomas*) here it is clearly an allegory of God's relationship first with the Jews and then with the Christians. To make sure we get the point and to underline his coming death as part of the divine plan, Jesus follows this tale with an allusion to one of the continuing motifs of the New Testament taken from Psalm 118, the rejected stone which becomes the capstone.

> The stone which the builders rejected
> has become the chief corner-stone.
> This is Yahweh's doing;
> it is marvelous in our eyes. (Ps. 118:22–23)

Perhaps this is the sort of talk that convinced Jesus' Temple adversaries to trap him any way they could. Initially, however, they only test him with quibbles over the Roman tribute and a query about a woman with several husbands in succession—whose wife will she be in heaven? They also ask which is the most important commandment, knowing full well the answer—which he gives them—from Deuteronomy. But after he passes all these tests and is on the way out of the Temple, someone calls his attention to the magnificence of Herod's recently completed Temple. "Look Master, what huge stones! What fine buildings." Jesus' reply is again probably supplied by the early Christians, "Not one stone will be left upon another." "When?" the disciples ask.

Apocalypse and Death

Though Jesus never really answers this question, or answers it in contradictory ways, he now begins the longest discourse in the Gospel. It is an apocalypse, essentially no different in form from Revelation or any one of several Christian/Jewish apocalypses of the second century. Supposedly delivered from somewhere on the Mount of Olives, its exact location is not known. Constantine, thinking he had discovered the spot in a cave on the side of the hill, built a church over it. The emperor's religious instincts, if not his geography, were correct; for in this "little apocalypse," as it is called, Mark at last tells us why Jesus must die, the "theme" of this Gospel.

When you hear of wars and rumors of wars, do not be alarmed . . . the end is still to come. For nation will rise against nation, and kingdom against kingdom; there will be earthquakes in various places; there will be famines. This is but the beginning of the birthpangs.

As for yourselves, beware; for they will hand you over to councils; and you will be beaten in synagogues. . . . Brother will betray brother to death, and a father his child, and children will rise against parents and have them put to death; and you will be hated by all because of my name. But the one who endures to the end will be saved.

But when you see the desolating sacrilege set up where it ought not to be (let the reader understand), then those in Judea must flee to the mountains; the one on the housetop must not go down or enter the house to take anything away; the one in the field must not turn back to get a coat. . . . And if anyone says to you at that time, "Look! Here is the Messiah!" or "Look! There he is!"—do not believe it. False messiahs and false prophets will appear and produce signs and omens, to lead stray, if possible, the elect. . . .

But in those days, after that suffering . . . they will see "the Son of Man coming in clouds" with great power and glory. Then he will send out the angels and gather his elect from the four winds. . . .

From the fig tree learn its lesson: as soon as its branch becomes tender and puts forth its leaves, you know that summer is near. So also, when you see these things taking place, you know that he is near, at the very gates. Truly I tell you, this generation will not pass away until all these things have taken place. Heaven and earth will pass away, but my words will not pass away. (13:7–31)

The fact that Jesus did not return, that he has never returned, has always been a problem. Edward Gibbon, the great eighteenth-century historian, wrote ironically of that disappointment, "the revolution of seventeen centuries has instructed us not to press too closely the mysterious language of prophecy and revelation." But so troubling was this failed revelation that over the centuries a kind of conspiracy of silence emerged, not only among Christians but among Christian scholars as well; and it lasted until the twentieth century. In *The Quest of the Historical Jesus,* Albert Schweitzer maintained that nearly all of nineteenth- century scholarship had been an attempt to deny this apocalyptic element in earliest Christianity. No one wanted to see the Gospel of Mark as a "thoroughly eschatological work," he said; that is, as a document whose theme was the "the end is near." Why? Because, said Schweitzer, the end *didn't* come and Jesus was *wrong*.

Schweitzer's emphasis on the Gospel's proclamation of the end of this world order—however one interpreted that notion—produced a revolution in the understanding of the New Testament, of which he was well aware: "To put it more prosaically, modern theology is at last about to become sincere. But this is so far [1907] a prophecy of the future" (*Quest,* 252). Today, nearly all agree that he was right *insofar as Mark's Gospel is concerned,* without regard to whether the historical Jesus believed the same way. Not only is Mark thoroughly eschatological; but this speech is exactly the sort of visionary discourse that was first a staple of late Judaism and then became characteristic of early Christianity. Seers of both religions were caught up in the notion that "the end" was near. Why? Clearly it was not a simple matter of politics or economics. In the first century of our era, the empire was entering upon its most peaceful and prosperous age. Where there was Roman rule, as we have seen, Jews were generally respected and honored, the benefactors of special legislation that excused them from emperor worship and compulsory military service. Yet here in Jerusalem and throughout Judea, as the Qumran documents demonstrate, there was a widespread belief that a cosmic catastrophe was about to occur.

Scholars have a sociological formula for such recurring apocalyptic moments. The "uncovering" or revelation of the end generally begins in a time of local chaos; the empire may be in fine shape, but Judea is in turmoil. An example closer to home is upstate New York in the 1840s. In the middle of the industrial revolution and the stampede westward, William Miller predicted that the Second Coming would occur between March 1843 and March 1844. When it didn't happen, he adjusted the date to October 12, 1844, a day subsequently commemorated by his followers as "The Great Disappointment." And we can come even closer. On June 19, 1992, in contemporary, distraught New York City, full of violence and change, a hard-pressed Hasidic group took out a full page in the *New York Times* to proclaim the prediction of Rabbi Menachem M. Schneerson, the Lubavitcher Rebbe: "Moshiach is coming and we must make preparations." Mr. Schneerson has subsequently passed on, but his followers continue to expect the worst.

For Mark's readers, the period of trouble was the war between the Jews of Palestine and their Roman overlords, a war that spilled over into a struggle between Jews and indigenous "Greeks" and often metamorphosed into a Palestinian civil conflict of one Jewish faction against another. It is *this* period which provides the details of Jesus' vision and therefore dates the composition of this passage to during and just after the years 66-70 C.E.

Under such threatening conditions, some people—literal Christians in the nineteenth century, or orthodox Jews in the first—begin to feel marginal and persecuted, unable to identify with any of the "players" of society. Small groups form wherever some relief from anxiety is promised. A particular kind of relief is often found in some "special knowledge" which predicts a time when life will be better, a time when the believer's one-down status will be redressed: "The folks in Hollywood and New York may have everything they want now. But just wait; we know what's in store." Fertile soil for the development of this special knowledge, say the sociologists, is a feeling of "relative deprivation." The word *relative* explains a lot. Apocalyptic groups don't actually have to be whipped in the synagogues; they need only *perceive* themselves as deprived in relation to others. The special knowledge that comes to them then works to restore emotional balance. Through their metaphysical beliefs, the group is transformed into a waiting, hopeful "eschatological community"; and the anxiety that brought the members together in the first place is replaced with a kind of happiness and security.

The particular content of the apocalyptic revelation that works this transformation may be as obvious as biblical "fundamentals" or as rarefied as early Mormonism; but its function is always the same: to overcome feelings of inferiority. If the message is short-term, so to speak—a prediction that the end will come within months or a year or two—the group is doomed to a swift comeuppance, the fate of the Millerites. Yet such doom rarely brings annihilation. One would expect communities of this type to dissolve upon the falsification of their prophecies, but one would be wrong. When the predicted date arrives and Jesus does not appear in the clouds—or whatever other phenomenon the group awaits—believers remain surprisingly faithful. And those who leave often join some other apocalyptic group; for the underlying socio-psychological factors that created their belief in the first place are almost certainly still in place. In time, of course, or under repeated disappointment, some cults disappear. Others, however, simply change their names (Millerites to Seventh-Day Adventists), adjust their theology, and become mainstream institutions which in turn spawn apocalyptic groups of their own.

What is particularly significant for a reading of the New Testament is that even today most eschatological communities are based on—or *give rise to*—the literary genre "apocalypse." Most treasure some document that embodies their beliefs; for though its message may have been brought to them orally by a seer, it is soon reduced to some permanent written form. And despite surface language, these documents are never much concerned with the future—that is, the time *after* the catastrophe. Most are intent on strengthening their readers for the coming hard times of tribulation. Even then, relatively little is generally said in exact description, but a good deal is made of who wins and who loses and why.

In the canonical New Testament there are at least three such revelations in addition to the passage in Mark already quoted; and dozens of others survive in the contemporary *koinē* literature. All were originally written for popular audiences and most are put forth in the name of someone important but long dead. All allude to other, earlier sacred literature and are written in some sort of symbolic code. In both form and content, Mark's little apocalypse is dependent on the book of Daniel, a coded apocalyptic work set in a fictional Babylon in the time of Belshazzar son of Nabonidus under a mythical Persian ruler "Darius." Actually the book was composed during the Maccabean revolt against Antiochus Epiphanes (168 to 164 B.C.E.). The mysterious figures of its text and what happens to them are meant to symbolize the Maccabees and Antiochus and what was happening to *them*. But its seventh chapter, written in Aramaic, not Hebrew, contains the following vision of the end.

> I was still watching in the visions of the night when I saw one like a son of man coming with the clouds of heaven; he approached the Ancient in Years and was presented to him. Sovereignty and glory and kingly power were given to him, so that all people and nations of every language should serve him; his sovereignty was to be an everlasting sovereignty which should not pass away, and his kingly power such as should never be impaired. (Dan. 7:13–14)

The phrase "Son of Man," which is at the heart of both Daniel's and Mark's apocalypse, has been much debated. Originally it seems to have been only a periphrastic way of saying "man," but it was used in late Jewish visions to indicate a humanlike, angelic figure. In Daniel it may represent

Michael, for instance, the leader of the "the holy ones of the Most High." Michael is the one who will defeat Israel's enemy, Antiochus Epiphanes, and will receive kingly power over the earth. An alternative view is that the phrase "Son of Man" represents the "loyal" Jews themselves, the Maccabean revolutionaries who will receive power with the coming victory. But for Mark, it is clearly a title belonging to *Jesus*–despite Jesus' own puzzling ambiguities about the matter. It is Jesus who, as Son of Man, will come with the clouds during the lifetime of the present generation.

In fact, when Mark's Jesus says such and such *will* happen, it has often already begun to happen. The birth pangs of the new age *have* started: wars and rumors of wars *are* occurring, people *have* been flogged in synagogues or arrested by Temple authorities. Families have been torn apart by political-religious strife, and the Temple has been desecrated; Christians have already fled to the mountains and perhaps across the Jordan; and most importantly, false Christs have arisen, some of whom even work wonders. But do not be misled; God has taken pity on humanity and has cut your troubles short. Soon after the gospel has been preached "to all nations," the sun will be darkened and the Son of Man will come according to the vision of Daniel. Though everything has gone wrong, in death Jesus will be "released" to return with the kingdom. This, then, is what Mark has all along been interested in, and he has taken the whole of chapter 13 to tell us about it.

But there is a very famous footnote. Right in the middle of his speech, while Jesus is telling us the sure signs of the end-time, he says, "let the reader understand" (13:14). *Reader? Jesus is speaking!* Perhaps Mark forgot he was writing dialogue. Perhaps he adapted this material from some already circulating pamphlet and failed to distinguish between direct and indirect discourse. No one knows. But as it stands the text is impossible; and yet some such direction "to understand" or "to interpret the code" occurs in almost every apocalypse. The authors of this sort of literature are always afraid their secret message will not get through. A case in point is Revelation 17:9ff.: "But here is the clue for those who can understand it. The seven heads are seven hills on which the woman sits. They represent seven kings. . . ."

Unfortunately, the "understanding" asked of the reader in the case of Mark 13 has never been completely recovered. The problem is this: Jesus says that the beginning of the end will occur "when you see the abomination of desolation usurping a place which is not his," a code phrase taken from Daniel 12:11, *where it is also code.* In Daniel it apparently meant some sort of desecration committed by Antiochus Epiphanes—pagan images brought into or affixed to the Temple perhaps (see 1 Macc. 1:54, 59). In

Mark, the phrase may refer to a similar wartime desecration either of the Temple in Jerusalem or of some other shrine. (Herod had long ago affixed a Roman eagle to the wall of the Temple, and Josephus describes a ritual wartime "desecration" in a synagogue in the north. Surely there were other such acts.) The trouble is, the actual abomination has never been identified.

Oddly enough, though the title Son of Man never caught on in Christianity, the apocalyptic expectation in which it was embedded *did*. While practically nobody prayed to the "Son of Man," everybody awaited his coming. Indeed, his imminent return became a core belief of the early Christians—though not, perhaps, the earliest. The word for this return in Greek is *parousia* (arrival), which soon became a cant term in Christianity. When this second coming failed to occur, Christians adapted to the circumstance just as the Millerites would do later; and as Christian readers of the Gospels still do. Recently, Christian thinkers have produced theologies of progress and liberation which see in the apocalypse a symbol for the advent of some future Peaceable Kingdom on earth. Indeed, the promise of some sort of ultimate justice tempered with mercy—though put off indefinitely—remains the basis for the one virtue most of us have left: *hope*.

In his prediction of an imminent return, however, Mark was probably already out of phase with the tradition (see 13:32, where he has Jesus *deny* that anyone has this knowledge). Even twenty years before Mark wrote, Paul was answering questions regarding the "delay" of the *parousia* and putting it off until the conversion of the Jews. Luke and Matthew, as I have said, also postpone the great day to some sort of vague future date; and the rest of the documents that make up the New Testament reflect the same adjustment until in 2 Peter (ca. 140 C.E.) the problem is finally made explicit:

> First of all you must understand this, that in the last days scoffers will come, scoffing and indulging their own lusts and saying, "Where is the promise of his coming? For ever since our ancestors died, all things continue as they were from the beginning of creation!" (2 Pet. 3:3–4)

But even in 2 Peter, anxiety about the delay is put into the mouth of unbelievers, as if the faithful would never think of such a thing. Why? Well, perhaps from the beginning Christian readers have always known that belief in the apocalypse was as much about themselves as about the world. This is easily understood. You don't have to be very troubled to equate your sorrows with cosmic forces of evil and to see in your own demise a pattern for the universe. You only have to be mortal. I have met fundamentalists who were perfectly well, socially secure, and happy, who nevertheless still identified with that old Jerusalem roofer whom Jesus cautioned not to come down and enter his house but to flee directly to the hills to await his end.

None of us knows the time of our own death; and therefore the prediction of the end is, in a way, *always true.*

Mark 14-16

The end of this long apocalyptic speech marks the beginning of those final days of Jesus' life which will occupy Mark 14, 15, and the eight verses of chapter 16. The whole is memorably introduced by the haunting lines: "It was two days before the Passover and the time of unleavened bread, and the high priests and the scribes sought how, with guile, they might catch and kill him." Appropriately, the imagery of death and burial begins to mount. Jesus is again dining with friends, for instance, when an unnamed woman suddenly appears and anoints him. As a child, and because of the crude translation in our Douay version, I always saw her opening a jar over his head, with the stuff running down over his long pre-Raphaelite locks like honey. I was astonished at this sticky business, but admired the woman very much; for, like the rest of Holy Angels Parish, I thought of her as the exciting, reformed whore, Mary Magdalene. I suppose my admiration was also influenced by her indifference to money. Unlike my Depression-strapped parents, "Mary Magdalene" didn't give a hang for frugality. The Lord also admired her and *praised* her, telling off those carping, miserable, pinchpenny grumblers who objected to such excess. Didn't they know what was coming for him? He'd told them often enough! Didn't they recall the crowd's shout of "Son of David" when he entered the city? Didn't even his friends know that he was their anointed king? Peculiarly enough, my childhood dislike of these disciples seems to have exactly agreed with how Mark intended his first readers to react.

Jesus concludes the scene with the thrilling: "Amen I say to you, wherever the gospel is preached in all the world, what she has done shall be spoken of as a memorial to her." I can also remember reading this as a child, and suddenly realizing that *I* was there in the text itself—a later-day person listening to that woman's memorial. There is a passage in Homer that affects me the same way. Toward the end of the war, Helen says to Hector: "No one in Troy has a greater burden to bear than you, all through my own shame and the wickedness of Paris, ill-starred couple that we are, tormented by Heaven *to figure in the songs of people yet unborn.*" In the manner of the Homeric poet, the author of this Gospel combined a stagey banquet, prudent, holier-than-thou disciples, and a symbolic anointing for burial into a story that people in ages to come would love to tell.

While Jesus is still in Bethany, there also occurs that hugger-mugger, secret society business concerning the approaching Holy Days. He tells his disciples:

> Go into the city and a man will meet you carrying a jug of water. Follow him, and when he enters a house give this message to the householder: "The Master says, 'Where is my room reserved for me to eat the Passover with my disciples?' He will show you a large room upstairs, set out in readiness." (Mark 14:13–15)

Has Jesus arranged this secret signal to avoid the authorities: a man rather than a woman carrying water, followed by a kind of password? Does this business *prove* that he's been in Jerusalem before? Has the melodrama something to do with his habit of spending his nights in suburbs? Nobody knows. Even the "Passover meal" is unclear. Mark describes it as a seder, assuming that Thursday was the 14th of Nisan, the first day of Passover. Yet it has always been difficult to imagine that the chief priests' interrogations and Jesus' crucifixion occurred during the Holy Days. In fact the idea is specifically rejected by the scribes and high priests in their debate over when to arrest Jesus, "It must not be during the festival . . . or we should have rioting among the people" (14:1–2). In John, as in the minds of the early fathers, the crucifixion occurs on the day *before* Passover, the "Day of Preparation" as it was called, when the lambs were slaughtered.

Mark may have been guided by a need to *think* of the meal as a Passover in which Jesus himself is the slaughtered lamb—though I don't remember anyone at Holy Angels ever saying this. In those days what interested us most about the Last Supper was the "consecration" formula. We all thought Jesus spoke Latin, of course: *hoc est enim corpus meum* (the *enim*, "indeed," always seemed odd and unnecessary), and therefore it came as a shock to learn later that Jesus probably spoke in Aramaic, but that his words were "recorded" in Greek! What was worse perhaps, these particular words had apparently never been spoken at all; for wherever I looked in the New Testament I found something different from what Father Sullivan used at the ten o'clock! It wasn't even clear whether Jesus accomplished the whole thing at once, bread *and* wine, or ate the meal in between. And in Mark, you may have noticed, he forgets to tell his disciples to perform the ceremony on their own. I suppose these curious and really unimportant discoveries—and others like them—disturbed my faith more than anything else, before or since. Through them I became aware for the first time that the people I grew up with and their religious leaders simply couldn't or didn't *read*—not even the priests. By contrast, the early fathers read their scripture accurately and thought about it seriously—if not in the way that I here call *sensible*.

After dinner, the company files out for the Mount of Olives; and on the way, the Lord predicts that they all will prove unfaithful and deny him, Peter famously dissenting. So dramatic is this scene that we are likely to forget that we are reading an artistic recreation of events written from the point of view of 70 C.E. In so doing we lose the double irony in Peter's words, "Even if it is necessary to die for you I will not deny you." By the time this passage was written, Peter had both denied him *and* died for him as a martyr in Rome.

Then they enter Gethsemane (it is not called a garden in Mark). Unacquainted as a child with the idea of the omniscient narrator and Mark's use of the techniques of fiction, I was troubled with the problem of "who heard the Lord at prayer?" I am *still* troubled by it, and I don't mean to hide the reason. Even though I am at pains to explain to you the intricacies of literary conventions, I myself, now in my sixties, an old man poring over the Greek text, have to force myself to acknowledge them. Christians of my generation find it emotionally difficult to read the Gospel sensibly even when we write books about doing just that. But however one reads it, the scene in the garden is powerful: Jesus addressing his father as *Abba* (and Mark, like Paul, preserving the Aramaic word), the metaphor of the cup of suffering he is sworn to drink but wishes to God he didn't have to, the wretched friends he has depended on (yet somehow *never* depended on). When Jesus finds them sleeping the third time, he says, "*apechei*," a Greek verb often translated as "the hour has come." In classical Greek, this expression would mean something like "it is distant from," as in "Peraeus is so many stadia distant from Athens." But in the *koinē* Greek of the New Testament it seems to mean "*to receive* (pay) *in full*"—Plutarch uses the word this way also. Perhaps it might be rendered here: "everything now will happen to the hilt" or "now everything goes smash."

If you happen to have gone to a Catholic grammar school and "did" the Stations of the Cross every Friday in Lent, you will always think of the narrative from this point on as "Jesus is Condemned to Death," "Jesus Falls the First Time," and so on up to "Jesus is Laid in the Tomb." It will always come back to me complete with memories of Sr. De Motha making me "kneel up" and fruitless scripture searches for Veronica and her veil and all those "falls." Well, the same sort of additions and embellishments had been added to the story by Mark's day; his passion account is also conceived as a devotional exercise, rather than a report of an execution. Just as we 1930s Catholics relished the folk inventions of the Stations of the Cross, so Mark felt free to recreate an imaginative "Death of Jesus." In so doing, he tended to see the details of the event through the holy haze of ancient "prediction."

Here is Mark 15:22–39 with quotations from, or allusions to, Psalms 22, 69, Isaiah 53, and Amos underlined:

> <u>He was offered drugged wine</u>, but would not take it. Then they fastened him to the cross. <u>They divided his clothes among them, casting lots to decide what each should have.</u>
>
> The hour of the crucifixion was nine in the morning, and the inscription giving the charge against him read, "The King of the Jews." <u>Two bandits were crucified with him, one on his right and the other on his left.</u>
>
> <u>The passers-by hurled abuse at him. "Aha!" they cried, wagging their heads,</u> "you would pull down the temple, would you, and build it in three days? Come down from the cross and save yourself!" So too the chief priests and lawyers jested with one another. "He saved others," they said, "but he cannot save himself. Let the Messiah, the king of Israel, come down now from the cross. If we see that, we shall believe." Even those who were crucified with him taunted him.
>
> <u>At midday a darkness fell over the whole land,</u> which lasted till three in the afternoon; and at three Jesus cried aloud, "*Eli, Eli, lema sabachthani?*" which means, "<u>My God, my god, why hast thou forsaken me?</u>" Some of the bystanders, on hearing this, said, "Hark, he is calling Elijah." <u>A man ran and soaked a sponge in sour wine and held it to his lips on the end of a cane.</u> "Let us see," he said, "if Elijah will come to take him down." (15:25–37)

Despite this artfulness, parts of the story are wonderfully believable—if only because they are so odd. Some passages seem to cut through the allusions to Hebrew Scripture and the "proof texts" and reach back to the very thing itself. The authorities take him with "swords and cudgels," for instance, as he comes out of the garden, which is—as he himself notes—strange. Hadn't he been sitting in the Temple every day preaching? And what about that strange young man who left his only garment in their hands and then ran away naked into history? No one would have invented *him*. Nor would anyone have dreamed up Simon of Cyrene, just come from the fields, who is the father of Alexander and Rufus, people the original readers apparently either knew, or knew *of*—otherwise why mention them?

But then in succeeding passages, we find ourselves back reading a "gospel" again, a narrative designed to make a point. Why is Pilate such a craven figure, for instance, so condescending to the Jewish authorities? He certainly wasn't this way in "real life." He doesn't even have a charge against Jesus, yet kills him to please the priests. And who are those "false witnesses" who tell contradictory stories we are never allowed to hear? And what is all this fiddle-faddle about a criminal to be released called "Son of a Father" (Barabbas) or some such name? Did serious Roman governors actually consult the mob in order to pardon revolutionaries charged with murder? The answer to all of these questions is that this account has been tailored to suit many interests, not all of which can be identified. It seems clear, however, that one goal was to take the onus away from the Gentile Roman authorities and place guilt squarely on the conservative Jewish leaders—a disastrous strategy we will find elsewhere in the New Testament.

But regardless of who was to blame for his death, why did Jesus die? In the plan of the Almighty, what purpose was served by the crucifixion? Albert Schweitzer, who thought Mark's Gospel an accurate portrait of the historical Jesus, conjectured that "the cessation of his miracle-working power [in Mark's chapter 10] of which He had become aware, revealed to Him that the hour appointed by God had come" (*Quest,* 132). Schweitzer thought that Jesus recognized this as a signal that the apocalypse was imminent in which he would *become* the Messiah. Beyond this, the death of the Lord seemed to have little significance.

Other New Testament writers, however, portray Jesus' death as a sacrifice for the sins of humanity. In this view, Jesus somehow "paid for" the transgressions of humanity and made us "capable" of immortality. Does Mark believe this? He has only two references to such a doctrine. At 10:45 Jesus says that the Son of Man came "to give his life as a ransom for many"; and during the Last Supper he says, "this is my blood of the covenant which is poured out for many." That's it. At no other point in this Gospel does the sacrificial idea, so important to later Christianity, appear. The question then is, Do these two isolated remarks constitute a theory of redemption? And if so, does the idea make any sense? Can the death of someone—even of a God—"ransom" me? What does *ransom* mean in this context? Perhaps the early church had some notion of humans as a "countryfolk of God" who were held hostage by demons and of Jesus as their heroic champion. We don't know.

I personally have never made much sense of redemptive theology. In Mark, thank goodness, I don't have to. Though the notion of sacrifice is in his tradition, Mark does not consider it very significant. Yet the idea will be made much of by other New Testament writers and by the church. Over the centuries, each Christian has had to resolve the matter individually; it depends a lot on circumstances. In pain, nearly everyone wants a savior, whether sacrificial or not, whether the idea makes sense or not—whether it is *just* or not. But thinking about God while you are in pain probably only guarantees a slanted view. Dietrich Bonhoeffer called such theology "torture chamber" religion. In good health and happiness and youth, the notion of a savior from sin seems foolish and radically *unjust.* Shouldn't God forgive everyone? Or no one? Bernard Shaw says somewhere that the Catholic

Church in particular got this matter of guilt and forgiveness precisely wrong. Instead of telling the penitent that his sins were forgiven, the priest should say, "What you have done is a historical fact, it can never be erased in any way. Now go and don't do it again." As I grow older, however, I am less and less sure that Shaw was right—which I suppose means that I have become more familiar with pain.

It seems to me that a conservative view of the passion according to Mark is that it was an attempt *to make sense* of the despairing death of one who, like the prophets of old, was caught up in God's inscrutable plan. Mark believed Jesus had come to preach the apocalypse and that in the process he was killed by those ignorant of his true identity. In a sense, then, Mark's Gospel is apocalyptic *without* any refined theological theory of sin and guilt. It says only "believe for the end is near." Yet I wouldn't claim to have the whole truth of this matter. In *The Churches the Apostles Left Behind*, Raymond Brown writes, "one can get some agreement about what Mark is saying, but not necessarily about why he is saying it" (p. 29).

When the Sabbath is over and the women come to embalm the body, a young man in white tells them that Jesus has been raised and that they should inform his disciples and the "Rock" [Peter] that "he is going ahead of you into Galilee! There you will see him, just as he told you" (16:7). But the women run away and tell no one. This, as we now know, is the abrupt ending of the "first" Gospel: no resurrection scenes, no meetings on the way to Emmaus, no visions in the upper room. Only the information that the risen Christ will appear in Galilee and the haunting line, "But they ran away and didn't tell anyone, for they were afraid."*

Both the joy and the sadness of the Enlightenment came very late to American Catholics. Not until the 1950s did we think of *secular* knowledge of the Gospel as anything but dangerous. But since higher learning was an essential part of our assimilation, we slowly began to experience at least the "sadness of knowledge." Some of us are still waiting for its joy. I don't

---

*Some later and less authoritative manuscripts have longer, "more satisfying" endings. They seem to have been created out of Matthew and Luke and some legendary material and are in a different style and vocabulary. One manuscript adds a dialogue in which the disciples apologize for the unbelieving age they live in, and Jesus reassures them that the age of skepticism is about over and commissions them to spread the word, adding some very dangerous signs as marks of the faithful—the ability to pick up poisonous snakes, for instance, or even swallow poison without harm. After this, he is taken up.

mean, of course, that very many of us suddenly took up the serious study of the two-source theory or form criticism or the development of dogma and were depressed by our studies. Initially, our sadness came only from the chance findings I have already mentioned. We discovered that Jesus made mistakes, for instance. In Mark he thinks that the priest who set out the showbread which David ate was Abiathar, when actually it was this man's father, Ahimelech. Or it dawned on us that biblical editors were fudging the truth with tiny footnotes reading: "some witnesses read . . ." or in the case of the false endings of Mark just referred to, "at this point some of the most ancient witnesses bring the book to a close, while others. . . ." I have already remarked on my own futile search for the consecration formula, which was followed by my discoveries that Isaiah 7:14 might well read "young girl," rather than "virgin," and that the story of the woman taken in adultery was written long after the composition of John.

As I have said, such youthful epiphanies were not, and are not, very significant theologically, but they seemed to confirm what I was already beginning to suspect, that the people who had originally taught me my religion were either fools or liars. To come to such a conclusion in maturity is one thing; to find it out as a child is quite another. A special sadness therefore still attaches to my old discoveries—my first *aggiornamento*—and it persists. To men and women of my generation, it is still not happy news that the Gospels are tendentious narratives written for communities that must have differed in belief much more than my Catholic family differed from the Methodist Vilbergs next door or the Quaker Mrs. Thiel across the street. Nor is it a pleasant thing to learn that the sacred writers used fictional techniques and assumed a cosmology of "firmament" and "demon" and "miracle," which—try as we might—we can never believe but only accept for "the sake of the tale." Nor is it always comfortable to read the Gospels as dramatic narratives in the manner of a "new critic." Remember your college literature text? Remember those "Study Aids" at the end of each selection? What are Peter's motives for X? Why does the author have angels appear just at Y? Is there anything *ironic* in the crucifixion? Try to see it from Jesus' point of view.

And Mark's Gospel makes everything worse. Even when we have come to grips with childhood illusions, reading it can be a startling experience. His "failed" Jesus is nothing like the figure taught to us. Instead he is man unsuccessful with family and friends and hated by the authorities both religious and civil. He communicates puzzles rather than moral dicta, preaches an apocalyptic kingdom that doesn't arrive, suffers a death that is cursed by scripture. At best, Mark's Jesus acts like those early prophets, Amos and

Hosea: antiestablishment visionaries who were fooled by their own epiphanies, splendid, short-tempered, erratically compassionate. Like Zephaniah, Jesus believed in the coming Day of the Lord, and like that minor prophet he was wrong. It is of Mark's Gospel that Werner Kelber asked, "What could possibly be the good news of such a story?" (*Mark's Story of Jesus,* 88).

To answer that question, some modern theorists—as we have seen— take the initial analysis of the Messianic Secret a step further. To these critics, Mark is not only contrasting Jesus' un-understanding disciples with his own later "eschatological community," but using these foolish and unfaithful disciples to represent the failed Jewish-Christian church in Jerusalem, which by the time he wrote has had to flee the city and has perhaps taken up with pseudo-Christs and fallacious ideas. This is sometimes called Mark's "corrective theology." Another possibility is that Mark and his *own* community have for some reason had to reevaluate their own view of what we now call "the historical Jesus." Burton Mack, for instance, comments that this Gospel was composed "in order to understand how history could go the way it had and the Jesus movement [Mark's] still be right about its loyalties and views" (*Who Wrote the New Testament,* 152). This is to say that Mark's group itself has had to struggle to see is that the resurrected Christ is now present in the community—which is the "good news." Jesus Christ *is* the gospel.

I for one have trouble imagining that this Gospel was built on such clever rhetorical devices or that its writer was all *that* concerned about theology down in Jerusalem. Yet the foundation of these theories—the solution to the Messianic Secret—seems accurate. On the evidence of the text, Mark must have held that, though Jesus' mission on earth appeared to be a failure, it had succeeded as a mystical presence in the hearts of his readers. The distinction Mark implies, therefore, between Jesus of Nazareth and the risen Christ was obviously useful to the early church.

Indeed, so useful was it that it has never left Christianity, being nearly identical to the early-twentieth-century distinction between the "Jesus of History" and the "Christ of Faith." Originally that pair of epithets was intended to allow liberal Protestants to neglect the Jesus of *scholarship*, a person who, especially in Mark, gets angry, makes mistakes, is ambiguous about who he is, and dies in despair. In his place, nineteenth-century Christianity concentrated on that postresurrection spiritual being folks prayed to and relied on—a creature not wholly different from the middle-class ideal of a father. That shift of emphasis has continued, of course, right down to today, encouraged by such "objective" readings of the New Testament as we are now engaged in. The most recent invocation of this distinction that *I* have encountered is in a piece by John Garvey in *Commonweal* for January 29, 1993, dealing with such objective scholarship: "The Christ of faith is the only Jesus who can finally matter to a believer."

The theological difficulty with this notion should be obvious. It makes the New Testament irrelevant to the faith, and it turns the faith into whatever happens to be considered true by a given group of people. Moreover, an emphasis on the risen Christ was attractive when most people believed in him as a matter of course; but today, most of us have no such confidence. Instead of feeling superior to the apostles, we see them as our *representatives*. Like them, we fail to understand. Yet we are nonetheless moved by the large outlines of the Gospel. Contrary to Garvey, our emotions are very likely to be with the historical Jesus, theology be damned. Martin Hengel has expressed it this way: "My view is that these brute facts have the character that Goethe once attributed to a Dutch painting: their truth hits us in the eye. The brute facts have . . . a concentrated, alarming evocative power just as they stand."

Yet these same "facts" are the source of that sadness with which I began this chapter. Having read Mark's Gospel, I have learned what the members of his community had, or thought they had: the true knowledge of the risen Lord and a confidence in their apocalyptic faith. But what good has this produced in me? Forgiveness, hope, joy, a sense that life is not some sort of bad joke, "a song to make death tolerable," as William Carlos Williams wrote? No, I haven't found that sort of thing—perhaps we *never* find such things in literature. What I found was *just a book*, a sad beautiful tale from a different age and culture, full of bravery and cowardice, with mystery, blind terror, and savagery to rival *Lear*. Mark is a kind of poem, a song with a memorable tragic splendor, like that of a Greek play. In his Peter lies our personal tragedy; in his Jesus—a man fated beyond his most despairing dreams, unable to solve the puzzle of himself or the world—lies the tragedy of mankind. There are no answers in Mark.

To deal with this sadness, Christian critics often maintain the circular view that in order to read any part of scripture correctly one must first *believe*. Recent apologists tend to soften this position verbally, but hold it all the more. Here is the late, respected Catholic journalist, Peter Hebblethwaite, in a *National Catholic Reporter* review of A. N. Wilson's *Jesus: A Life*: "Understanding the New Testament presupposes some sort of commitment to the person and the cause of Jesus as well as to the believing community we call *church*." But this argument seems to me "the last refuge of a scoundrel"—though certainly Hebblethwaite was a scholar and a gentleman. What I mean is: surely Christian belief must begin *somewhere!* And where else would it begin but in the earliest Gospel? If I cannot read Mark prior to belief—if I cannot read it in "neutral," as it were—where *can* I begin the Christian pilgrimage?

But now I hear a critic whisper that there *is* no neutral, that Derrida or Gadamer or Wittgenstein or *somebody* has conclusively shown that all we ever have is an interpretation of a text, never a text. It is this sort of contemporary hermeneutics that Charles Davis must have had in mind when he told the Canadian Society of Biblical Studies that "objective" historical criticism of scripture has "lost all value for theology." Davis's view is that theology has to be separate from and prior to the reading of these enigmatic texts, a position which is the same as Hebblethwaite's, but with a learned gloss—a more forthright statement of what Garvey was saying.

But must we really begin by first accepting some sort of interpretive and denominational religious scheme and then go on to ratify that scheme page by page, reading the Gospel as one long proof text for what we *already* believe. No, thanks. We've been down that street. And even if we were so minded, would it work? Is reading the New Testament really so intimately connected with faith as the preachers traditionally have said? Surely some of you readers are Christians committed to the interpretation current in your believing community. (I sometimes think I am myself.) Has our *sensible* reading of Mark altered that commitment? Did your belief render the sad tale joyful or turn defeat into triumph? Let me suppose that I have convinced you that Mark's Jesus was a kind of failure who worked a few unimpressive miracles, proposed no innovative ethics, lost the esteem (or at least the loyalty) of his companions, was deliberately ambiguous before the authorities, had in any case no intention of founding a religion, and finally predicted an apocalypse that never happened. Did all that change your view of *Him?* Or did you find this Jesus—what shall I say—more attractive, more admirable, more lovable now that you recognize his failure? Do you perchance even think more highly of him now, the way you might think of a deliberately tragic figure: Othello, for instance, who also died for love?

What I am suggesting is that a sensible reading of Mark reveals a better Gospel than we have heretofore known, a Gospel for which no apology is necessary, the good news of a failed Jesus who paradoxically triumphs. In what proved to be almost his last letter from prison, Dietrich Bonhoeffer described this "failure" of the crucified Jesus in classical yet modern Christian terminology:

> The God who lets us live in the world without the working hypothesis of God is the God before whom we stand continually. Before God and with God we

live without God. God lets himself be pushed out of the world on to the cross. He is weak and powerless in the world, and that is precisely the way, the only way, in which he is with us and helps us.

Theological paradox is one thing; devotion is quite another. One may therefore ask, Is it in fact possible to reverence the figure portrayed by Mark, to use him in some public "liturgy," to (let me bold) *pray* to him? Clearly, Bonhoeffer thought so; but he did not live long enough to argue the point. Increasingly I think so too. Unfortunately this notion seems radically illogical, blending together as it does literary, historical, supernatural personages. Sensibly, the Gospel of Mark is just a book.

CHAPTER 2

The Achievement of Matthew

The Two-Source Theory and Q

The way we have just read the Gospel of Mark has been a long time coming—for good or ill. Even the corrected text we have read, which stops abruptly at 16:8 and lacks any evidence of the Lord's resurrection, is relatively "new." This last often shocks the devout more than any other notion. But the fact that the New Testament is periodically corrected is only one of the many results of the science of textual criticism, which had its remote origin and chief impetus in the Reformation; for the Protestant reformers considered an accurate Bible their religion's first requirement. "The true Christian pilgrimage," wrote Luther, "is not to Rome, or Compostela, but to the prophets, the Psalms, and the Gospels." He believed it was a pilgrimage open to all, because "the Holy Spirit is the plainest writer and speaker in heaven and earth, and therefore His words cannot have more than one, and that the very simplest, sense which we call the literal, ordinary, natural sense" (see W. G. Kümmel, *The New Testament: The History of the Investigation of its Problems,* 22–23).

Luther was terribly wrong about this simplicity, but the concept of a "Bible-based" theology was a powerful motive for his fellow humanists to turn away from Jerome's Latin translation, the "Vulgate," and to search for a more accurate text. Because the Reformation happened to occur simultaneously with the renaissance of ancient learning, this search, in fact, had already begun. A Greek text was produced in Spain in 1514, and another was published two years later in Holland, by Erasmus. It was Erasmus's version, first issued in 1516, that Luther used for his monumental German translation. This text was based on only a handful of late manuscripts, which in retrospect have no great authority; but nevertheless it was a beginning—a beginning that remained "authoritative" until the end of the nineteenth century.

At present, an editorial committee must have in mind about five thousand documents or parts of documents. Of these, seventy-six are fragments written on papyrus and preserved by the Egyptian climate. The oldest, a tiny fragment of John's Gospel, dates from the first half of the second century. The Chester Beatty papyri include almost an entire third-century codex (book) of Paul's authentic letters—eighty-six pages. From the fourth century there survive three almost complete Greek texts on vellum, and hundreds more date from later centuries. All of these "witnesses," as they are called, contain errors: copyist's mistakes, deliberate "corrections," inclusions as text of what were marginal comments by a previous scribe, and so on. But beyond these kinds of problems there is the peculiarity that as far back as textual scholars can now go, they never come to a single "textual tradition." This is to say that these manuscripts all seem to derive from at least three different "types," which in some cases—the book of Acts, especially —can be startlingly different. In addition to the Greek witnesses, there survive parts of extremely old translations into Syriac, Old Latin, and Coptic which represent underlying Greek texts that may be authoritative. As this wealth of variant material has appeared, especially the great finds of the nineteenth century, it has gradually dawned on scholars that because of the number of significant, differing manuscripts, the text of the New Testament will always be in flux. That does not imply, however, that it cannot be constantly improved and better understood.

As early as 1678, for instance, a French priest, Richard Simon, rightly concluded that the authorial superscriptions of Matthew, Mark, Luke, and John had been attached to previously anonymous manuscripts sometime in the second century—they had no independent authority. Simon also noted that the story of the woman taken in adultery (John 7:53–8:11) did not appear in the earliest and best manuscripts, but "floated" among late copies of various Gospels, and that the so-called Johannine Comma: "For there are three that bear record in Heaven, the Father, the Word, and the Holy Ghost; and these three are one" (1 John 5:7, 8) was the work of a late trinitarian editor. It would be a mistake, however, to think of these early discoveries as neutral, scientific findings. Simon wanted to show, he said, that

> the great changes that have taken place in the manuscript of the Bible completely destroy the principle of the Protestants and the Socinians who only consult these same manuscripts of the Bible in the form they are today. If the truth of religion had not lived on in the Church, it would not be safe to look

for it now in books that have been subjected to so many changes and that in so many matters were dependent on the will of the copyist. (Kümmel, *New Testament,* 41)

This is still the basic Roman Catholic position. But that is to look far ahead; for now, we should note that most of the scholars who have made progress in biblical studies, regardless of denomination, were similarly concerned to prove that *their* version of the faith was the truth.

Simon's method and findings were far too startling, and too technical, to have had an immediate effect, but they became the foundation of modern textual criticism. As that discipline developed, it confronted disagreements not only among manuscripts but among the Gospels themselves. In asking why, scholars adopted an increasingly "critical" or rational approach to the texts, which produced startling results. The first of these was the solution to the so-called Synoptic Problem.

From the days of the earliest Greek fathers, it had been noticed that the first three Gospels were in some way connected. Looked at together, or "synoptically," they told very much the same story. No wonder. Nearly all of Mark appears in the other two, as against 65 percent of Matthew and 53 percent of Luke. Moreover, passages that are repeated in two or more Gospels are frequently nearly identical, showing that the authors were in part, at least, using a common and *written* Greek source. (We must remember that the characters in the Gospels are supposedly speaking Aramaic; therefore, the presence of verbal identity in Greek can only mean direct copying from manuscript to manuscript.) It was also noted that when these three Gospels differed they often contradicted each other—as with the infancy stories and genealogies in Matthew and Luke. Therefore the authors must have written in isolation from each other.

Yet the problem remained, Who copied from whom? To get at the truth of the matter, Jakob Griesbach printed a text in which he placed Matthew, Mark, and Luke in parallel vertical columns creating the name "synoptic." It was an invitation to study these Gospels in detail and to solve what was in essence purely a logical problem. Yet the beginning of the solution was suggested only in 1810 by Johan Eichnor and completed by Christian Weisse in 1838. Variously called the "Markan Hypothesis" or the "Two-Source Theory," and occasionally modified, it has become the basis of nearly all of contemporary New Testament scholarship. Here is a simplified version of the theory.

The two-source theory holds that Matthew and Luke are independently rewritten versions of Mark and that though these later evangelists also had unique materials of their own, they also made use of another common

The Two-Source Theory

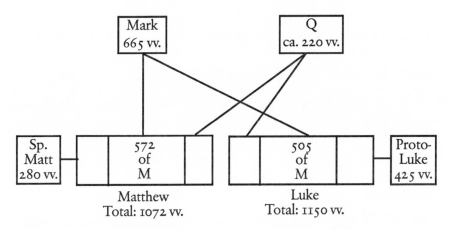

source. This second, common text has come to be designated Q, probably from the German word *Quelle,* or *source.* It represents the material found in both Matthew and Luke, but *not* found in Mark: about forty-eight separate pericopes (or units), in the neighborhood of two hundred verses.

There are, however, a few passages that appear in all three Synoptics in which Matthew and Luke agree *against* Mark, suggesting to most scholars that the later evangelists may have used a version of Mark slightly different from the one we have, or that here and there Mark and Q overlapped. There is also extant a fragment of the passion story called the *Gospel of Peter,* which some claim underlies the passion stories in *all* of these Gospels. These problems and others remain in debate without substantially affecting agreement about the basic relationships of the documents.

Some people have trouble imagining the theoretical Q, which is so important to this theory, and therefore they consider the whole analysis fanciful. But discovering a hypothetical document lying split up and scattered in two other existing Gospels is really no different from finding Mark's Gospel in those same documents—similarly split up and reworded. Nor is it different, as we shall see, from finding the Epistle of Jude embedded in 2 Peter. In the last two cases, however, we happen to have both original and rewrite; in the case of the Synoptic Gospels we have only the two rewritten versions and must reconstruct the common source from whatever both writers chose to use.

Belief in the reality of Q has been remarkably strengthened by the discovery in 1945 of a first-century document of the same type. The *Gospel of Thomas* is not Q, but it is in exactly the form that scholarship had predicted for Q: a non-narrative compilation of the sayings of Jesus. About a third of its contents is paralleled in the New Testament, and about half of this is also found in Q. Indeed, the *Gospel of Thomas* contains sayings of Jesus that are in some instances older than the versions preserved in the canonical Gospels. Some scholars therefore call it the "Fifth Gospel."

Since Q is both important and a little remote from everyday experience, college professors are fond of asking their students to cite "Q passages in Mark" or comment on "Mark's influence on Q." Anyone attempting to answer these questions fails the quiz—as I hope the diagram makes clear. By definition there is no relation between Mark and Q. But that is only because we do not have a copy of Q. If someday we actually discovered one, we would be able to see which verses Luke or Matthew omitted from their Gospels—if any—and whether these corresponded to anything in Mark. Without such a copy none of that is possible. Theoretically it is even impossible to say which member of a pair of Q passages represents the earlier, less-tampered-with version—the text in Matthew or the one in Luke. It is also theoretically impossible to say of any passage that appears in only *one* of the later Synoptics that it *was* or was *not* in Q. I say "theoretically" because scholars do in fact make these judgments. One meets such scholarly expressions as, "X is closer to the Q version of this statement," or "Y is almost certainly Q." The first means that of two parallel passages, one (again in the author's opinion) seems closer to the style and content of Q. The second means that though a passage is found only in one of the Gospels, it seems the kind of thing that *would have appeared* in Q. You will also discover that nearly every writer will assume, for reasons well established in the general study of ancient documents, that the version of a Q saying found in Luke is closer to the original.

The Q sayings were evidently compiled about the time Paul wrote his letters, twenty years or so before the composition of Mark; and from their similar sequence in Matthew and Luke it can be argued that they were originally grouped according to topics. Under some such title as "The Sayings of the Living Jesus," the author listed 114 "verses," beginning, it is thought, with two or three passages by or about John the Baptist, followed by the beatitudes and Lord's Prayer, and finally prophecies of the judgment. Obviously such an order is highly conjectural, since, as I have pointed out, it is impossible to say definitely what was in Q that the evangelists did *not* use. Nevertheless, it seems very likely that the collection contained no passion story at all; what survives has no allusion to Jesus' suffering and death on the cross, no notion of a sacrificial death, no resurrection. Instead of these traditional subjects of theology, the collection seems to be "permeated," to use Howard Clark Kee's word, with an apocalyptic expectation of "the end." Q is an antiestablishment document. It contains John the Baptist's remark that those who are listening to him are "a generation of vipers," certain orthodox types, apparently, who have come out from the city to hear him, Pharisees and Temple lawyers. Such men also had their counterparts in the Galilean towns of Capernaum, Chorazin, and Bethsaida, upon whom John also declares "woes." These "city types" are the enemies not only of the Baptist but of Jesus as well; for the Q compiler always thinks in terms of the Palestinian countryside, where his people live in small villages and mistrust the townsmen whom they symbolize as the chaff thrown into the bonfire at harvest time. In Q's "John sayings," this harvest has already begun; the axe lies ready at the root of every tree that has not brought forth good fruit. It is not, of course, *every* city dweller who is the enemy, only the successful, the rich, those in high position, the "first" who will be last, the well-fed, even the "laughers."

> But alas for you who are rich; you have had your time of happiness. Alas for you who are well-fed now; you shall go hungry. Alas for you who laugh now, for you will mourn and weep. (Luke 6:24–25)

Ideally, however, Q people do not judge, lest they be judged. Instead they *pray* for their enemies among the unrepentant rich and well-fed; and they ask God to change their hearts. Yet like Mark, they don't really expect this to happen; for they are convinced that Israel has habitually destroyed God's messengers. They think of their opponents as the descendants of those who not only killed the prophets but now have the effrontery to build them memorials. Consider this speech of Jesus from Q as it appears in Matthew 23: 33–35—one of a series of "woes."

> You snakes, you vipers' brood, how can you escape being condemned to hell? I send you therefore prophets, sages, and teachers; some of them you will kill and crucify, others you will flog in your synagogues and hound from city to city. And so, on you will fall the guilt of all the innocent blood spilt on the ground from innocent Abel to Zechariah son of Berachiah, whom you murdered between the sanctuary and the altar. [Jesus intends this to refer to the first and the last of the "prophets." But Q has him make an error: the Zechariah killed in this way was the son of Jehoiada, who died before 800 B.C.E. See 2 Chron. 24:20–21.]

Clearly, the Q people thought of Jesus as a prophet, but of what sort? Perhaps the most promising clues to their Christology come from contrasting their sayings with the rest of the New Testament. Though the Q community would appear to be overwhelmingly apocalyptic—something like 85 percent of the sayings preserved in Matthew and Luke have Jesus announcing the "end"—its sayings know neither a Son of Man who returns on the clouds or a Son of Man who hangs on the cross. The Q people use this title all right, but for them it seems to refer to their itinerant, mistreated leader, Jesus, a prophet who preaches the kingdom and for whom they would die. Nowhere is Son of Man connected with the heavenly figure from Daniel.

Moreover, Q never refers to Jesus as the Messiah; and though he seems to have worked a few cures, these are treated matter-of-factly and differ in no way from the cures of his followers. Certainly the details of the miracles hold no interest for the Q compiler. In fact, the most celebrated Q miracle (and its only narrative) may not be one; for the centurion's slave regains his health offstage with no interaction from Jesus. In Q, this story may be intended to express a simple hortatory openness to the Gentile world, ending in: "I tell you, nowhere, even in Israel, have I found faith like this" (Luke 7:9). Finally, Q people seem to have looked upon the death of Jesus only as the inevitable and tragic validation of his role as prophet, involving no sacrifice and no redemption. To put it positively, Jesus' role in Q is somewhat parallel to his role in Mark: to announce the coming of the kingdom and to live spiritually in each member of the group—or at least in each of their traveling preachers—even after his death.

> To receive you is to receive me, and to receive me is to receive the One who sent me. (Matt. 10:40)

Sometimes this indwelling of spirit almost amounts to a *thing*; note the word "peace" in the following:

> When you come to any town or village, look for some worthy person in it, and make your home there until you leave. Wish the house peace as you enter it, so that, if it is worthy, your peace may descend on it; if it is not worthy, your peace can come back to you. (Matt. 10:11–14)

Q folk are poor in everything except the Lord.

> . . . I am sending you out like lambs among wolves. Carry no purse, or pack, and travel barefoot. Exchange no greetings on the road. (Luke 10:4–5)

And here is the Q version of the Lord's Prayer. Note that in the context I have provided one should probably take the term "daily bread" literally.

> Father, thy name be hallowed;
> thy kingdom come.
> Give us each day our daily bread.
> And forgive us our sins,
> for we too forgive all who have done us wrong.
> And do not bring us to the test. (Luke 11:2–4)

By the time this passage was composed—perhaps in the 50s—Q people must have already been brought to the test: dragged into the synagogues and hauled before rulers, where, so they were counseled, they were to rely completely on the Lord. To people in authority, as to us today, they would have seemed very odd, even dangerous: members of an apocalyptic Jewish cult without an apocalyptic text; not legalistically inclined regarding the holiness code, rather lax in fact, yet completely devoted to spreading the word of the coming kingdom despite torture and death; opposed to the Jewish establishment in Jerusalem and in the other cities of Judea and Galilee, but open to Gentiles. Were these the kind of Christians Paul originally persecuted and sought for in Damascus? Were they the people who stirred up trouble in the Jewish community in Rome under Claudius? We cannot say for sure. But whoever they were, they have profoundly shaken the scholarship of the New Testament.

The disruption has occurred in the following way. Within the last decade, two scholars, John Kloppenborg and Arland Jacobson, have independently concluded that Q was formed in two major stages yielding two sorts of Q people and two underlying theologies. This situation has most recently been analyzed by Burton Mack in his *The Lost Gospel* (1993) and in *Who Wrote the New Testament?* (1995). Mack likens the original group of Q sayings to those of an itinerant "cynic" of the Hellenistic period, pointing in particular to the idealized portrait of such a teacher given by Epictetus in his *Discourses* (3.22)—though Epictetus, who was a contemporary of the Gospel writers and knew about the new Christian movement, did not himself make such a comparison.

The parallels are striking. Replying to an acquaintance attracted to that philosophy, Epictetus warns him that when you become a Cynic you have to change your life. First of all you have to recognize the all-pervasive role of God in the universe; for only if the divine power looks favorably on your new endeavor—if in fact you are an "elected" Cynic—will you succeed. You cannot "pretend" to this high calling, which demands that you consider the body and its pains as nothing. Nor must exile mean anything to you, for God is everywhere. You will endure beatings and revilings, love your enemies; feel no rage, no envy. Since all will despise you, you will have only your self-respect for comfort. You will only look to overcome what is called "good" or "evil" which are within you. You will be alone. "Where will you find me a Cynic's friend?" You will have no wife nor children—all humans are your family. You will in fact be God's spy, going about in adversity with a clean and oiled and smiling countenance. For the Cynic exhibits the qualities of his soul—"even his squalor ought to be cleanly and attractive." He is "free" in the sense that the heroes of all existentialist literature are free—

Camus' prisoner, for instance—or, as in ancient Zen teaching, *free* of all attachment, even to pleasure and pain.

Mack gives a good many reasons why such teaching and such teachers might have been found in Galilee in the first century, people he provocatively describes as "non-Christians," that is, followers of Jesus who thought of him simply as a teacher—not a Messiah, not the *christos*, not the resurrected one. Mack even prints a reconstruction of these people's original compilation of Jesus' sayings—a selection from Q which reads like the book of Proverbs or some other wisdom literature directed at living righteously through the rejection of the "things of this world."

At some later point, he argues, another author inserted into this original collection a whole series of apocalyptic predictions, including the Son of Man sayings. It was this later version, Mack argues—with obvious parallels in thought to Mark—that the two later Synoptic writers used as a source. But by that time (85–90 C.E.) belief in the imminent return of the Lord had faded; and therefore, while adopting all this apocalypticism, Matthew and Luke both had to tone it down and postpone the second coming to the end of time.

If true, this thesis seriously undermines the notion commonly accepted since Schweitzer that the earliest Christian preaching was apocalyptic. As I said in the introduction, however, my primary purpose is not to delve behind the text of the New Testament or to examine its sources but to read the canonical text intelligently. What is important here, therefore, is the use the evangelists make of Q, rather than its genesis.

It turns out that both Matthew and Luke preferred to keep source material in the same order in which they found it. This is true for their use both of Q and of Mark. Therefore, when one ignores intervening material, the Q sayings are found to be in the same order, even though Matthew inserted them sporadically throughout his Gospel and Luke placed them neatly in two so-called interpolations 6:20–7:35 and 9:51–13:34. With regard to Mark, specialists suggest that the order of incidents in both Gospels follows Mark from 6:6 on. Both evangelists try to improve Mark's Greek, and each eliminates passages he considers embarrassing or theologically repugnant. Mark 3:20; 7:31–37; 8:22–26; and 14:51, for example, are missing from both. In the first, Jesus' family thinks he is mad; the second and third contain those very primitive miracles I have commented on in the previous chapter, and the last describes that young man who runs away naked before the crucifixion. Presumably neither Luke nor Matthew could make any more sense of it than we can.

A final element in the two-source theory comes into view if one lifts out from the two later Synoptics all the material drawn from both Mark and Q. About one-fifth of Matthew and one-third of Luke remain, material for which no common source has ever been found; and, since these verses diverges widely, none is expected. What is this residue? There are first of all the two independent infancy narratives and genealogies, then the resurrection stories, followed by parts of Matthew's Sermon on the Mount (and Luke's Sermon on the Plain), individual versions of the Lord's Prayer (if they are not considered to be from Q), and differing accounts of the Ascension. Overall, the greatest degree of variation occurs in the infancy stories and the resurrection material; the least disagreement, though it is still noticeable, is found in the passion story.

In each case, these unique materials must be assigned either to the use of differing oral or written traditions or to authorial invention. This is an ever-present phenomenon in the Synoptics, one that the casual reader is likely to miss and the pious reader gloss over. A trivial example will suffice. Compare in detail Mark 2:15–17 with Luke 5:29–32. Here are two versions of the same pronouncement story ending with the idea that Jesus, like a doctor, did not come for the healthy (virtuous) but for the sick (sinners). The two "punch lines" are nearly identical. Mark has: "It is not the healthy that need a doctor, but the sick; I did not come to invite [to the kingdom] virtuous people, but sinners." Luke has: "It is not the healthy that need a doctor, but the sick. I have not come to invite virtuous people, but to call sinners to repentance." But in Mark, Jesus is speaking to some Pharisees who happen to observe him *at table in his own house in Capernaum* with "many bad characters." In Luke, he says this while attending a "big reception" held in his honor at the house of Levi. It is the innocuousness of the changed setting that is so striking. Luke clearly feels free to alter the context of the pronouncement as he feels fit in order to make a better story. But he also feels free to change Jesus' words. He is creatively editing a theological tale; he is not writing biography.

A s one may imagine, the discovery of these relationships among the Synoptic Gospels was only grudgingly accepted by Christian scholars and with a good deal of trauma. The notion that the evangelists were author-editors, rather than divine voices or impartial witness-reporters, seemed at first to be just another stage in the rational attack on scripture that had been going on since the eighteenth century. But the two-source theory has been constantly challenged for over one hundred years and has stood the test of time. Today it is fundamental to all New Testament scholarship. Yet it is remarkable how little known this idea is to the person in the pew, whose well-trained clergy seem reluctant to inform their congregations of the "facts" of the Bible, often promoting an unthinking fundamentalism in denominations that traditionally hold no such view.

This split between the scholarly view of the New Testament and the piety of the people has a long and checkered history. The early Greek fathers made a lot of very rational and courageous observations about Christian scripture, but by the beginning of the fifth century and the fall of the empire, these began to be ignored. Instead, the Roman fathers canonized the contents of the New Testament in both senses of the word: scripture was limited to the present twenty-seven texts in Jerome's translation, and the whole made sacred and normative. To be sure, few educated Christians in those days ever thought these documents "inerrant," in the manner of today's fundamentalists, but obvious contradictions in the sacred texts *were* embarrassing. To maintain an appearance of consistency Augustine invented (or borrowed) a fourfold method of interpretation guaranteed to get him out of any intellectual jam, while St. Thomas and the later Roman Catholic Church insisted on the necessity of "official" interpretation. Though he rejected this idea, Luther in fact exercised similar authority. In the various prefaces to his translation of the New Testament, for instance, he expressed doubts about the canonicity of Jude and Revelation, and he declared that James was not of apostolic origin. He called it "an epistle full of straw."

It was only in the eighteenth century that a consistently historical and rational view was adopted. In England, John Locke had laid it down that the content of revelation ("propositions above reason") could not contradict the plain dictates of sense, an idea John Toland then applied in his famous *Christianity Not Mysterious*. Initially, such works were intended as friendly attempts to "make sense" of the scriptures, but in time—as I have suggested above—other sorts of commentaries appeared. The most celebrated attack on the traditional reading of the New Testament was published by the German poet and critic Gotthold Lessing in 1774–78 as the "Wolfenbüttel Fragments." The actual author of these essays was Hermann Reimarus, a professor of oriental languages at Hamburg Academic Gymnasium who had been dead for nearly ten years. One of these so-called fragments, "The Aims of Jesus and His Disciples" is the beginning of modern interpretation of the New Testament. It is "not only one of the greatest events in the history of criticism," wrote Schweitzer, "[but] a masterpiece of general literature" (*Quest*, 15). Reimarus held that Jesus was a Jew and intended to stay a Jew and had no desire to found a new religion, that he had no notion of himself as a "suffering" Messiah who was to be sacrificed for the sins of humanity (an idea invented by the apostles) and that his basic gospel was apocalyptic, "repent for the end is nearly here." Reimarus also voiced many other views now widely accepted: that the Gospel titles Son of Man and Son of God and so forth all have only their simple (Judaic) meaning, that all allusions to the Trinity are later interpolations, that baptism was no part of Jesus' preaching (nor did he ever baptize anyone) that all the postresurrection materials found in the Gospels are inventions of the later evangelists, and finally that the miracles cannot be used to "prove" the truth of the Christian religion because they require as much proof as the proposition they are intended to demonstrate—a variant of the David Hume argument I have already discussed.

Reimarus was not *wholly* correct. He wrote before the realization that Matthew and Luke are independent revisions of Mark and therefore wasted a lot of time catching them in contradictions. He also had an unnecessarily low opinion of the evangelists, assuming that they were all liars who were disappointed that Jesus had not given them an earthly kingdom, and that having stolen Jesus' body and proclaimed a risen Lord, they tried to dupe their silly disciples for money. What has been truly lasting in Reimarus's work is the notion that each evangelist was an actual author, rather than a reporter, and that he told his tale in his own way for his own purposes. This "dangerous" notion, like the two-source theory of which it is a part, has been tested over and over again for a hundred years.

Paradoxically, during much of that same period a whole scholarly industry was devoted to discovering the "historical Jesus" by reading the Gospels as biographical reports! Even in 1906, when Schweitzer proved this search fruitless, it was still hard for many Christian scholars to accept that we cannot write a life of Jesus. It is difficult for some even today. Since the end of World War II, however, study of the editing, rewriting, and original composition in Matthew and Luke has produced a body of knowledge widely accepted even by the clergy. This so-called redaction criticism, from the German word for editor, *redaktor,* maintains that by studying Matthew and Luke in relation to Mark and Q we can arrive at the theological aim of each evangelist and therefore the concerns of the community for which each author wrote.

The Gospel of Matthew

It comes as a surprise to some people that from very ancient times a whole section of academia has been continuously studying and editing and commenting on the sacred texts of the Christian religion. I know Christians, good people but almost hopelessly ignorant of books and bookmaking, who have no inkling that anything like this has ever gone on. For such folks to read the Gospel According to Matthew as a rewrite of the Gospel According to Mark is difficult, if not impossible. The fact that Matthew traditionally stands first in the New Testament and that it is obviously the core text for the Christian liturgy makes the hurdle all the higher.

Yet now that you have read Mark closely, you must realize why, after fifteen to twenty years, it failed to satisfy—why somebody *had* to rewrite it. As the German scholar Willi Marxsen comments, "Mark's gospel could fulfill its task only in the period of its origin. A few years later it was already 'out of date.'" By the 90s, any feeling of hostility or superiority to the church in Jerusalem must have disappeared along with the disappearance of that church itself. Moreover, no one any longer needed encouragement to remain strong for the imminent arrival of the Lord. Instead, what was needed was an explanation of why he hadn't come. What had happened after the discovery of the empty tomb and what were they to expect in the future? "Thus it is *absolutely* necessary," says Marxsen, "for a later copyist to add a conclusion" (*Mark the Evangelist: Studies on the Redaction History of the Gospel*, 210).

As we have seen, the copyists did this—producing, in fact, three or four different endings. But merely adding a conclusion did not satisfy; the whole Gospel needed to be rewritten. Two of these rewritten versions have survived from two different Greek-speaking areas of the empire. In whatever localities Matthew and Luke worked, it is clear they wrote for communities that had somewhat different understandings of the Christian tradition. But they shared its dilemma. The *parousia*, or arrival of Jesus in the sky, was now indefinitely "delayed," and with that fact had come a wealth of questioning. What had occurred at Jesus' birth and resurrection? What was the status of Jews who opted for Jesus? What about those "sayings" in that pamphlet which was circulating? Not to mention the puzzles that arose over the teachings of independent preachers of the stamp of Paul. In sum, what was the new church to believe?

Clearly, what we might call the "belief circumstances" in these later communities were now different. Apocalyptic thought had lost its immediate relevance. The special knowledge or *gnosis* that had brought the group together in the first place was now too narrow to hold the new, larger numbers of believers, as people of various social classes joined the movement and as the feeling of social deprivation that may have originally motivated the group began to weaken. The problem now was how to broaden belief so that more and more could be accommodated. Yet paradoxically, because of the passage of time, it was also necessary to emphasize the historic and respectable roots of the whole spiritual enterprise. One solution to this problem is what I call "The Achievement of Matthew."

To understand Matthew's accomplishment it is necessary to keep in mind one overriding circumstance. Unlike Mark, Matthew addressed people who still thought of themselves as Jews, and he understood himself as a Jew writing for them. He is therefore intent on showing that Christianity is a natural development from the old ethnic religion, a development that is superior, respectable, and long-term—the fulfillment of prophecy. One result of this intention is that the Gospel of Matthew is nearly twice as long as Mark. It adds an infancy story (chapters 1–2) intended to show that from birth Jesus was indeed the fulfillment of Jewish messianic hopes, and it introduces a great deal of Jewish-oriented preaching material tucked into what look to be five successive sections, each composed of an "action" passage (journey, miracle, etc.) followed by a "parenetic" (teaching) passage. Each of these five sections ends in the phrase, "When Jesus had finished these sayings . . ." (3:1–7:29; 8:1–11:1; 11:2–13:53; 13:54–19:1a; 19:1b–26:1). Coming after these two major additions and the structural revisions they necessitate is Matthew's account of the passion. The text closely follows Mark's story, but concludes with a new and independent version of the resurrection and commissioning. That the whole is consciously organized is indicated not only by those key repetitive phrases but by the formulas used to mark "proof text" passages. These are quotations lifted out of context from the still not completely settled Jewish scriptures and applied to events of Jesus' life to prove that he was the fulfillment of the ancient religion (1:23; 2:15, 18, 23; 4:15–16; 8:17; 12:8–21; 13:35; 21:5; 27:9–10).

The Gospel begins with a genealogy of "Jesus Christ"—given as if *christos* were a proper name. Matthew traces Jesus' ancestry from Abraham to David and then through the royal line of Judah to Jaconiah (who was king in the Babylonian exile) and then to Joseph, husband of Mary. Each of the three sections is made up of fourteen ancestors—a number numerologically equivalent to the Hebrew *D-W-D*, that is, "David," though three kings must be dropped to achieve this. This list is different from the genealogy in Luke, a fact that indicates the writers' independence—no two authors writing across from each other in the Jerusalem Public Library would have produced these two genealogies—and their different emphases.

The two legend-like nativity narratives demonstrate the same thing. The only constants are Joseph, Mary, and the virgin birth in Bethlehem under Herod. All else is not only different but *very* different. Unfortunately, festive department store windows and unscholarly Christmas cards have shuffled the two sets of details in our minds. To prove to yourself that Matthew and Luke have two separate, largely legendary accounts, therefore, you probably need to read the stories successively at one sitting. We "will wait on you"—as Billy Graham used to say, as he gave his altar call to the upper deck at Yankee Stadium.

Beyond their obvious differences, you will have observed that both of these opening accounts, but especially Luke's, are written in a kind of "fairy-tale" prose style. This manner of writing is sometimes called "Septuagint Greek," from the Greek translation of Hebrew Scripture made about 250 B.C.E. In both Matthew and Luke, this initial style contrasts strongly with the rest of the Gospel. I am not suggesting that these two evangelists adopted a deliberately archaic Greek for their nativity stories. Rather, it seems likely that this language represents their separate sources. Moreover, the events in these infancy stories are never referred to again. In Matthew, nobody later knows anything about the slaughter of the innocents or the visit of the astrologers; in Luke no one is subsequently aware that Jesus and John the Baptist are related. In neither Gospel is there even any further reference to a virgin birth! Indeed this miracle does not *exist* anywhere else in the New Testament, neither in Paul nor Q nor Mark nor John, nor in the later documents; and only Matthew sees it as the fulfillment of a prophecy at Isaiah 7:14 in the Septuagint. (Yet as I write I have a 1963 Cambridge University Bible commentary before me which reads, "There is no adequate reason to doubt that the virgin birth is historical.")

Why were such tales told? Like the genealogies, both infancy stories may have originally been attempts to refute allegations of illegitimacy, and/or add grandeur to Jesus' humble birth. This will seem less strange if one reflects that in the Hellenistic period, a virgin birth was awarded to several important ancients including Alexander the Great, who was delighted with the story and frequently repeated it. Writing at roughly the same time as Matthew, Plutarch tells us that Alexander's mother, Olympias, had dreamed of being impregnated by a thunder bolt (Zeus) the night before Alexander's conception. Others saw her sleeping in the garden with a snake (Zeus Ammon). Olympias herself modestly denied her son's divine parentage; but her coquettish rejection of the idea seems to suggests the opposite: "Does Alexander never stop slandering me to Hera?"

In Matthew, the story of the virgin birth is consonant with the ruling purpose of the whole infancy tale: to legitimize Jesus as the messianic, Davidic heir. Dreams and angels conspire to stage-manage a plot in which Jesus of Nazareth must be born in David's hometown of Bethlehem, "From Bethlehem shall come a governor for Israel" (Micah 5:1); and like David also he will be pursued by a murderous king. Perhaps more importantly, these stories also echo the Moses saga in a curiously inverted way. As Elaine Pagels has pointed out, Jesus will first experience an exodus *to* Egypt, which is for him a safe haven or promised land. He is escaping a murderous enemy who is *not* Pharaoh, but a Jewish king—one who slaughters children nevertheless. Then, Matthew having turned the table right side up again, Jesus returns in triumph from Egypt *to* the promised land, "I called my son out of Egypt" (Hosea 1:1), where he will put forth a "law" from a "mount."

Neglecting all this Jewishness and abandoning their high school physics, slightly addled Christians take these stories literally and go in search of Matthew's Star of Bethlehem. Centuries of work hours have therefore been spent checking out supernova, the periodic returns of Halley's Comet and planetary conjunctions, in ignorance of the simple fact that none of these remote lanterns could lead even the wisest of wise men to a particular house on earth. This doesn't mean, however, that the story of the star has no meaning. Matthew (or his source) was probably thinking of astrological matters. Perhaps there existed a national horoscope of Judea in which some sort of new light would be "rising," that is, appearing just before dawn against the particular background of planets and fixed stars associated with the land of Israel. There was in fact a conjunction of Jupiter and Saturn in Pisces in 7 B.C.E. This is a good date, for it fits the tale's chronology, in which Jesus has to be born before Herod's death in 4 B.C.E.; but the light from such a conjunction of planets could have "led them"—or us—only in an intellectual sense. Matthew may also have had in mind a remark made by the pagan soothsayer Balaam at Numbers 24:17, "A star shall come forth out of Jacob, a comet arise from Israel. He shall smite the squadrons of Moab and beat down all the sons of strife." There is also a late Jewish *midrash*, or commentary, which speaks of a miraculous star that foretold the birth of Abraham even as astrologers were visiting Terah. Supposedly these earlier wise men went off to Nimrod with the news that "a lad has been born who is destined to conquer this world and the next." One should be careful, however; this story is late enough to have *itself* been influenced by Matthew.

And then there are those angels who keep bringing the news—which is precisely the alpha and omega of an angel, since the Greek word means "messenger." What is it with these angels? One shows up in a dream in Bethlehem to announce the child's sacred conception; another tells Joseph to take the family to Egypt; a third tells him to return. All such functionaries in Matthew—or are they only one?—are anonymous. Only in very late Judaism and subsequent Christian writings do angels have names. A reader is likely to recognize only Gabriel, Michael, and Raphael (in Tobit). Uriel, Remiel, Raguel, and Sariel are in the Apocrypha, and "Lucifer" seems to be a misunderstanding of a passage in Isaiah. A few other exotic angelic names in the ancient writings called "pseudepigrapha" are familiar only to specialists. But eventually the church will imagine whole hosts of angels, both dutiful and fallen—so many they couldn't be named, but had to be massed, like tulips, into Archangels and Seraphim and Thrones and so on.

In any case, angels are characteristic of Matthew. In Luke, as we shall see, an entirely different but equally legendary and "Jewish" set of images will provide a kind of Gentile hymn of feminine devotion to Jesus—a major theme of that Gospel. But why should *any* Christian writer make use of such material in 85 or 90 C.E.? The answer for Matthew, I believe, is that his Gospel is written in a time when serious diversity of belief begins to appear in Christianity. Among Matthew's intended readers were people still close to late Judaism, people who would respond to Jesus' connection to David and echoes of the Moses saga—as well as a tenacious reaffirmation of the law. Matthew knew of other Christians, however, Greek converts, who rejected the Jewishness of Jesus' reform, people who were *not* completely certain that he was the Messiah and certainly not convinced, as we shall see, that the Torah was still operative in their lives. This division in the church had been apparent since the 50s, when Paul described and deplored conflicts between Gentile-oriented and Jew-oriented Christians. Like Paul, Matthew is aware of the tension, but in contradistinction to Paul, he writes a document that celebrates tradition-keeping, Jewish Christianity. Indeed, Matthew is at pains to "correct" non-Jewish views of the Jesus story.

The fact that Jesus is the Messiah, therefore, far from being kept secret, dominates Matthew's Gospel from the beginning and accounts for all its Davidic and folkloric trappings. There is no Messianic Secret and no need for dull and disloyal disciples. By the time this text was written, Jesus' followers—now almost always called "apostles"—have become revered as the founders of the religion. It follows that they should be rehabilitated. You may recall that in Mark, after the miracle of the loaves and fishes, Jesus walks out onto the lake and climbs into the boat next to the disciples. Mark then typically comments, "At this they were dumbfounded for they had not understood the incident of the loaves; their minds were closed" (6:52).

Matthew rewrites the latter part of this passage as follows:

Peter stepped down from the boat, and walked over the water towards Jesus. But when he saw the strength of the gale, he was seized with fear; and beginning to sink, he cried, "Save me, Lord." Jesus at once reached out and caught hold of him, and said, "Why did you hesitate? How little faith you have!" They then climbed into the boat; and the wind dropped. And the men in the boat fell at his feet, exclaiming, "Truly you are the Son of God." (14:29–33)

Notice how this version, while still including a weakness of faith, actually restores the disciples to honor, making Peter both human and heroic. But it does much more. It provides a paradigm of Christian salvation, and in the phrase Son of God universalizes the Messiah concept. When Mark repeats this incident at 8:14–21, intensifying dramatically the disciples' lack of understanding, Matthew copies him but adds a final sentence: "Then they understood that they were to be on their guard . . . against the teaching of the Pharisees and Sadducees." In Mark, the disciples do not understand the parables and ask to have them explained. In Matthew, when Jesus asks, "Have you understood all this?" they reply, "Yes." At Mark's transfiguration, as we have seen, Peter and his friends do not "know what to say." In Matthew this line has silently been dropped.

Amplified by the sayings of Q, Jesus' preaching is presented in Matthew as five schematic sections which seem intended to demonstrate successively (1) that Jesus' role as Messiah means not the abandonment of the law but its perfection, "The Sermon on the Mount"; (2) that the new, reformed religion was first preached to Jews but now belongs to the whole world, "The Mission"; (3) that Jesus described his dream of a kingdom in memorable parables, "The Kingdom"; (4) that the means of bringing about this kingdom are a fully empowered organization, "The Church"; (5) that eventually, at the end of this present dispensation, Jesus will return as Mark had predicted, "The Apocalypse."

The first of these five sections (3:1–7:29) begins with Jesus' baptism and continues through the temptation in the wilderness, the "calling" of the disciples, and their first preaching and healing tour in Galilee, to culminate in the long Sermon on the Mount. Mark provides the skeleton of this section, including the introductory scene of John the Baptist at the Jordan and the quotation from Isaiah about a voice in the wilderness; but when Jesus comes to the river to be baptized himself, Matthew adds:

John tried to prevent him, saying, "I need to be baptized by you, and you come to me?" But answering, Jesus said to him, "Let it be so for now, for it is suitable for us to fulfill all righteousness." Then John allowed him to come. (Matt. 3:14–16)

In the early days of the church this whole business of baptizing, especially John's baptizing of Jesus, was a sore spot; Matthew's treatment is typical. You may be so familiar with these lines that you don't realize that they don't mean anything. *Why* is this strange baptizing a "fulfillment of righteousness"? John himself doesn't seem to think so! The phrase has puzzled thoughtful Christians from that day to this.

There now follows a good deal of Q material: the generation of vipers speech, which I have already spoken of, as well as the expanded temptation in the desert with its character, *Diabolos*, out of Job, and its ministering angels. But when Jesus returns from the wilderness, Matthew again adds two typical verses of his own: "Having left Nazareth he came into Capernaum on the seacoast in the district of Zebulum and Naphtali. This was to fulfill the passage in the prophet Isaiah which tells of . . ." (Matt. 4:13). The allusion is to Isaiah 9:1–2, where these two tribes are mentioned (along with the land of Galilee) as having a "great light" come to them, probably the birth of a Davidic prince. To a modern reader of Isaiah, the verses have absolutely no connection to Jesus. But, as I warned you in the introduction, Matthew feels perfectly free to apply them to Jesus anyway, as if Isaiah had written with Christianity in mind.

The largest and most important part of Matthew's first "book" of preaching material is, of course, the famous Sermon on the Mount (5:1–7:29), which includes the beatitudes, the Lord's Prayer, and many other monuments of the Christian religion. Roughly based on Q material and parallel to Luke's Sermon on the Plain, it also makes use of some Q verses that appear in Luke 11–13. But Matthew has so expanded and reworked this sermon that it is no longer possible to say what is source material and what is authorial. He has eight or nine beatitudes, for instance (5:3–11), where Luke has only four (6:20–22). In order to make the situation clearer, I have italicized the "underlying" Lukan version in the following translation, which is my own. Is Matthew simply varying something he has found in Q, or does he have some undiscovered source?

> *Blessed are the poor* in spirit *because theirs is the kingdom of the heavens.*
> *Blessed are those who mourn [weep]* because they shall be comforted
> *[laugh]*
> Blessed are the gentle because they shall inherit the earth.
> *Blessed are those who hunger* and thirst for righteousness *because they shall be fed to the full.*
> Blessed are the merciful because they shall be treated with mercy.
> Blessed are the clean of heart because they shall see God.
> Blessed are the peacemakers because they shall be called the children of God.
> Blessed are they who are persecuted for the sake of righteousness because theirs is the kingdom of heaven.
> *Blessed are you whenever men reproach you and persecute you and speak all sorts of evil against you because of me. Rejoice and be glad, because your pay is great in the heavens for thus did they persecute the prophets*

who were before you. [This is a little stronger in Luke, but essentially the same.]

First of all it should be noted that these are not discrete, conditional promises as in "all those who do this particular thing will receive that particular blessing, while those who do this other . . ." and so on. Like similar blessings in the Hebrew Scripture, these describe a single mental attitude or condition to which attaches a single eschatological promise: the kingdom of heaven. In fact "blessed," though traditional, is probably not a good translation; in this context the Greek means something like "happy are they who."

In any case, it is only when we compare the two versions that we realize how the Gospel of Matthew has dominated Christian thought. Raymond Brown has written:

> People who know by heart the Lucan form of the Lord's Prayer could probably hold meetings in a telephone booth; the number of people who know Matthew's form of the Lord's Prayer is coterminous with the number of Christians in the world. Those who are even aware that Luke has four beatitudes are very few, while Matthew's eight beatitudes have been committed to memory and heart by countless believers. Only students are aware that Luke has a Sermon on the Plain, while even for non-Christians Matthew's Sermon on the Mount is the quintessential message of Jesus. (*The Churches the Apostles Left Behind,* 124–25)

But *is* it a quintessential message? Or have people made these lines into a largely unread shibboleth which stands for whatever they themselves happen to believe and whatever way of life they prefer? In fact, haven't the evangelists themselves set the example for such subjectivity? As you can see from the italicized words, the "condition" for being happy or blessed in Luke is being poor and put-upon. In Matthew happiness goes to the "poor in heart"—whatever that may mean. Luke celebrates the hungry; Matthew those who "hunger *after justice*." Assuming that the Lukan versions are closer to Q, why does Matthew convert these sayings into quite conventional notions from Judaic piety and the psalms? The answer may lie in a technique of biblical study called "form criticism," which attempts to reconstruct "the situation in real life" (*Sitz im Leben*) in which a given text originated. What situation in "real life" would elicit these changes and additions to Q? Many scholars think that that situation is described in the passage immediately following in Matthew 5:17ff., in which the author is also embroidering around a Q saying (which I have italicized).

> Do not think that I have come to abolish the law or the prophets; I have come not to abolish but to fulfill. *For truly I tell you, until heaven and earth pass*

away, not one letter, not one stroke of a letter, will pass from the law until all is accomplished. Therefore, whoever breaks one of the least of these commandments, and teaches others to do the same, will be called least in the kingdom of heaven; but whoever does them and teaches them will be called great in the kingdom of heaven.

It is important to read carefully what Matthew's Jesus says here about people who, like Paul, had in fact set aside the law. Are they condemned to Gehenna? Cast into outer darkness? No. Preachers of such un-Jewish theology will take only a *lower* place in the kingdom of heaven. What Matthew's Jesus objects to is their inferior *but still acceptable* version of Christianity. The *better* way of being a Christian, Matthew believes, is to hold to the law even more firmly than those who still remain in the synagogues unconverted, "the Pharisees and doctors of the law." In a very modern moment, however, Matthew's Jesus accepts other views. Matthew seems aware that for twenty years or more, both in the Near East and as far away as Rome, there have been radical Christians who have preached the *end* of the law. He puts into Jesus' mouth an objection to this doctrine—but only a mild one.

With its insistence on a continuity with Judaism, however, this passage provides a foundation statement for the great "two-book" religion that ecclesiastical, historical Christianity will become; and it may have been intended to function in just that way. More immediately, it is a window into Matthew's own world. Can we ask where? Well, somewhere in a city where Greek is the common language (Aramaic is used in the countryside) and where there is a sizable population of Christians who are converts from Judaism. These conditions seem to exclude Palestine but suggest someplace like southern Syria, where converts from Judaism retained their customs and their sense of Torah while mixing with Gentile Christians. Because the clearest earliest reference to this Gospel comes from Ignatius, bishop of Antioch, this chief city of Syria is often taken as the probable place of the composition of this Gospel. As I have suggested, these Christians sound much like those Paul preached to twenty years or so earlier in that same city, as he tells us in Galatians. The first readers of Matthew may have been an Antiochean group still Jewish-oriented, a group that was perhaps still in dialogue with scribes and Pharisees, who simply couldn't stomach Paul's rejection of the law.

The Gospel of Matthew was meant to instruct such people in a version of the "good news" that is superior both to traditional Judaism and to the Gentile interpretation of the Way. Its beatitudes are intended to interiorize, spiritualize, and thus "perfect" the law given by Moses. The same attempt "to perfect" the law is evident in the so-called antitheses which follow.

These sayings take the form, "You have been told [Torah] . . . , but what I tell you is . . ." [Matthew's Gospel]. "You have been told that murder is bad, I tell you anger is just as bad; you have been told adultery is bad, I tell you lust is just as bad," and so on. To many these statements have always sounded unrealistic, acceptable only under the extreme conditions predicted by an apocalypse; but such a view poses a problem. Unlike Mark, Matthew accepts the "delay of the *parousia*" and rejects the notion that dire circumstances are to be expected in the immediate future. It would seem, therefore, that Matthew cannot be preaching an interim of perfection. A solution may lie in the "Jewishness" of these verses (5:23–24), which assume that the Temple cult is still functioning: "leave your gift at the altar etc." One should recall that within that Jewish world teachers were in the habit of setting "fences" around the Torah, rigid man-made admonitions intended to protect one from ever breaking a God-given rule. The most famous of these is the prohibition against eating meat and dairy products together (a rule made by humans) in order to avoid any chance of eating an animal cooked in its mother's milk (a God-given rule). Perhaps Jesus preaches that you should avoid anger ("except with good cause," add some manuscripts) to make sure that you never injure or murder another, you should suppress desire in order never to commit adultery, and so on. In effect, such dicta make up an idealized, extreme ethic which is nevertheless interpreted realistically. In this same way, Christians have always managed to preach sainthood, but accept—even be grateful for and surprised by—a bare obedience to the law. That something like this must be the case is indicated by Matthew's repetition of those curious hyperbolic figures of Mark: plucking out an offending eye or cutting off an offending hand. These can *only* be "poetic fences." *We* understand this; *Jesus* understood it too.

On the other hand, some Q admonitions may have originally been meant literally: to turn the other cheek, to let the fellow who sues you for your shirt have your coat also, and to go another mile with the Roman soldier who forces you to carry his pack for the statutory distance. Originally, all such sayings must have had a certain radical, primitive—perhaps even comic—reality, and they may stand very close to the actual words of Jesus. But in Matthew, as in our modern churches, these admonitions are consistently lumped with the hyperbolic "fences" to take the sting from them and to produce a kind of genially charitable Christianity. In fact, Matthew's Gospel is a studied reinforcement of traditional—what might be called "middle-of-the-road"—values, right down to the qualification of Mark's radical ban on divorce: "except for unchastity."

A good many people are shocked when they discover this "middle-class" element within the New Testament. They seem to believe that though they themselves are bereft of heroic virtue, early Christians and Jesus himself must have exemplified a gospel of radical perfection. Yet Jesus' ethic as presented in Matthew is both realistic and traditional. Jewish scholars have made this point so often they are weary of it; but the same is true if we view it from a Greek point-of-view. Like the ethics of Aristotle or Epictetus, some of Matthew's injunctions deal with what we might think of as etiquette, rather than morality. In Matthew, we are enjoined to perform charitable acts in secret, for instance, and keep a smile on our faces when fasting, that we should pray only in private and even then briefly. Such suggestions would have seemed quite proper to his Hellenistic audience; for lists of virtues of the day typically reflect such a mixture of morals and manners.

Perhaps we should note in passing that where Jesus' ethical thought differs from that of pagan thinkers, the pagans sometimes have the better of the argument. Contrast the notions of *pride* as they generally appear in the Gospels and in Aristotle. The former borders on self-abasement; the latter is justified as a right estimate of one's worth. In fact, Christian ethicians have almost always urged the Aristotelian view, while protesting that they follow the New Testament. On the other hand, Jesus' aphorisms against "stress" sound at once truly modern and truly ancient: Don't worry about what you are to eat, drink, or put on; imitate the birds. Can you do anything about these things, anyway? Notice the flowers: they are not anxious, etc. All these ideas are quite wonderfully phrased and as true as any folk wisdom.

We should not leave this first preaching section of Matthew's Gospel without commenting on his version of the Lord's Prayer, the well-known, liturgical version of that text. Though modern Christians rarely notice it, this prayer is an apocalyptic invocation which asks for the early return of the Lord. Also its forgiveness of *debts*—a good translation which is preserved in many English versions, rather than Luke's "sins"—may have been the original monetary meaning for the Q people. In a similar way, one should note the unapologetic demonology of "save us from the evil one." Finally, it should be noticed that the beloved, "For thine is the kingdom and the power and the glory forever. Amen" is a liturgical flourish added in some later manuscripts.

Jesus finishes this first discourse at 7:28–29. He then comes down from the heights and enters Capernaum, where begins the second panel of Matthew's material, 8-11:1, consisting of a series of miracle stories drawn from Mark, Q, and the author's own sources. Perhaps I have already said enough about miracles, but I must pause briefly over Matthew's version of that story which caught our attention in the previous chapter, the one about the woman who suffers from a hemorrhage. You may recall that in telling this anecdote Mark allows himself to enter into the thoughts of both the woman *and* the Lord and that he also conceives of a miraculous power which runs out of Jesus without his control. In repeating the story, Matthew seems at pains to follow his source as closely as possible; he even retains the odd organization by which this story is set within another miracle account. But Matthew does not allow himself to get inside Jesus' head, and he eliminates entirely that electrical power.

The real interest in this second section, however, is neither miracles nor revision techniques, but the important and illuminating commissioning scene Matthew constructs: the summoning of the Twelve, their list of names, and their rules for the road (10:1ff.). Matthew takes over Mark's prohibitions and then adds further restrictive rules which suggest that earliest Christianity may have been much more ascetic, much more radical than has been generally believed. In addition to going out without money and with only one cloak, the disciples are now forbidden sandals and staffs. Are we looking at an actual way of life in these injunctions? Most scholars think we are—the way of life of the Q people or their preachers.

It is here that Jesus gives an order that occurs nowhere else: "Do not go along the roads to the gentiles, and do not go into any Samaritan city. But go rather to the lost sheep of the house of Israel." (He will make the same point to the Canaanite woman in Matt. 15:24). Most readers are astonished at this injunction because it so clearly jars with the famous ending of Matthew's Gospel, "Go therefore to all nations and make them disciples . . ." (28:19). Perhaps Matthew has inherited two contrasting passages reflecting the division of the early church into a "Jewish" and a "Greek" camp—the one centered in Jerusalem (until 70 C.E.), the other in Antioch or even Rome. A more profound analysis may be that the two sayings represent the contrast between Jesus of Nazareth and the risen Christ. When Jesus was alive and preaching in Palestine, he thought his mission was to pull together the disaffected elements of Judaism to create a reform movement. Only after he had been murdered by the Jews of Jerusalem—Matthew is unfortunately very clear about assigning the blame—did his followers extend the mission to include the sort of mixed community Matthew is writing for. Either way, this text conflates two periods in the life of early Christianity: the time of Jesus and the time of the risen Christ.

I realize such an explanation will not satisfy all readers, primarily because of its implication for Christology. Explanations of this type imply that the Synoptic Jesus was in some *fundamental* way different from the risen

Christ, a more radical form of the distinction between the Jesus of history and the Christ of faith. This form of the notion was first promulgated by David Friedrich Strauss in 1832. Strauss held that in the Synoptic Gospels Jesus is not aware of being the Christ, as exemplified in his use of such titles as Son of Man and Messiah. Even the most casual reader notices that Jesus often speaks of these personages in the third person and equivocates when someone asks if *he* is the Son of Man or the Messiah. Following Strauss, scholars have suggested that it was the postresurrection *tellers* of these tales, the evangelists, who appropriated the titles. Apparently, though these writers had traditions about Jesus in which he spoke as if the Son of Man and the Messiah and so on were a third party—or at least that he was not *yet* such a personage—they also had a firm faith that he *was* the Christ. In trying to square their tradition with their faith, they muddled their texts. Matthew tries from the beginning to present a Jesus who is the Messiah, though he leaves the ambiguity in Jesus' speech. The effect is as if he were portraying Jesus from both a pre- and a postresurrectional point-of-view. Such conflation of time becomes clear when Jesus gives his followers warnings that they will be betrayed to the Sanhedrin and the synagogues, where they will be whipped—sufferings that never occur in the Gospels and clearly come from the later days of the church.

In this Gospel Jesus also says to the apostles, "You shall not get through the cities of Israel before the Son of Man comes." This is the passage of Matthew that set the young Albert Schweitzer on his lifelong study of scripture. In the first chapter of *Out of My Life and Thought*, Schweitzer recalls that, having been drafted for military service in the autumn of his first year at the university, he had taken his Greek New Testament along on maneuvers in his haversack. "On a certain rest day which we spent in the village of Guggenheim," he writes, "I concentrated on the tenth and eleventh chapters of Matthew, and became conscious of the significance of what is narrated in these chapters by him alone, and not by Mark as well." Schweitzer noted that when Jesus says, "You shall not get through the cities of Israel before the Son of Man comes," he "doesn't expect to see them again"! No writer of a later generation would ever have had the temerity to put words into Jesus' mouth that were so clearly "belied by the subsequent course of events," Schweitzer thought. Therefore, when we find Jesus saying that the Son of Man will appear in the clouds before the generation listening to him has passed away (Mark) or that the Son of Man will appear before the apostles will have finished preaching to the cities of Israel (Matthew) we are dealing with the speech *of Jesus himself*. Schweitzer concluded that Jesus really expected the apocalyptic end to occur very shortly; it was the foundation of his preaching—but *Jesus was mistaken.*

Today these same passages are thought to be creations of the early church, even by such conservative scholars as John Meier—written by "people seeking to reassure themselves of Christ's coming in glory as the years passed and with no parousia in sight." Yet the logic of Schweitzer's argument is still striking. Why would even *these* Christians invent such unfulfilled sayings? Schweitzer tells us that he spent a good deal of his remaining years at the university puzzling over such passages, which he believed to be the key to understanding the Synoptic Gospels. His overall view may be summarized as follows: that Jesus' thought was wholly governed by the conviction that the end was near at hand, that he conceived of this end as commencing with the return in the heavens of the Son of Man and that he, Jesus, was not entirely convinced—and certainly didn't preach—that he himself was that apocalyptic figure. The Son of Man was to usher in a new state of supernatural existence, which Jesus described, perhaps only metaphorically, as a banquet. It was in that coming supernatural state that Jesus would be manifested as the Messiah. One's entrance to that state was obtained through unquestioning love. Noting that nineteenth-century research had failed to see this obvious situation because of its own preoccupation with liberal Christianity and modern Christology, Schweitzer came to a very wise conclusion about the origins of Christianity.

> The error of research hitherto is that it attributes to Jesus a spiritualizing of the late Jewish Messianic Expectation, whereas in reality He simply fits into it the ethical religion of love. Our minds refuse at first to grasp that a religiousness and an ethic so deep and spiritual can be combined with other views of such a naive realism. But the combination is a fact. (*Out of My Life and Thought,* chapter 4)

I will not try to settle the question; I present these matters only to illustrate what it means to read the Gospels in the light of scholarship.

The third section of the preaching material (11:2–13:53) begins with that enigmatic visit from John's disciples, who ask if Jesus is really the one who is to come. (Doesn't John remember whom he baptized?) This scene is followed by a series of "woes"—actually curses—which Jesus calls down on the cities of Galilee because they have been unimpressed by his miracles and by those controversy stories in which he has distinguished his doctrine from that of the Pharisees. These anecdotes again largely follow Mark, except where Matthew pauses to insert a proof text or a typical "hedge-perfection" statement of the type already discussed: "I tell you, on the day of judgment you will have to give an account for every careless word you utter..." (12:36–37). Here too is a collection of parables. But Matthew, having noted Mark's curious idea that Jesus uses these riddles to *hide* his meaning from the crowd—lest they understand—is at pains to correct it. He therefore goes back to Isaiah and quotes the entire passage Mark had referred to but in a variant Greek form. He does this in order to affirm that Jesus' hearers fail to understand because they *themselves*—not the Lord— have hardened their hearts. Here is Matthew's version of Isaiah.

> For this people's mind has become gross; their ears are dulled, and their eyes are closed. Otherwise, their eyes might see, their ears hear, and their mind understand, and then they might turn again, and I would heal them. (Matt. 13:15)

Typically, Matthew then adds another proof text from Psalm 78 as a conclusion to the speech—as if it also had been written by Isaiah.

> I will open my mouth in parables
> I will utter things kept secret since the world was made. (Matt. 13:35;
> quoting Ps. 78:2)

On the surface these "secrets" seem to be descriptions of that kingdom of heaven spoken of in the following parables. Jesus first compares the kingdom to a field of wheat into which an enemy has planted weeds, then to a mustard seed that grows into a large bush, then to yeast that enlarges the dough, then to a treasure of great price, a pearl, and a fishing net. Though in the traditional English versions each of these comparisons begins with "The Kingdom of Heaven is like ..," none of them describes *the kingdom of heaven*. Similarly, the images of the pearl of great price and the treasure in the field tell us only that the kingdom is valuable and hidden, not what it is. On the contrary, the comparisons to the mustard seed and the yeast seem to refer to the slow, steady spread of the faith and by implication the delay of the parousia. The saying about the yeast is particularly remarkable in that it converts a substance that generally has a negative image in Judaism into something positive. In its original context, this must have been done quite deliberately for shock value—like the drinking of symbolic blood (nonkosher) at the Last Supper.

In all such very old and possibly authentic sayings, Jesus seems to be describing the growth of some new understanding or new status, which is perhaps what he always meant by the notion of the "kingdom." Most interesting in this regard is the long metaphor of the sown field.

> The kingdom of heaven is like this: A man sowed his field with good seed; but while everyone was asleep his enemy came, sowed darnel among the wheat, and made off. When the corn sprouted and began to fill out, the darnel could be seen among it. The farmer's men went to their master and said, "Sir, was it not good seed that you sowed in your field? Then where has the darnel come from?" "This is the enemy's doing," he replied. "Well then," they said, "shall we go and gather the darnel." "No," he answered, "in gathering it you might pull up the wheat at the same time. Let them both grow together till harvest; and at harvest-time I will tell the reapers, 'Gather the darnel first, and tie it in bundles for burning; then collect the wheat into my barn.'" (Matt. 13:24–30)

Originally this story was probably meant to account for the fact that the worldly fortunes of believers and unbelievers do not differ—only their fortunes in the afterlife. Six verses later, however, Matthew has Jesus go inside and produce an interpretation which in its mythological detail strikes most scholars as deriving from Matthew's community of the 90s, rather than Jesus' world of the 30s.

> The field is the world; the good seed stands for the children of the Kingdom, the darnel for the children of the evil one, and the enemy who sowed the darnel is the devil. The harvest is the end of time, and the reapers are angels. As the darnel is gathered up and burnt, so at the end of time, the son of man will send his angels who will gather out of his kingdom every cause of sin, and all whose deeds are evil; these will be thrown into the blazing furnace, where there will be wailing and grinding of teeth. Then the righteous will shine like the sun in the kingdom of their father. If you have ears, then hear.

Let me emphasize that both parable and interpretation are unique to Matthew. What do they accomplish? To put it mildly, here is the whole of orthodox—one might say *Calvinistic*—eschatology: life on earth, the devil, judgment day—everything *except* a description of heaven. From one point of view, the Great Church to come will never recover from this vision; from another it would never have been "great" without it.

The fourth section of Jesus' preaching begins as he returns to Nazareth (13:54), where the people are "resentful of him" and where he does not perform many miracles "because of their lack of trust." Now the Pharisees and scribes come out from Jerusalem to quarrel with him. They want to know why Jesus' disciples do not ritually wash their hands before meals and they have been offended by his saying, "Listen and understand, it is not what goes into the mouth that defiles a person, but it is what comes out of the mouth that defiles." You may recall that Mark had glossed this remark with, "Thus he declared all foods clean," understanding it to be a rejection of the dietary laws. Matthew, as might be expected, has Jesus interpret his own remarks in a more traditionally Jewish way.

> Do you not see that whatever goes into the mouth enters the stomach, and goes out into the sewer? But what comes out of the mouth proceeds from the heart, and this is what defiles. For out of the heart come evil intentions, murder, adultery, fornication, theft, false witness, slander. These are what defile a person, but to eat with unwashed hands does not defile. (Matt. 15:17–20)

There follow further curses on the Galilean cities and the feeding–boat trip business is repeated, four thousand hungry picnickers, as opposed to five thousand in the first version. This and the passion story are the only extended passages included in all *four* Gospels. Afterwards, Jesus goes northwest toward Tyre and Sidon, where, meeting a "Canaanite" woman, he cures her demon-possessed daughter and—as noted above—repeats the notion that he "was sent only to the lost sheep of Israel."

The crux of this whole section, however, is the unique exchange Jesus has with the disciples at Caesarea Philippi; verses 7–19 occur only in Matthew. They will become famous. Jesus has asked his disciples who people say the Son of Man is, and Peter has replied, "You are the Messiah, the son of the living God."

> Then Jesus said: "Simon son of Jonah, you are favored indeed! You did not learn that from any human being; it was revealed to you by my heavenly father. And I say to: you are Peter, the Rock; and on this rock I will build my church, and the powers of death shall never conquer it. I will give you the keys of the kingdom of Heaven; what you forbid on earth shall be forbidden in heaven, and what you allow on earth shall be allowed in heaven."

Quite apart from the later historical significance of this passage, it should be clear that it is perfectly consonant with Matthew's interpretation of the Jesus story as the fulfillment of messianic hope in an ongoing *church*. Only here and in Matthew 18:17 (which we will shortly look at) does the word *ekklēsia* ever appear—in *all* the Gospels. Matthew not only conceived of a reform of Judaism, but a reform which begins to look a lot like an American denomination. It has its own head, Peter, whose name, *Kephas*, in both Aramaic and Greek punningly denotes "rock." It has its own *authority*, emphasized in this Gospel at the time Jesus first reads from scripture in the synagogue and confirmed "six days later" by the Transfiguration. What Matthew has achieved, in fact, is the composition of a foundation story for a church which already existed by the time this passage was written. This is made clear in the advice Matthew's Jesus now gives about a brother who does wrong:

... go and take the matter up with him, strictly between yourselves, and if he listens to you, you have won your brother over. If he will not listen, take one or two others with you, so that all facts may be duly established on the evidence of two or three witnesses. If he refuses to listen to them, report the matter to the congregation; and if he will not listen even to the congregation, you must treat him as you would a pagan or a tax-gatherer. (Matt. 18:15–17)

I know present-day people in a small Hutterite community who precisely follow these directions as if they indeed came from the mouth of Jesus rather than the pen of Matthew. When asked what sort of fault merited this treatment, an elder replied, "Oh, pride, for instance." He seemed to think himself quite capable of making such a judgment.

The fifth and last segment of the Lord's public career occupies 19:1b to 26:1. The narrative again follows Mark closely, including Jesus' final prediction of his death, his entry into Jerusalem, all the way to his apocalyptic sermon on the Mount of Olives. But Matthew attempts to add dignity to Jesus' entrance into the city by seeing it through the eyes of the very late (160 B.C.E.?) Jewish prophet called Deutero-Zechariah, who describes the Messiah entering the city in triumph as follows: "Rejoice, rejoice, daughter of Zion, shout aloud, daughter of Jerusalem; for see, your king is coming to you, his cause won, his victory gained, humble and mounted on an ass, on a foal, the young of a she-ass" (Zech. 9:9). This is a poetic text which uses the basic Hebrew device of repeated parallelism: there is *one* donkey: a colt, the foal of a she-ass. Strangely enough, Matthew doesn't understand this tradition and therefore, having quoted the prophet, makes Jesus ride on two animals at once: "The disciples went and did as Jesus had directed, and brought the donkey and her foal; they laid their cloaks on them and Jesus mounted . . ." (21:6–7). As a child I remember being immensely puzzled by this passage, but afraid to ask about it. Today my wonder persists. How could anyone as scripturally oriented as Matthew make such an blunder? A Greek scribe?

In this last preaching section there also appear Matthew's revision of Mark's doctrine on divorce and a series of "long" parables. Finally, when the apostles ask what they will receive for all their devotion, Jesus describes an eternal life in a heaven in which "the Son of Man is seated on his glorious throne"; around him will be the apostles "on twelve thrones judging the twelve tribes of Israel." The same apocalyptic view will return near the end of the Gospel when Jesus depicts the Day of the Judgment (25:31ff.). For this "royal-court" conception of the afterlife, Matthew is probably indebted to a contemporary, anonymous Jewish work, the *Similitudes of Enoch*; more remotely, this image is found in Daniel.

Jesus now tells the enigmatic parable of the vineyard owner who pays the same wages whether one works all day or only starts at three in the afternoon. The employer insists he has acted righteously since all freely agreed to their wages when they hired on. This story, which is peculiar to Matthew, has always bothered people—my mother could make nothing of it—for it flies in the face of our most rudimentary notions of work and justice. For this very reason, however, all critics think it very close to Jesus' own words—except for v. 16, which doesn't fit. I do too. Indeed, I think it one of the finest things in the New Testament: the basic hope of the Christian message, an unmerited grace that is the same for all. If there is such a thing as salvation I am sure it works in this way—surprising, gracious, quirky, forgiving, aristocratic, uninfluenced by our piddling human notions of justice.

As the little party now approaches Jericho—and despite what Jesus has just told them—the disciples continue to fuss over who will be first and who will be last. Once there, Jesus cures two blind men and then goes on to Jerusalem, entering as we have seen in a kind of triumph, even though he has never been there before. In the city, he goes immediately to the Temple, where he debates with Pharisees at length (chapters 21–23). Chapter 23 is especially curious—perhaps outrageous—an uncalled-for diatribe on the "scribes and Pharisees," made up from Q and Matthew's own material. Curiously, the writer has Jesus speaking to the Pharisees in the 30s when a Jesus-inspired "reform" of Judaism pure and simple was still possible, but he has him denouncing them in a way that is appropriate only to 85 or 90 C.E., when the rabbis had rejected Christianity and were already gathering at Jamnia to produce their *own* reformation.

Apart from these imaginary "Pharisees," however, Matthew's Gospel is typically inclusive and realistic. As we have seen, his Jesus recommends ideal, even quixotic behavior while at the same time establishing procedures to deal with the realities of church life—including punishment by shunning. It is this combination of idealism and realism that is Matthew's achievement. Echoed in Greek father after Greek father from Ignatius on, Matthew's habit of mind produces the Great Church. Reverberating down that church's checkered history, "the church's book," as it came to be called, has always been indispensable to mainstream religious institutions. Only cults are pure; a church is a mottled creation.

This last preaching section now concludes with the long discourse Jesus delivers on the Mount of Olives, directly across from the Temple (24:1–36). It is Matthew's version of Mark's "little apocalypse," and differs from that speech by drawing directly on Jewish-Christian experience during the siege of Jerusalem: "Many will fall from their faith; they will betray one another and hate one another. Many false prophets will arise" (Matt. 24:10–11). Though duly admonishing the reader to prepare for the end, Matthew is careful to delay the *parousia* until the kingdom of God is proclaimed to the whole world. The last judgment itself, an idea that seems to have arisen in late Judaism, but with no clear parallels anywhere else in Hebrew Scripture, is described as follows:

> When the Son of Man comes in his glory, and all the angels with him, then he will sit on the throne of his glory. All the nations will be gathered before him, and he will separate people one from another as a shepherd separates the sheep from the goats, and he will put the sheep at his right hand and the goats at the left. Then the king will say to those at his right hand, "Come, you that are blessed by my Father, inherit the kingdom prepared for you from the foundation of the world. . . . Then he will say to those at his left hand, "You that are accursed, depart from me into the eternal fire prepared for the devil and his angels." (Matt. 25:31–42)

As we shall see, this same idea—without all its operatic trappings—is present in Paul. In a recent book, *The Origins of Christian Morality*, Wayne Meeks comments: "It is remarkable how this belief in a universal judgment became standard among the earliest Christians, those who were previously gentiles as much as those who were Jews . . . the expectation of a universal judgment before the omnipotent deity powerfully supports a theocentric notion of sin and both individual and communal responsibility" (pp. 123–24).

But for all its inclusiveness, we should note that Matthew's Jesus provides only *two* moral bins for, say, ten billion souls—if the end were today: everybody now living and all those who once were alive. What is the distinction between? Astonishingly, it is simply *love*—and not even love of God! Those who loved their neighbor and those who did not; for unknown to them, Christ was their neighbor. After laboring all this time to have his Jesus found a visible church, complete with hierarchy and rules and whatnot, Matthew concedes—again through Jesus—that ultimately, salvation is a matter of ethics, not belief. This is what Schweitzer believed about the combination of a cultic naive realism and an idealized ethic of love—not only believed it, but lived it.

Thus ends Matthew's account of Jesus' public ministry. The Gospel itself, of course, concludes with the passion story and a resurrection account. The latter is wholly Matthew's own, but I will defer comment on it for comparison with the quite different resurrection material in Luke. For the passion story, Matthew follows Mark's text very closely. Let me simply note some changes that seem significant.

As we have seen, in the Gethsemane scene Matthew's disciples are at least partly rehabilitated, and that embarrassing young man who runs away naked after Jesus' arrest is eliminated. But Matthew does very little additional tinkering. He adds the moral that those who take to the sword will die by it, and he tells an independent story of how Judas, suffering remorse, returned the thirty pieces of silver and then hanged himself. (There seems to have been a good deal of variety in the legends concerning Judas.) Perhaps the only *important* variation in Matthew's passion is in the treatment of Pilate. In this Gospel alone do we have the intervention of the governor's wife, who in good Matthew-like fashion has "suffered much" from a *dream* about that "innocent man." And only here does Pilate wash his hands as a symbol of his being "guiltless of this blood." Fortunately, only here in Matthew also do we hear the horrible shout of the crowd, "His blood be on us and upon our children."

At the moment of Jesus' death there are other typical decorations: an earthquake, and the bodies of "sleeping saints" come back to life. Taking this last with mock seriousness, A. N. Wilson lumps the awakened dead with the young man in Nain, Jairus's daughter, and Lazarus, to conclude: "Those Christians who insist upon the literal and historical truth of Jesus's resurrection must ask themselves what happened to all these other resurrected bodies which walk the pages of the New Testament with such apparent naturalness. Did they like Jesus, ascend into heaven, or did they have their dying to do over again?" (*Jesus: A Life*, 6).

I have called this chapter "The Achievement of Matthew," defined as the writing of a foundation story for the Christian church. Matthew rewrote Mark's apocalyptic account into a document that could explain to his readers just what sort of reformed Judaism they practiced and why. Presumably such a Gospel was necessary in a world in which these Jewish-Christians increasingly met other kinds of people who had been differently influenced by Jesus of Nazareth. In attempting to hold this variety of beliefs together, Matthew's Gospel reveals to us a period in the development of Christianity in which the initial cult is about to become a religion. The problems he deals with, therefore, are those that are particularly acute when the group is on the verge of losing its pure, separatist status and is beginning to consider two relationships. What should be our stance regarding fellow believers who have a somewhat different faith? And what should we think about "the world"? How should Jewish-Christians react to Christians who hold to a Gentile, somewhat "Pauline" faith, on the one hand, and to the pagan civilization of the Roman Empire, on the other?

Similar problems are common to all emerging religious groups. The first phases in such a transition are always defensive. In Matthew's community, and presumably in many another Christian groups, this meant claiming strict, Judaic orthodoxy. The judaizers we will meet in Paul's Letter to the Galatians exhibited the same phenomenon. This claim is always tempered, however, by a certain tolerance—a stance, I have argued, that becomes basic to all later successful versions of the faith. Nevertheless, a core of beliefs—eventually to be condensed into a creed—will gradually emerge. Since the "First Gospel" is still read as authoritative in many churches, it might be useful for Christian readers to pause at this point to ask themselves how much of this core they still believe. Again, like Billy Graham, we'll wait on you, but it will be helpful and expeditious if you are as concrete as possible. Don't ask yourself whether you believe in some vague and ultimate cataclysm; try to imagine Matthew's judgment coming on an actual day— say Monday, July 22, 2034. Do you believe that at, say, 10:15 that morning, Jesus will show up in the sky sitting on a throne with angels in one or more species around him and all the nations (Brunei; Kuwait; Miami; Racine, Wisconsin)—all who live and all who ever lived gathered before him? Where will they sit? Who will provide the PA system. Some older fellows will have strange hair covering and rather heavy jaws and so on; nearly all will be terribly surprised—never having heard of Christ or Christianity. Nevertheless, the whole assembly will be divided into two categories: saved or not saved—forever. The goats will go to some sort of fiery end, and the sheep . . . Yes, what *about* the sheep? We never have heard—nor will we ever hear—the details of their happy fate. To the end, the kingdom remains mysterious.

Believe me I am not trying to be blasphemous, or to sound like the village atheist. What I hope I am doing is reading the New Testament seriously, assuming that it means what it says—as Schweitzer tried to do so long ago. If you have been doing that with me, you may have discovered that something has gone wrong with your "belief system," as we now say. You may have realized that as a contemporary Christian you have both a concrete "mythology" *and* a vague set of intellectual beliefs. Palestinian sheep and the goats, on the one hand; and "authenticity" or the "ground of my being" on the other. The situation is not new. When Rudolf Bultmann, who began publishing in the 1920s, finally in 1941 wrote of the need to "demythologize" the New Testament, it was because he had made this same sort of realization. It was not so much that he was trying to lead his fellow Christians in an existential direction (though he was trying to do that too) but that he was attempting to catch up with the wide disbelief that had *already* taken place. By the 1920s, many ordinary Christians, though they still paid lip service to visions of thrones in the sky and simple, two-part divisions of humanity and so on, actually no longer considered the New Testament a description of either present or future reality. In fact, its "mythology," as Bultmann called it, may not have represented the belief of educated Westerners since the late eighteenth century. Twentieth-century Christians have been able to maintain the mythology of their religion—what Schweitzer called its "naïve realism"—only by never thinking about it. The time had come to rationalize actual belief into something that made contemporary philosophic sense and to recognize the rest for what it was: myth.

It can be argued, of course, that without such a mythology there would have *been* no Christianity, that it was impossible for any religion to win out and prosper in the Hellenistic period without an account of salvation and heaven and hell, and that that impossibility remained until the eighteenth century. But what about today? Is demythologizing possible? Desirable? Or have the dark events and "crooked thoughts" of our time, as Samuel Beckett calls them, had the effect of discrediting rationality and the *sensible* reading of the scripture? Haven't the paradoxical "triumph" of science and the failure of popular education combined to *return* us to our operatic past? Are not the people you know personally even more prone to mythological thinking than ever before? Isn't there a marvelous inertia in religion unknown to other fields of human endeavor, so that we keep our stories, no matter what?

As usual, let me avoid answering these very large questions. I wish to point out only that the achievement of Matthew was to put together the following set of beliefs, which turned out to be supremely useful to the visible, fallible church: (1) a two-book religion that provides a mythical history of humanity from creation to the end of time and beyond; (2) a church with a theology and rudimentary organization—including a leader; (3) a metaphysics of heaven and earth and hell compatible with pagan opinion; (4) a noble ethic that at its best is nondiscriminatory, yet remains narrow enough to be hypnotically attractive; (5) the promise of eternal salvation based on a reinterpretation of the apocalyptic vision of Daniel.

Matthew's achievement makes a sharp contrast with the sadness of Mark. Mark writes from a mystical belief in a risen Christ—a Christ who had been misunderstood by his immediate followers and, perhaps, the communities of Christians they had founded. Matthew rewrites Mark's story from the viewpoint of one of those later communities, a living, visible church. The first is a romantic and ultimately futile exercise in belief; the second shook the world. The fact that Matthew's mythology has lost its appeal nowadays does not lessen its ancient glory and triumph. Nor does the inability to put that old Christianity and its church together again lessen the need and longing for it—in some of us at least. This two-book religion will not go away, and yet it is no longer literally believed; the church persists even in a churchless age.

In the safety of the university hallways—especially after examinations— my seminarian students sometimes get after me.

"You're going to hell, Beeching, you know that?" they'll say grinning, but only half joking.

"You young fellows are going to have to reinvent this church," I reply. "Do you know *that* ?" Their faces become briefly serious.

CHAPTER 3

_____

The Sacred History of Luke-Acts

The Gospel of Luke

It is time to pause. A book, like a highway, should have resting places where readers can stop, get a cup of coffee and a map, places in which to take stock of where they've been and where they're going. Apart from the details of literary conventions and authorial-editorial relations and so on, what is it that we have been reading? What have these two Synoptic writers *really* been talking about?

I raise this question before we begin the two-volume work Luke-Acts, because at 25 percent of the entire New Testament this work is so much larger than Q or Mark or even Matthew and so much more ambitious that we otherwise might lose our way in it. Therefore let us take a breath and try to digest what we have *already* read. What have the Q people and Mark and Matthew been trying to tell us?

The story is deceptively simple. Some thirty to fifty years ago a wonder-worker went about Galilee, the upper coast of Palestine, and Samaria—ending in Judea at Jerusalem—proclaiming the imminent arrival of what he called the "kingdom of God," or as his more Jewish-oriented audiences chose to phrase it, "the kingdom of heaven." This Jesus of Nazareth had had a predecessor, perhaps competitor, John, who was killed by the authorities. John preached repentance for sin and had "baptized," or *dipped* people into the Jordan as a sign of their changed status. Jesus also preached repentance, but unlike John, he talked about the "Son of Man" of contemporary Jewish apocalyptic literature, a being often identified with the "anointed one," or Messiah, the Son of David, who would "restore" Israel. To some at least, it seemed that Jesus *was* that Son of Man and Messiah. On an unknown charge arising out of this situation—the details are lost—Jesus too was eventually executed. His followers then began to claim with an ever stronger voice that not only had Jesus been the Messiah of the suffering sort foretold in Deutero-Isaiah but that he had risen from the dead and would soon return on the clouds as the Son of Man foretold in Daniel. His arrival, or *parousia,* would confirm and realize the mysterious "kingdom of God" which he had preached and had begun to institute.

That's what all this fuss is about, and from the beginning it has been a very vague fuss. Yet if you were raised in a traditional Christian community, you have probably been unaware of the extreme ambiguity of Jesus' story. As we have been reading Mark and Matthew, you may even have silently supplied whatever interpretation of this story is—or was—current in your denomination. You may have been thinking in terms of your immortal *soul* and a *heaven* (as an eternally happy place for humans), or *hell,* or *grace,* or even the *sacraments.* But these terms almost never show up in the subject indexes of scholarly works about the New Testament, not even *faith,* which in its modern religious sense is found only infrequently in the Gospels. (The Gospels always speak of *pistis,* which means trust.) You may have consciously been looking for these familiar religious ideas—echoing my Catholic students who often say, "But where's the Blessed Virgin?"—and have been disturbed at their absence.

We are, of course, just about to come to the "Blessed Virgin" in Luke's great infancy story; but in the sense the Catholic students mean—"Mother of God" and "Queen of Heaven"—we will never "come to the Blessed Virgin." Like *soul* and *grace* and *sacrament,* like *pope* and *mass* and *feast* and *mortal sin* and *vigil light* and *priest* and *cardinal,* like *double predestination* and *salvation by faith alone* and *born again,* we will never find *her* in the Synoptic Gospels. All such ideas are products of the early church; and religious faith is belief in *them,* rather than the events described in scripture. Even when these evangelists share a term and when modern scholarly tests suggest that that term occurred in Jesus' own preaching—*kingdom,* for example—its meaning is generally ambiguous or vague.

Part of our difficulty lies in the artificial way we approach these documents. The twenty-seven texts that make up the New Testament were never intended to be read one after the other, comparing each to each and searching them out for a consistent theology. As we have seen, the Synoptic authors wrote about the "Way" independently, at different times in different communities with different presuppositions. But we shouldn't exaggerate. There were Christians before there was any part of the New Testament, and they had a lot in common. After all, the Q people and Mark and

Matthew are telling roughly the same *tale*; each meant something similar when he used the words *love* or *believe* or *bless* or even *way* or *Lord*. In considering the coming of the *kingdom*, for instance, each inherited from the Old Testament an ancient idea of a future time in which God's rule would be more evident, less opposed by wicked people and nations, a time of peace and prosperity and dignity—not a heaven or an afterlife or immortality, but "better times." But during the period of the Second Temple, when the long-expected return of prosperity and peace failed to arrive, these better times linked to the notion of a Messiah who would bring them about had been pushed so far into the future that the idea of a natural Kingdom began to merge with that of a supernatural realm.

Influenced as we are by later Christian belief, it is very difficult to understand the precise meaning of the word *kingdom* in the New Testament; and consequently an enormous literature has accumulated about it. It is true that by the time of Jesus, Pharisaic Jews had promoted the notion that the rule of God would not appear until the end of time when people would rise from the dead, and this form of the idea is present in Matthew. But it is not always clear whether such a resurrection includes human immortality. Do the blessed live on forever? For the Synoptics in general, the preponderance of usages seems to suggest a kingdom of, and in, *this* world. The blessed are mortal—at least eventually. Of course, each of the early Christian communities may have differed not only on the meaning of the *kingdom* but on the means of getting there. The Q people were to enter the kingdom through poverty, suffering, and radical devotion. Theory suggests that Mark's community saw itself as *already* in possession of the risen Christ and that this would guarantee *their* entrance into a kingdom (however conceived) which would very shortly arrive. Matthew's Gospel assumed that the kingdom was delayed, but that entrance into it would ultimately depend on the love of one's neighbor—though privileged places would be afforded those who follow the Torah.

None of these views clearly addresses later religious questions such as: Is the kingdom forever? Do nonbelievers participate? And the same is true of the rest of the message. Why did Jesus have to die? Who was he? What ultimate value is to be placed on Jewish traditions? What is the point of baptism? What exactly is the significance of the common meal? Oddly enough, none of these questions seems to arise in a forceful way for the characters in these narratives. When Jesus asks who men think he is, for example, he seems as interested as the disciples in the answer—but he doesn't pursue the matter.

And yet, clearly there is a kind of subtext here that we should pay attention to. Apparently all the evangelists and their readers *want* something that life outside the "Way" does not provide. This is why they are writing and reading these documents. But what? Food, riches, freedom from pain, status? Certainly. Like members of other cults, they want these personal acquisitions. Companionship, a sense of belonging? Sure. Like any member of a religious group each wants all the collective or social advantages. But was this *all* Christianity held for its first believers? I will return to this question when we have finished Luke-Acts.

B y tradition, Luke's Gospel was written by the "beloved physician," supposedly a companion of Paul (see Col. 4:14; Philem. 24; 2 Tim. 4:11). But that story dates only from the time of Irenaeus, about 180 C.E. and is not consistent with the evidence. The author of Luke-Acts is not familiar with Paul's theology, for example, nor is he aware of the details of Paul's life as they appear in his own letters. In fact, whoever Luke was, he tells us himself that he is an objective historian who has composed his accounts at some distance from their subjects, not as a friend of their hero. Beyond that, we can say only that Luke-Acts was written sometime after the fall of Jerusalem in an area predominantly Gentile and Greek-speaking. There is a growing tendency to date this two-volume work in the first quarter of the second century, despite the fact that Paul's letters were accessible sometime in the early 90s, but the whole matter is quite speculative.

As Matthew's narrative was Jewish-oriented, so Luke's is governed by a consistently Gentile point-of-view imposed on the whole chronology of Jewish history. Time for Luke is "all-time," and space is coterminus with the Roman Empire. Though the church remains consciously proud of its Jewish roots, it now stands alone. Luke 16:16 is often taken to be an aphoristic summary of this view: "The law and the prophets were in effect until John came; since then the good news of the kingdom of God is proclaimed, and everyone tries to enter it by force." Sometimes called the "hinge of history," this verse seems to divide all past time into two differing periods in humanity's relation to the divine; but in actuality, the division is in thirds: the time before Jesus, the time of Jesus, the time after Jesus. In the third "dispensation," the path to salvation has become less dramatic if not less heroic. Righteousness is now a diurnal affair, a matter of patience to the grave: "And to all he said, 'If anyone wishes to be a follower of mine, he must leave self behind; day after day he must take up his cross and come with me'" (9:23). We have read this passage in both of the other Synoptics, but Luke has added "day after day." What this long and wide point-of-view amounts to is a theory of "sacred history," a theoretical interpretation of the past; and like other theories of history—Marx's or Toynbee's or Spengler's—Luke's idea is both breathtaking and almost certainly wrong. What is important for us, however, is not its veracity but how it structured his Gospel and the book of Acts. The last stage of time, the time of the Holy Spirit, *our* time, provides this evangelist with his background and point-of-view; that is, Luke writes—as we do—from the perspective of the institutional church.

Let us begin our reading of Luke's Gospel with a literal translation (mine) of its first sentence:

> Since many have taken in hand to compile a narrative concerning those matters which have been accomplished among us, insofar as those who were eyewitnesses and servants of the Word from the beginning have transmitted these matters to us, so it seemed good to me in turn, having looked into everything carefully, to write to you in an orderly way, your excellency Theophilus, so that you might learn the full truth about the reports of which you have been informed.

We have read nothing like this in the New Testament: a verbose, one might say bureaucratic, prose directed at some sort of official, real or imaginary (*Theophilus* means God-lover). Unlike Mark and Matthew, Luke acknowledges himself with the personal pronoun, at the same time making clear, as I've said, that he is *not* an eyewitness but a member of a later generation. He also implies that the stories he has reviewed differed somewhat and that now he is going to give us a more orderly, perhaps a more truthful, account. The whole giant sentence is a kind of "proof text" of the theory that the evangelists were creative author-editors; for here we finally see one at work.

Unfortunately, we do not have any explicit statement of the "order" Luke had in mind. Nor do sophisticated intention and style persist very long, in fact not even through the very next sentences:

> In the reign of Herod king of Judea there was a priest named Zechariah, of the division of the priesthood called after Abijah. His wife, whose name was Elizabeth, was also of priestly descent. Both of them were upright and devout, blamelessly observing all the commandments and ordinances of the Lord. But they had no children, for Elizabeth was barren, and both were well on in years. (1:5–7)

Readers of the Hebrew Scripture will immediately recognize the stereotypical subject of an older, barren couple who are promised a son. Readers of its Greek version, the Septuagint, will recognize the simplified, Semitic

Greek, which is in fact called "Septuagint Style." Even in English it is obviously quite different from the opening sentence. It will be *this* style that will continue throughout Luke's infancy story. As I suggested regarding the parallel story in Matthew, this language represents an underlying source. Apparently one of those "who had taken in hand" to write about Jesus had produced a story of his birth filtered through the eyes of the Greek Old Testament, and Luke has now appropriated it for the opening of his Gospel.

The tale begins as the story of two kinswomen, Elizabeth and Mary; Mary lives in Nazareth, and Elizabeth in the "uplands of Judah." To both, the archangel Gabriel (mentioned in Daniel) has promised a child, splendid in the eyes of God. When Elizabeth's child is born, his aged, priestly father recovers the speech he lost as a punishment for his disbelief in such an eventuality. When Mary's child is born, a heavenly host sings: "Glory in the highest to God!"

Placed carefully within this double tale are bits and pieces of ancient literature. The phrasing of Gabriel's annunciation to Mary, for instance, is remarkably paralleled in a fragment from Qumran that is earlier than Luke and also speaks of the coming of a "Son of God." And the three great songs in this story, though they come down to us in Greek, were clearly modeled on Hebrew or Aramaic originals. After the church became Roman, the opening words of these songs became titles: the *Magnificat*, the *Benedictus,* and the *Nunc Dimittis.* The *Magnificat* appears in the text when Mary first tells her cousin of God's miracle. It is a hymn of praise in the tradition of one sung by Hannah in 1 Samuel, a poem that must originally have told of the joy of God's chosen people in their election and in the careful brooding of the Almighty over their checkered history: the beating down of the arrogant and the raising of the lowly. By changing only the context rather than any individual words, Luke or his source fashioned a celebration of one of Christianity's most beloved mysteries. As with the other songs that follow, this is in my translation.

> My soul magnifies the Lord,
> And my spirit rejoices in God, my savior.
> Because he has seen the humility of his handmaiden,
> All generations shall henceforth call me blessed. (1:46–48)

Mary now visits her cousin and stays in Judea for three months before returning home; perhaps she has remained for the birth of Elizabeth's child, John. In any case, eight days later when it comes time for the child's circumcision and naming, his father, Zechariah, sings a psalm that also has parallels in thanksgiving songs discovered among the Dead Sea Scrolls.

Beginning with *Benedictus,* or "blessed," it speaks of the messianic hopes of both Israel *and* Christianity:

> Blessed be the Lord God of Israel,
> For he has sought out his people and rescued them. (1:68)

In the final stanza the ancient prophecy that Elijah would return to proclaim the Messiah is brought round to apply to this very child, John, the herald of Jesus who is destined:

> to give light to those who sit in darkness and the shadow of death,
> to guide our feet into the path of peace. (1:79)

Now Luke must manage to get Mary to Bethlehem before she delivers her *own* child, which means that having begun the story in Nazareth, he must find a pretext for moving south—for Luke accepts the tradition that the Messiah will be born in the town of David. He therefore tells us that a census has been declared which demands that Joseph and Mary return to Joseph's home. (There was a census in the area about 6 or 7 C.E., but that is far too late if we wish the birth to jibe with Matthew's account; Herod died in 4 B.C.E.)

The last scene from Luke's story of Jesus' infancy and the occasion for the final and most dramatic song of all is the circumcision. After the turtledoves and the pigeons have been sacrificed for the purification of the child's mother, Simeon, an old man destined by the Almighty to see the Messiah before his death, takes the babe in his arms and, realizing that God's promise does not fail, sings the *Nunc Dimittis:*

> Lord, now may you release your servant in peace according to your
>   word,
> Because my eyes have seen my Savior whom you have prepared
>   before all peoples,
> A light for the revelation of the gentile
> And the glory of your people of Israel. (2:29–32)

With Jesus now safely born of Mary, let us pause again to consider this "new thing" we have encountered: the mother of the Lord. Strange as it may seem, we have now read pretty much all of what the New Testament knows about her. According to Acts, Mary will be with the apostles in the upper room right after the ascension; and in Galatians, Paul has a passing reference to her, but not by name: "But when the fullness of time had come, God sent his Son, born of a woman, born under the law, in order to redeem those who were under the law, so that we might receive adoption as children" (Gal. 4:4-5). Paul's point is that Jesus was human (born of woman), rather than a ghost or spirit as some were then saying; he has no interest in *who* Jesus' mother was. Then in John there will be the Cana story of water changed to wine and the scene of Mary and the "disciple whom he loved" standing at the cross. Beyond this, nothing.

Yet from such unpromising beginnings Mary will emerge by 431 as "Mother of God" (*theotokos*); and by the Middle Ages she will be the object of an entire devotional cult, including her own "hours," amulets, pins, novenas, and the rosary. By our time she will have appeared (generally with a message) in some two thousand places throughout the world, many of which have continued to support her local shrine long after the Virgin's departure. Her influence on the church's view of sexual matters—virginity, purity, chastity—has been profound; indeed, in a kind of apogee of this thinking, the church came to hold that Mary was "ever virgin" despite the "impossibility" of this idea—as a female student once helpfully informed me. Until very recently, at least, one could argue that many Roman Catholics were more devoted to the BVM (Blessed Virgin Mary), as we called her, than to her Son. Some Catholics, following St. Jerome, still wish to proclaim her "co-mediatrix of all grace" and speak of "death through Eve, life through Mary."

A good deal of this Mary business has remained at the folk level, of course, but not all. In 1854 Pius IX proclaimed that alone among mortals Mary was conceived without original sin, and in 1950 Pius XII announced that she had been bodily assumed into heaven. By that time her feast days filled the liturgical year: Solemnity of Mary (January 1), Purification (February 2), Annunciation (March 25), Visitation (May 31), Assumption (August 15), Nativity (September 8), Immaculate Conception (December 8), on the last of which Catholics had to attend mass.

How come? James Joyce has somewhere written (or put into Stephen's mouth) the idea that Mary was the appealing image that the cunning Italian intellect thrust on unsuspecting Europe. I'm not sure what role Italians played in it—they came a little late for this sort of theology—but there is wisdom in this remark. Though Judaism and Islam were satisfied with a simple male monotheism, most people, ancient and modern, prefer to have a goddess along with their god. In my youth, Catholic men would seriously explain that they prayed to Mary because as a woman she was more compassionate than the Lord, who represented justice. In saying this they also managed to suggest that, being a woman, she was also more easily fooled into granting petitions the Lord would instantly recognize as con jobs.

B ut to return to the Gospel according to Luke. In his opening sentence Luke was quite forthright about the composite nature of his work—something we had to infer regarding Matthew. But clearly both of these later Synoptics use multiple sources. When we examine their texts in detail, however, we find dramatic differences in the *way* they use them. A glance at the diagram near the beginning of the previous chapter will reveal that of Matthew's 1,072 verses, 370 are drawn from a private source; while of Luke's 1,150 verses, 535 are peculiar to him. (In each case the remainder are from Mark and Q). These figures mean that we may expect a more idiosyncratic story from Luke, though not necessarily a more inaccurate one.

Luke also differs from Matthew in the way he puts all these materials together. He not only uses less of Mark's narrative (omitting entirely Mark 6:45–8:26 and 9:41–10:12), but he bundles what he does use into three blocks (Luke 3:1–6:19; 8:4–9:50; and 18:15–24:11). Nevertheless, Luke keeps close to Mark's order of events. He also orders the Q material the same way but presents these Jesus sayings in two blocks, 6:20–8:3 and 9:51–18:14, the so-called lesser and greater interpolations.

All this applies only to Luke's Gospel, of course, and ignores the fact that this author wrote a second volume. About Acts we cannot be so neatly quantitative, though it is evident that various sources underlie it as well. But we must try to keep in mind that Luke set out to tell the story of the faith beginning (in the genealogy) from Adam. In this scheme, the Gospel tells only the first part of the story, setting the stage for the glorified history of the early church in the book of Acts, which universalizes the new religion and orients it toward the empire. Such a large canvas is naturally as full of sources as it is of new characters. Chief among these latter is the "Holy Spirit," who brings about Mary's pregnancy, descends upon Jesus at his baptism, and is acknowledged by him in the synagogue at Nazareth. He is present also when Jesus begins his public ministry in Galilee "in the power of the spirit"; and on his death, this spirit is said to return to heaven, only to descend again on the apostles at Pentecost. Precisely what or who the Holy Spirit is, is left for later theologians. Luke himself sometimes thinks of it as the "Spirit of God" and sometimes the "Spirit of Jesus"—once actually using this phrase (Acts 16:7).

The difference this new character makes in the Gospel can be observed in Jesus' first appearance as an adult in Nazareth. Here is the way the scene is handled in Mark, but Matthew's version is nearly identical:

> When the Sabbath came he began to teach in the synagogue; and the large congregation who heard him asked in amazement, "Where does he get it from? What is this wisdom he has been given? How does he perform such

miracles? Is he not the carpenter, the son of Mary, the brother of James and Joses and Judas and Simon? Are not his sisters here with us?" So they turned against him. Jesus said to them, "A prophet never lacks honor except in his home town, among his relations and his own family." And he was unable to do any miracle there, except that he put his hands on a few sick people and healed them; and he was astonished at their want of faith. (Mark 6:1–6)

In Luke, however, Jesus returns to Galilee, "armed with the power of the Spirit."

> So he came to Nazareth, where he had been brought up, and went to the synagogue on the Sabbath day as he regularly did. He stood up to read the lesson and was handed the scroll of the prophet Isaiah. He opened the scroll and found the passage which says, "The spirit of the Lord is upon me because he has anointed me; he has sent me to announce good news to the poor, to proclaim release for prisoners and recovery of sight for the blind; to let the broken victims go free, to proclaim the year of the Lord's favor." He rolled up the scroll, gave it back to the attendant, and sat down; and all eyes in the synagogue were fixed on him.
>
> He began to address them: "Today," he said, "in your hearing this text has come true." There was a general stir of admiration; they were surprised that words of such grace should fall from his lips. "Is not this Joseph's son?" they asked. Then Jesus said, "No doubt you will quote the proverb to me, Physician, heal yourself! and say, 'We have heard of all your doings at Capernaum; do the same here in your own home town.' I tell you this," he went on; "no prophet is recognized in his own country. There were many widows in Israel, you may be sure, in Elijah's time, when for three years and six months the skies never opened, and famine lay hard over the country; yet it was to none of those that Elijah was sent, but to a widow at Sarepta in the territory of Sidon. Again, in the time of the prophet Elisha there were many lepers in Israel, and not one of them was healed, but only Naaman, the Syrian." At these words the whole congregation were infuriated. They leapt up, threw him out of the town and took him to the brow of the hill on which it was built, meaning to hurl him over the edge. But he walked straight through them all, and went away. (Luke 4:16–30)

Placed near the beginning of Luke's account of Jesus' teaching career, this passage seems to form the real prologue to the Gospel. Jesus has now been baptized—though whether by John or someone else is unclear—has fasted, and has been tempted in the desert. He enters his hometown not, as in Mark, announcing the imminent coming of the kingdom but simply taking his turn at reading from the Torah in the Sabbath synagogue. Astonishingly, he applies the verses of Isaiah (61:1–2) directly to himself. At first there is a general approval of this claim, even though Jesus is recognized as a fellow townsman. But then, perhaps because he admits that, as it stands in Mark, "he was unable to do any miracle" in Nazareth, he tells them that they will mock his inability. And he quotes 2 Kings (from the Greek text) to show the unworthiness of Israel compared to the Gentiles—thus putting the blame for his failure on his neighbors. This is too much; the people of Nazareth try to kill him. As is common in Luke, however, Jesus mysteriously escapes. One suspects that this anecdote was well known in the early church and laden with meaning. Indeed, the same two folk sayings are given together in the *Gospel of Thomas* §31: "Jesus said, 'No prophet is accepted in his own village; no physician heals those who know him.'" In any case, the whole Gospel story is here in capsule form: Jesus' mission to the Jews, its failure, his turning to the Gentiles, even his murder.

There follows a series of events from Mark, beginning with the healing of the demon-possessed man in the synagogue at Capernaum and the curing of Simon's mother-in-law. Jesus preaches from a boat to crowds on the shore and cures a leper and a man who is paralyzed, as "the Lord's healing power" is with him. Then he feasts with the tax collector Levi. As in the other Gospels, Jesus makes the point that he has come for the sake of the sinful rather than the righteous and that he rejects, for the period of his life, the practice of fasting. In so doing, Jesus predicts both his death and the struggles of the early church: "Can you make the bridegroom's friends fast while the bridegroom is with them? But the time will come when the bridegroom will be taken away from them; that will be the time for them to fast" (Luke 5:34–35). As many have noticed, this passage also legitimizes the *resumption* of fasting in the early church.

But at 6:18 Luke turns to his Q material and his private source to put together a sequence not found in Mark. Called the "lesser interpolation," it begins with a "sermon on the plain," the counterpart of Matthew's Sermon on the Mount. Here are those "realistic" four beatitudes we have already looked at. The inheritors of the "kingdom" are to be the poor, the hungry, those who weep, and those who suffer for the Son of Man. To this typically Q perspective, Luke also adds four "woes" not found in Matthew. Those who will *not* inherit the kingdom will be the rich, the well fed, the happy, the well-thought-of. As if to take some of the sting from these remarks, Luke reiterates the Q dictum to love your enemies and pray for those who hate you, and this sentiment is then expanded into a very "hard" ethic based on those same pithy Q sayings we saw in a weakened form in Matthew: turn the other cheek, give both coat and shirt, etc. What good is it to love those who love you in return? Don't lend to those who can pay interest. Give without stinting. For Q and Luke, real virtue, as St. Thomas will say, is to love the unlovable.

At the end of this sermon, we have the Q story of the curing of the centurion's servant. Jesus is on the way to help with the sick man, when the officer sends word to him: "Do not trouble further, sir; I am not worthy to have you come under my roof. . . . But say the word and my servant will be cured" (7:6–8). Pointedly, Jesus says he has not found such faith in Israel. Suitably generalized, this Roman's saying will takes its place in the Christian liturgy as *Domine, non sum dignus ut intres sub tectum meum sed tantum dic verbo et sanabitur anima mea,* "Lord, I am not worthy that you should come under my roof. Say but the word and my soul shall be healed." A good prayer.

The rest of the "lesser interpolation" can most profitably be read as part of Luke's major concern for women—unexampled elsewhere in the New Testament. We have already noted this sympathy in connection with the infancy story, but that is only the beginning. If you lift out of Luke's Gospel all that is neither Mark nor Q and view it as a whole—I have my students do this—you will find that almost every remaining anecdote deals in some way with women. In a place and at a time when ordinary women were little better than slaves, this is highly unusual. At 7:11ff., for instance, we have Jesus raising the only son of the "widow of Nain," with Luke's editorial remark, "When the Lord saw her his heart went out to her." At 7:36ff., while Jesus is banqueting with a Pharisee, a woman "who was living an immoral life" anoints his feet with myrrh, wets them with her tears, and dries them with her hair. Jesus defends her with the typically Lukan remark, "And so, I tell you, her great love proves that her many sins have been forgiven; where little has been forgiven, little love is shown" (7:47). And the following scene, which concludes the lesser interpolation, is a passage describing the role of women in Jesus' entourage:

> With him were the Twelve and a number of women who had been set free from evil spirits and infirmities: Mary, known as Mary of Magdala, from whom seven demons had come out, Joanna, the wife of Chuza a steward of Herod's, Susanna, and many others. These women provided for them out of their own resources. (8:2–3)

Skipping ahead to chapter 10 within the "greater interpolation," we find Luke returning to this theme. At 10:38ff. Jesus visits Martha and Mary. While there he hears Martha's complaint that her sister simply attends to his words and doesn't help with the food. Jesus, however, sides with Mary as Luke apparently tries to show that Christian women have a right to discipleship and should not simply be kitchen menials. My mother didn't read it that way. Indeed, this was one of the very few anecdotes of scripture to which she was adamantly opposed. Mother could never see why the Lord (she called him this without any affectation) approved of that simp Mary who only posed at his feet and refused to help with the dishes.

"Just like a man," she would say.

In Luke's Gospel, even casual shouts from the street ring with the feminine: "While he was speaking thus, a woman in the crowd called out, 'Happy the womb that carried you and the breasts that suckled you!'" (11:27). At 13:10ff., though it is the Sabbath and people object, Jesus cures a woman who apparently suffers from osteoporosis. Then at the very end of his life there are the women who have accompanied him to Jerusalem and have the good sense to obtain spices and perfumes before sundown Friday evening when the shops close: Mary of Magdala, Joanna, Mary the mother of James, and others. (Like everyone in the Gospels, none of them takes seriously the notion that Jesus will actually arise from the dead.)

What is one to make of this emphasis on the feminine? Is it simply Luke's idea that Jesus cared for the socially unempowered—to use today's jargon? Or is there something more to it? I have no very good answer to this question, but I would suggest that one of the great attractions of Christianity has always been its radical democracy; on the spiritual level we are all supposed to be equal, beggar and pope, Lazarus and Dives, man and woman— though to be sure this doctrine has rarely if ever been implemented.

Another reason has occasionally been suggested: that Luke herself was a woman.

Coming back to chapter 8, we find Jesus telling the parable of the sower and then giving its allegorical interpretation to the disciples—as in Mark. There follow other Markan sayings concerning the hidden that shall be made clear and then a journey across the lake to Gerasa and the madman whose name is legion; once back in Galilee, he cures the woman with the hemorrhage. At the beginning of chapter 9, as we have seen in the other Gospels, Jesus sends out "the Twelve" as missionaries who take nothing with them; and as in those other accounts, they return almost immediately.

Luke continues to follow Mark in this way until 9:51, the beginning of the "greater interpolation," a long journey to Jerusalem made up from Q and Luke's own source. Going directly south into Samaria—contrary to the injunction in Matthew 10:5–6, "Do not take the road to gentile lands, and do not enter any Samaritan town." Jesus now delivers more hard sayings, "Let the dead bury the dead," for instance, and the wonderful, "No one who puts a hand to the plow and looks back is fit for the kingdom of God" (though the Jesus Seminar assigns this remark to the early church).

As he goes along he now sends out seventy (or seventy-two) disciples, two by two, to go as missionaries ahead of him. One wonders, of course, where such a great number of "friars" have come from so suddenly; but never mind, these numbers simply represent the traditional number of Gentile countries, and Luke seems to mean that the Twelve have been sent to the Jews, while the seventy-two are sent to the Gentiles. Jesus repeats to these men the rules for the road he has delivered to the Twelve in 9:1ff., but with some variation. The essence of what he says is given in the statement: "Whoever hears you hears me, and whoever rejects you rejects me, and whoever rejects me rejects the one who sent me" (Luke 10:16). As I have said, scholars like Burton Mack make a great deal of this saying from Q, assuming that the earliest Jesus preachers—like Jesus himself—were *filled with the spirit*. When *they* spoke, Jesus and the spirit spoke; revelation was an ongoing business. That this belief continued into the early church is very clear from attempts to control it by Paul, his imitators, and the writers of an early church manual called the *Didache*. The later authors all recommend "testing the spirits," as they called it, a technique for judging the sincerity of itinerant preachers. This whole issue indicates the emergence—perhaps the inevitable emergence—of orthodoxy.

Unaccountably, all these disciples—like the apostles before them—return almost immediately. When they brag that even the demons "submit to us," Jesus exults, saying "I thank you, Father, Lord of heaven and earth, for hiding these things from the learned and wise and revealing them to the simple" (10:21). This very un-Jesuslike boast is the only such passage in the Synoptics—a classic cultic exultation; and one wonders what *Sitz im Leben* (setting in life) called it forth. Were there already skeptical elements in Luke's community, intellectuals who sneered at all this popular religion? Were some Christians restive under the new orthodoxy? We don't know; but it is disturbing that the same sort of anti-intellectualism pops up in late Jewish writings and appears in Paul's first letter to the Corinthians.

The so-called "greater interpolation," in which these last anecdotes occur, is conceived as a very long journey to Jerusalem and death, to be paralleled in Acts, some think, by Paul's long journey to Rome. That this is a very artificial construction—no actual journey would exhibit so many occasions for wonders and teachings—is not always appreciated even by those who read the New Testament regularly. I once heard an excited preacher tell his congregation how intelligent it was of the Almighty to lengthen out what should have been a brief excursion down to Judea in order that Jesus might accomplish so much. And indeed, this journey contains some of the most memorable and moving stories in the entire New Testament. The anecdote of the Good Samaritan is here, calculated to universalize the

"Way" into a worldwide religion, now that Christianity has been rejected by the Jews—it is no accident that the men who pass by the suffering wayfarer are a priest and a Levite. Other stories exhibit Luke's concern for prayer, not so much the form of prayer, as its frequency and intensity; he even tells two tales of people who *pestered* God into doing the right thing by them. There is the judge who is constantly visited by the same widow. "Although I have no fear of God or man," he says, "yet this woman is so great a nuisance that I will give her justice before she wears me out with her persistence" (18:1–8.). And then there is my favorite, in which a man simply *embarrasses* God into giving in; it seems to come right out of the suburbs of the twentieth century.

> He also said to them, "Suppose one of you has a friend and goes to him in the middle of the night to say, 'My friend, lend me three loaves, because a friend of mine on his travels has just arrived at my house, and I have nothing to offer him'; and the man answers from inside the house, 'Do not bother me. The door is bolted now, and my children and I are in bed; I cannot get up and give it to you.' I tell you, if the man does not get up and give it to him for friendship's sake, persistence will be enough to make him get up and give his friend all he wants. (11:5–9 [*Jerusalem Bible*])

Stand in his front yard in the middle of the night and shout out your needs, and God will be shamed into giving you what you want. This is the familiar anthropomorphic God of Yiddish folklore, the God of Chagall and Isaac Singer—irascible, unpredictable, lovable—the divine being behind such a saying as, "If God lived in this *shtetl* (village) we'd break his windows." Here at last we have the God of thieves and ne'er-do-wells, a God who protests that he won't get out of bed, but finally does.

It is in fact *this* God who still bothers me; not the rational God of traditional philosophy but the irrational, personal God of existentialism. Isn't it odd that Kierkegaard's God, who *necessarily* transcends reason and human concepts of justice, turns out also to be the God of the *shtetl*? The voice making impossible demands on Abraham, the householder exasperated by the scene in the front yard, the preacher foolish enough to go up to Jerusalem to die, the arbitrary, unreasonable, *failed* God seems plausible to me when all other conceptions of the divine have gone the way of Nineveh.

Inevitably, the long journey repeats a wealth of Q material. Here is the Lukan version of the Lord's Prayer in the Scholars' Version used by the Jesus Seminar:

> Father, your name be revered.
> Impose your imperial rule.
> Provide us with the bread we need day by day.

Forgive our sins, since we too forgive everyone in debt to us.
And please don't subject us to test after test.

Jesus also has a long, six-part condemnation of the Pharisees comparable to Matthew's chapter 23 and issues some hard sayings. More characteristic of Luke, however, are the "lost parables" of chapter 15. In these an idiosyncratic shepherd leaves ninety-nine sheep to look for one, and a housewife who has lost a dime (as I once heard a priest refer to the coin) lights all her lamps and sweeps the house until she finds it. And here too is one of the world's great tales, the story of the Prodigal Son. I delight in asking my classes, "Whose story is it?" In the midst of their own youthful rebellion, students almost always think it is the prodigal's tale. A few, more thoughtful or sensitive than the rest, will finally admit that the parable may be even more pertinent to the poor dutiful brother who has remained at home and must now drum up some love for his worthless, returned relative. Finally, peering down at them from the lectern, I say, "The day will come, my young friends, when you will suddenly, with blinding clarity, see that this parable is actually about that distraught and joyous old father." The students look at each other with disbelief. They think they will never grow old.

This God of Luke who broods over us and sweeps the world to find us has, however, one very obvious peculiarity: he doesn't like money. Luke's Jesus hates riches and believes that wealth automatically corrupts. Luke himself seems to think about money in a way no poor person ever thinks of it; and—as you might suppose—there is a theory that this evangelist was brought up in comfortable circumstances and reacted against them. Perhaps so; this notion at least has the merit of explaining his fairly good Greek. In any case, the hatred of money, which is everywhere in the primitive Q, is also typical of the sophisticated Luke.

For the Jesus of this Gospel, the condition of being well-to-do *itself* condemns one; sin in the ordinary sense is not necessary. To be sure, Jesus sometimes inveighs against *greed* instead of wealth, but generally it is money pure and simple which is evil. Is this notion also hyperbole, a hedge around a measured, moral principle, or does Luke actually intend to introduce a kind of asceticism or even a "social gospel" in the modern sense? Consider the remarkable story of Lazarus and the rich man in 16:19–31. At death, the rich man goes to the tormenting fire of Hades, while Lazarus is swept up to Abraham—for no better reason, apparently, than the disparity in their IRS returns. When the rich man has the temerity to complain, Father Abraham says, "Remember, my child, that all the good things fell to you while you were alive, and all the bad to Lazarus; now he has his consolation here and it is you who are in agony." Such a view of life and afterlife suggests not so much a moral principle but the pagan image of a wheel of fate: bound on a wheel endlessly turning between good and evil, humanity inevitably travels through both. The rich man has been through happiness and luxury; now it is Lazarus's turn.

There is an ancient Western example of the persistence of this belief. In Rochester Cathedral southeast of London, on the choir wall opposite the bishop's throne, there is a painting of men clutching the wheel of fortune. What appears to be an angel relentlessly pushes it forward, while some human figures, having lost their grip, grab frantically in air as they begin to fall. The guidebook says; "Some mystery surrounds why such pagan imagery should be present here; perhaps it is a stern warning to those who reject the sure path offered through the redeeming love of Christ. . . ." But the imagery is perfectly accurate; it is the same conception we find in Luke. Both are portraits of the human condition. The error occurred only when Luke transferred this insight to the heavens and the ancient British painter chose a Cathedral wall for his picture. Having been concealed and protected for centuries behind a pulpit, Rochester's "wheel of fate" is sometimes said to be the oldest painting in England. One might add, "And the most truthful."

The story of Lazarus and the rich man is also notable as the only parable in the Gospels that directly images the afterlife. If Luke meant us to take the story literally, he may have assumed the reality (as did Matthew) of the states that will become "heaven" and "hell," whether "everlasting" or not. But does "carried away by the angels to be with Abraham" mean what Sister Josepha thought it meant? Does torment in Homer's "Hades" mean you know what? And if these meanings are correct, why haven't we heard more about them in the rest of this Gospel? I suspect that much of this is simple storytelling for Luke; for generally he seems hesitant about such things In chapter 17, for instance, he gives us his version of the "little apocalypse." It *begins* with the notion that the kingdom is *already* here.

> You cannot tell by observation when the kingdom of God comes. There will be no saying, "Look, here it is!" or "there it is!"; for in fact the kingdom of God is among you. (17:21)

More than thirty years before Luke wrote, the same mystical intuition—that the followers of Jesus had already attained salvation and "lived in Christ" had produced an entire theology. Paul's letters are full of what scholars today call "vertical eschatology," the idea that union with God takes place immediately (vertically) upon conversion—whatever may occur at the end-time (horizontal eschatology). But the Synoptic writers, though they preserve echoes of this idea as in the passage just cited, generally follow a later tradition. They believe that the kingdom will arrive with the *parousia*, but that *that* happening has been postponed to a far distant future. We will see later that these two understandings of the kingdom, one that it comes at the end, the other that it is immediately accessible, will travel uneasily yoked through all the history of Christendom.

But uneasiness was there from the beginning. Matthew repeats Mark's expectation of the end (Mark 13) pretty much unchanged, but lengthens out the time till Jesus second coming by means of parables like the field sown with weeds. Luke, on the other hand, deals with the issue by careful editing. At the risk of trying your patience, I give Luke's version of the Markan apocalypse with his additions in boldface and his omissions in brackets. You may recall that people have asked Jesus when the end will be and what will be its signs:

> He said, "Take care that you are not misled. For many will come claiming my name and saying, 'I am he,' and 'The Day is upon us.' **Do not follow them.** And when you hear of wars and insurrections, do not fall into a panic. These things are bound to happen first; **but the end does not follow immediately.** Then he added, 'Nation will make war upon nation, kingdom upon kingdom; there will be great earthquakes, and famines and plagues in many places; in the sky terrors and great portents. [These are the birthpangs of the new age.]
>
> **But before all this happens** they will set upon you and persecute you. You will be brought before synagogues and put in prison; you will be haled before kings and governors for your allegiance to me. This will be your opportunity to testify. . . .
>
> **But when you see Jerusalem encircled by armies, then you may be sure that her destruction is near.** [But when you see "the abomination of desolation" usurping a place which is not his (let the reader understand)] Then those who are in Judea must take to the hills; those who are in the city itself must leave it, and those who are in the country must not return. . . . there will be great distress in the land and a terrible judgment on this people. They will fall at the sword's point; they will be carried captive into all countries; and Jerusalem will be trampled down by foreigners until their day has run its course. (21:8–24)

These changes seem intended to keep an apocalypse for those who still want one, but postpone it to some unspecified time in the future. They also separate the fall of Jerusalem from Daniel's apocalyptic vision and eliminate his coded references.

Yet I do not wish to convey the idea that Luke was generally a careful editor or that he was above writing in code himself. Before we go on to the passion story and resurrection material, then, let us consider some of the problems in reading this evangelist: his opacities, his contradictions, his deliberate omissions, and finally his double view of time. Consider first this impenetrable passage from Luke 13:

> At that very time there were some people present who told him about the Galileans whose blood Pilate had mixed with their sacrifices. He answered them: "Do you imagine that, because these Galileans suffered this fate, they must have been greater sinners than anyone else in Galilee? I tell you they were not; but unless you repent, you will all of you come to the same end. Or the eighteen people who were killed when the tower fell down on them at Siloam—do you imagine they were more guilty than all the other people living in Jerusalem? I tell you they were not; but unless you repent, you will all of you come to the same end." (13:1–5)

No one has ever understood this. The difficulty lies not only in the historical allusions to some violent act of Pilate or to some dreadful building accident (did even Luke's first readers know about these matters?). The problem is worse. Jesus is here affirming two contradictory things: that earthly mischance is unconnected with moral behavior and that it can be avoided by moral behavior—repentance. The solution may be that the phrase "same end" refers to damnation—but he doesn't say that. When a disciple asks how to deal with a stranger who has been exorcising demons in Jesus' name we have: "But Jesus said to him, 'Do not stop him for whoever is not against you is for you'" (9:50, from Mark). But just a few verses later Jesus says, "He who is not with me is against me, and he who does not gather with me scatters" (11:23, from Q). One might think that such confusions arose from Luke's desire to write a Gospel that would preserve as much of Mark and Q as possible, while still hewing to his own beliefs and his own versions of things. But he is quite capable elsewhere of simply omitting what he doesn't like. He leaves out the whole of Mark 6:45 to 8:26, by which he avoids sending Jesus into places like Tyre and Sidon and the Decapolis and keeps the focus on the symbolic journey to Jerusalem. He also tells the story of the loaves and fishes only once, and he finesses some of Mark's harsh criticism of the disciples. Where Matthew saw judaizing Christianity as the preferred variety of the faith, Luke considers it an early and honorable, but now abandoned, "denomination." Consequently he omits as unnecessary Mark's gloss on Jesus' explanation of why his followers don't wash their hands before eating, "By saying this he declared all foods clean" (7:19).

Finally, Luke conflates time. At 10:4 he has Jesus command his disciples not to carry anything with them on their missionary excursion; but at 22:38, with his own death imminent, Jesus says, "'When I sent you out without a purse, bag, or sandals, did you lack anything?' They said, 'No, not a thing.'

He said to them, 'But now, the one who has a purse must take it, and like-wise a bag. And the one who has no sword must sell his cloak and buy one.'" This passage—unique to Luke—expresses the time difference not only between the few months that have elapsed in the narrative, but the melancholy decline between the heroic age of Jesus and the actual state of Christians at the time when Luke is writing. In *Acts*, where he is portraying the beliefs of the Gentile church, Luke creates a divine vision in which Peter is *commanded* to eat of all things of the earth, kosher or not.

The story of the passion of the Lord, which Luke now begins with Jesus' entrance into Jerusalem (19:27), seems to have taken a settled shape very early and stands like a rock of solidarity in the tradition. Matthew's retelling strays very little from Mark's account. Luke's version, while still quite faithful, raises more questions. Yet even in its earliest form, the passion story seems to have been worked over by editors who saw its events as fulfilling all sorts of prophecies and allusions. But the story has great power, and the variations the later writers introduce are slight and often seem only intended to lighten the original, grim account. In Luke's Gethsemane, for instance, the disciples fall asleep "from grief" and Jesus' prayer is answered by "a ministering angel." Jesus' despairing cry from Psalm 22, "My God, my God, why have you forsaken me," is totally eliminated.

In addition to this sort of thing, however, there is a modicum of *theological* editing. What has particularly caught the attention of scholars is Luke's rejection of *any* sacrificial understanding of Jesus' death. You may recall that when I earlier took up this idea, I made the point that Mark has only two references to such a sacrifice: "For the son of Man did not come to be served, but to serve, and to give his life as a ransom for many" (Mark 10:45) and the reference to the "blood shed for many" at the Last Supper. Luke moves the first to the context of the Last Supper and reduces it to "I am among you like a servant," and he eliminates altogether Jesus' statement about the sacrificial shedding of blood.

What then *does* Luke consider the meaning of the death of the Lord? To answer that question—and because we have now reached the final Synoptic version of the passion story—let me briefly set Luke's account against the stories the other two evangelists tell. Mark and Matthew begin this final tragedy with Jesus dining at the house of Simon the leper, outside the city in Bethany, where a woman anoints him as if for burial. Luke omits this scene because he has told the story earlier, locating it in the home of "Simon the Pharisee." But his variant account of the Last Supper is harder to explain. In neither of the other Synoptics does Jesus enjoin the disciples to repeat the ritual of bread and wine—a puzzle to those who will later claim that the church's "sacrament" was founded by the Lord—and in Luke Jesus first drinks from the cup and then eats the bread. The only other text in which Jesus asks the disciples to repeat the ritual is 1 Corinthians 11:23–34, which has the conventional eucharistic order. If the ceremony was well established by the time Paul describes it in the 50s, why should this sort of variance show up in the Gospels?

At the end of the meal, Luke omits Jesus' important statement in Mark and Matthew that, "I shall go ahead of you into Galilee." As we shall see later, Luke prefers the area of Jerusalem for resurrection appearances. And he alone tells us that Pilate, finding no case against Jesus, and discovering that he was a Galilean, sent him to Herod Antipas, who happened to be in town. Herod "was delighted," Luke says, because he had heard of Jesus and hoped to see a miracle. But Jesus will say nothing to him, and therefore the king and his men mock him and send him back to Pilate who, as in the other Gospels, acquiesces to the crowd. Luke omits the crowning with thorns and the other mistreatment by the soldiers but adds, as we have seen, the weeping women.

As Jesus takes up his cross in the city streets, he expresses pity and compassion for the women of Jerusalem. The author may have in mind not so much the women watching the actual crucifixion, but those who Luke knows suffered from famine and even resorted to cannibalism in the siege of the city in 70 C.E. Consider the passage yourself:

> Daughters of Jerusalem, do not weep for me; no, weep for yourselves and your children. For the days are surely coming when they will say, "Happy are the barren, the wombs that never bore a child, the breasts that never fed one." Then they will start saying to the mountains, "Fall on us," and to the hills, "Cover us." (23:28–29)

Then at the crucifixion, Jesus turns this same pitying gaze on those who are torturing him: "Father, forgive them; they do not know what they are doing." To the Good Thief he says, "I tell you this: today you shall be with me in Paradise." Finally he returns to God the Spirit which had descended upon him at baptism, "Father, into thy hands I commit my spirit," and dies (23:34, 43, 46). Luke omits the splitting Temple veil and Matthew's meteorological decorations, and the scene ends with the centurion saying simply, "Truly, this was an upright man." In Mark and Matthew the crucifixion is conducted in near silence; but Luke gives Jesus speeches found nowhere else in the Gospels; even in Luke they exhibit great variation from manuscript to manuscript. Three of these, combined with three others from John and the despairing quotation from Psalm 22 given in Mark and Matthew, have come to make up the so-called Seven Last Words, a perfect illustration of the working of popular piety, which proceeds by accretion, blurring the distinctions among the Gospels.

These small distinctions aside, however, it is clear that Luke and the other two Synoptic writers accept an underlying order of events in the passion and death of the Lord. According to all three, Jesus' body is buried before sunset in a tomb belonging to a well-to-do disciple, Joseph of Arimathea; and Jesus' women followers take note of the grave. But when we come to the postresurrection material—no canonical Gospel describes the actual *resurrection*, though the same cannot be said for the apocryphal writings—the situation is different. First of all, only Matthew and Luke *have* such material; and, like their infancy stories, their accounts of the risen Lord are independent and unrelated narratives. (Again it is profitable to read them successively and at one sitting.)

In Matthew, there is first a scene in which the "chief priests and the Pharisees" ask Pilate to place a guard at the tomb to prevent tampering, for they "recall how that impostor said while he was still alive, 'I am to be raised again in three days.'" In a second, later scene—after the reader is convinced Jesus has been raised—these same chief priests bribe the soldiers to say that the disciples have stolen the body "while we were asleep." Aside from this obvious attempt to rebut a contemporary rumor, we find that Matthew exhibits the risen Christ twice: to the women in the cemetery and to the disciples at the Ascension.

In Mark, you may recall, when the women arrive at the cemetery the grave is open, the body gone, and a young man in white calmly gives them instructions. In Matthew, however, we have the following typically overwrought passage:

> Suddenly there was a violent earthquake; an angel of the Lord descended from heaven and came and rolled away the stone, and sat down on it. His face shone like lightning; his garments were white as snow. At the sight of him the guards shook with fear and fell to the ground as though dead. (28:2–4)

When Matthew's women hurry away to do this angel's bidding, they find Jesus in their path; and, as an indication of his new status, Matthew has them kneel. But the risen Christ simply repeats the angel's message: "Do not be afraid. Go and take word to my brothers that they are to leave for Galilee. They will see me there" (28:10). The scene that would then logically follow, the women telling the news to the apostles, is not given us; Matthew makes a quick cut to the priests fussing over the missing body and then another to Galilee, where the eleven have rather unconvincingly "made their way . . . to the mountain *where Jesus had told them to meet him*" (28:16). The disciples now kneel when they see Jesus, while he utters another remark typical of Matthew, "Full authority in heaven and earth has been committed to me." The whole concludes with a commissioning scene which universalizes this reformed Judaism, postpones the *parousia*, and contains one of the very few trinitarian statements in all the Gospels:

> Go therefore to all nations; make them my disciples; baptize them in the name of the Father and the Son and the Holy Spirit; and teach them to observe all that I have commanded you. I will be with you always, to the end of time.

Luke's resurrection account, on the other hand—which rests on a lot of very early and hard to judge manuscript variations—omits the operatic earthquake at the beginning but adds an additional angel. (In case you haven't noticed, Luke likes twos). The message itself is also changed: Jesus has been raised all right, but the disciples are *not* to go to Galilee. They are to wait in Jerusalem. After Luke's women report this to the disciples there is another of those abrupt cuts.

Suddenly we are somewhere on the road to Emmaus (a village never definitely located). Unrecognized, Jesus appears to a disciple named Cleopas and his friend, who are walking along in conversation. In a clear but clumsy bit of dramatic exposition, Jesus asks them what they are debating, and they reply, the news of the last few days. In the two ensuing speeches we get a summary of Luke's interpretation of Jesus' mission:

> "What news?" he said. "About Jesus of Nazareth," they replied, "who, by deeds and words of power, proved himself a prophet in the sight of God and the whole people; and how our chief priests and rulers handed him over to be sentenced to death, and crucified him. But we had been hoping that he was to be the liberator of Israel. What is more, this is the third day since it happened, and now some women of our company have astounded us: they went early to the tomb, but failed to find his body, and returned with a story that they had seen a vision of angels who told them he was alive. Then some of our people went to the tomb and found things just as the women had said; but him they did not see."
>
> "How dull you are!" he answered. "How slow to believe all that the prophets said! Was not the messiah bound to suffer in this way before entering upon his glory?" Then, starting from Moses and all the prophets, he

explained to them in the whole of scripture the things that referred to himself. (24:19–27 [Revised English Bible])

This is not dialogue; it is Luke's attempt to rebut two contemporary objections to Christianity: that Jesus was a failed revolutionary and that he could not have been the Messiah because he suffered and died on the cross. Later, when Jesus breaks bread with these men, he is suddenly revealed in his true identity and vanishes—an anecdote suspiciously symbolic of the Eucharist. When the story of this meeting is brought to the rest of the disciples in Jerusalem, we are told that they already know of the resurrection and that the Lord has already appeared to Peter. Suddenly, Jesus appears in the room terrifying them; but he calms them by eating some cooked fish, apparently demonstrating that he is not a ghost or spirit—a folk belief we will meet again in John. Luke's point apparently is to show that he who was dead is now alive, that Jesus really *has* been raised from the dead.

Jesus now gives them a lecture that we are spared—presumably the same sort of thing he said on the road to Emmaus—and then leads them out to Bethany, a few miles east of the city. There he "parts" from them, though some manuscripts add "and was carried up into heaven." As we have seen, there were at least two traditions regarding the place of the ascension. Matthew holds to Galilee. Luke, however, has Jesus ascend from somewhere east of Jerusalem: Bethany in his Gospel, the Mount of Olives in Acts.

I know of no one today who thinks either of these resurrection accounts contains much in the way of fact. When you think about it, how could they? To attempt to describe a situation unparalleled in human history, before or since, is to fail. Apart from the obvious sermonizing and the attempts to score off old debating opponents, these narratives establish only that the early church believed its founder had been raised from the dead.

The Acts of the Apostles

The Acts of the Apostles is without precedent or successor in the New Testament. It is a work of Hellenistic history, full of odd personalities, made-up speeches, moralizing, wonders, and wonder-workers. Many commentators treat this book in a rather summary fashion, therefore, looking closely at only one or two of the speeches given to Peter and discussing at length only the controversy over the "Jerusalem Council." This treatment is the more understandable, since a close reading of the text often ends in embarrassment for a contemporary Christian. Unfortunately, the book of Acts is permeated with a quirky, folkish notion of the supernatural, wherewith even the most despicable or trivial magic worked by the disciples is proof of the faith, while similar miracles wrought by others are examples of demonology. Paradoxically, the *non*magical activities of the "apostles" are often gritty, realistic, and unedifying. Indeed, as the book proceeds, the life of the church less and less resembles the life of its founder.

In its opening sentence, the author contends that Acts is the second-volume continuation of Luke's history.

> In the first part of my work, Theophilus, I wrote of all that Jesus did and taught from the beginning until the day, when after giving instructions through the Holy Spirit to the apostles whom he had chosen, he was taken up to heaven. He showed himself to these men after his death, and gave ample proof that he was alive; over a period of forty days he appeared to them and taught them about the kingdom of God.

Despite this statement, there have always been some who question whether the author of Acts really did write the third Gospel. They point especially to those startlingly different accounts of the ascension, which I have already mentioned. Other difficulties arise when one tries to explain the many repeated passages in the text, especially the thrice-told tale of Paul's conversion, and the mysterious "we-passages" in the descriptions of Paul's sea voyages. All of these suggest multiple authorship or incomplete editing by a second party or both. It is not so much that Luke—whoever he was—didn't write a good bit of this text, but that we don't know who was responsible for what he *didn't* write.

Nor do we know much about its publication, except that it was available sometime before the year 100. The name "Acts of the Apostles" dates from the late second century; but there is no evidence that this superscription is original, and it doesn't particularly fit the contents. The earliest readers apparently referred to this document as a "commentary" or "witness," and even in those days it seems to have existed in two manuscript forms, neither of which can be given priority. Every extant text right down to today's is therefore eclectic, a scholarly reconstruction from the two ancient variants.

What sort of story does it tell? From a vantage point of sixty or seventy years later, Acts describes an idealized early church in the first blush of the "waiting time" of the delayed *parousia*. It celebrates the glamorous early days of the church and attempts to show that Christianity is not a threat to the empire. Acts also promulgates a theology of a Holy Spirit—the ongoing presence of God in his peoples' lives. This is the Holy Spirit which brought about Jesus' birth in the first place, counseled him in life, returned to heaven at his death, and now guides his followers.

The first half of the work, sometimes called the "Acts of Peter," describes the movement of the church out from Jerusalem into Samaria and the coast. The second half, the "Acts of Paul," is an account of that apostle's long journey westward to Rome. To appreciate fully the *symbolic* value of this narrative, one should recall that fusion of time I've already commented on. Even as Luke was writing about Jesus' heroic career of fifty years earlier, he was already setting Judaism aside as noble but outmoded. Now in this later work he displays the Gentile church in its geographical and intellectual development. With Jesus gone, this is a curiously lonely business, and there is an inevitable loss of grandeur. Acts does not begin with the stark drama of postresurrection Jerusalem and end in some cocktail party in the sophisticated suburbs south of Rome; but it is an insensitive reader who does not feel the fading of some tragic splendor.

The theology of this story is carried principally by the speeches it is famous for. Occupying more than a fifth of the text, and placed in various mouths to be delivered on various occasions, these declamations—as the reader soon recognizes—are all by Luke and represent *his* version of what the new religion is all about. As we have seen, much the same can be said of the speeches in all the Greek historians, with the possible exception of Xenophon, who as military commander actually delivered some of the speeches he records. In Thucydides especially, the speeches are deliberately composed in the same way to express the historian's view of the developing issues in the war. For the sacred writer, this technique has the advantage of putting the "right ideas" into hallowed mouths. It also presumably contributed to the success of the work; for Luke's understanding of the maturing religion became for many later generations the "meaning" of Christianity, an interpretation which goes by the cumbersome name of "Hellenistic Jewish mission Christianity."

This version of the faith seems to be the kind of Christianity that grew up among the earliest Gentile converts, people often called "Godfearers," a Greek term designating Gentiles who had come to admire Jews and to associate themselves with the synagogues of the Diaspora. For them, the idea of Jesus as "Messiah" or "Son of Man" must always have had less meaning than it had for the early Jewish converts. The title *Messiah*, translated literally as *Christos*, the "anointed one," eventually won out—at the expense of its royal meaning—so that *Jesus Christ* became a proper name. More frequently, it appears, Gentile Christians simply called Jesus "Lord," a usage that can be seen in the Aramaic *Mar,* which Paul sometimes invokes in the complimentary close of his letters: *Marana tha*—"Come Lord!"

"Lord" was also, however, the usual term for the dying and reborn god of the fertility religions then so popular in the Hellenistic world. In their earthly phases, these gods were sometimes thought of as "divine men" who went about preaching and working wonders somewhat in the manner of Jesus as he is portrayed in the Synoptic Gospels. The whole situation and its carryover to Christianity is well illustrated by the episode in Acts 14:8ff. where Paul cures a lame citizen of Lystra (in modern Turkey).

> When the crowds saw what Paul had done, they shouted, in their native Lycaonian, "The gods have come down to us in human form!" And they called Barnabas, Jupiter, and Paul they called Mercury, because he was the spokesman. And the priest of Jupiter, whose temple was just outside the city, brought oxen and garlands to the gates, and he and all the people were about to offer sacrifice.

Paul dissuades them from such blasphemy in a typically Lukan speech about true and false gods—meant to instruct the reader, of course, not the Lycaonians. But in fact this little epiphany must have been repeated, actually or in people's minds, time and again throughout the empire. In fact, in 8:10ff. people behave in just this way toward the magician Simon Magus. "All of them, high and low, listened eagerly to him. 'This man,' they said, 'is that power of God which is called The Great Power.'" The similarities between such men and Jesus are not simply a matter of working wonders. Christianity shares with the fertility religions not only a dying and reborn god, but a sacrificial meal, sacred texts, the notion of immortality, paradise, and hell. So close are the parallels that as early as 160 or so Justin Martyr was arguing that the devil had arranged these correspondences in order to cast doubt on the true religion.

But whatever the exact relation may have been between the fertility or mystery religions and Christianity—the argument continues into our own day—it is clear that Christian theology in the first century began to lose certain Jewish elements and take on others typically Greek. In Acts, the notion of an apocalypse which entails (for Greeks) the offensive or ludicrous idea of a bodily resurrection nearly disappears (cf. Acts 7:2). In its place, Gentile Christians gradually accept the Hellenistic idea of soul and body along with the whole panoply of Platonic thought.

But that is to get far ahead of the story; here in Acts and at the end of the Synoptic tradition, Greek idealistic philosophy lies off in the distance, a cloud no bigger than a person's hand. Jesus has just disappeared into the heavens and his little band has begun its career as a church. Sometime during the ten days between the ascension and Pentecost, Peter delivers his first speech to the brotherhood in Jerusalem, said to be about 120 people. Since it deals with the housekeeping task of restoring the apostles to the sacred number twelve, this speech gives Luke an opportunity to tell still another variant story of how Judas met his end. Then on Pentecost, Peter, along with the restored number of apostles, receives a new baptism of fire from that "Holy Spirit" mentioned earlier. From this point on the speeches of Acts will be high-flown and full of magical authority; the apostles will even "speak in tongues." Unfortunately, Luke seems unaware that on occasion earlier Christians had babbled in this way—people in Paul's communities did it, as do Pentecostal folks today, sometimes on television. Or perhaps he knows about this odd custom but is reluctant to attribute it to his heroes. In any case he misinterprets "tongues" to mean that while the apostles speak in their own Galilean dialect of Aramaic, each member of their audience hears his own language—an unprecedented linguistic and, of course, symbolic miracle.

What is the burden of this universal speech? In effect, Peter gives a theological *interpretation* of the Gospel of Luke. Jesus of Nazareth, he maintains, was a man *chosen* by God to be the Messiah, and this choice was made clear by the wonders he worked on earth. But by God's "deliberate plan" he was yielded up to the Jews of the city who killed him, using "heathen men" (Romans) as their instruments. Jesus was then later raised from the dead and now sits at the right hand of his Father in heaven, where he has once again received the Spirit, which he had yielded up on the cross.

What should Peter's audience do about all this? If they repent and are baptized in the name of Jesus of Nazareth they *too* will receive that Spirit. When Peter finished these remarks, three thousand people, Luke tells us, "were added to the number of believers"; and they chose "to hold everything in common," keeping up a daily attendance at the Temple, sharing their meals "with unaffected joy." This is the picture the author wishes us to have of those earliest days of the Christian community.

> Now the whole group of those who believed were of one heart and soul, and no one claimed private ownership of any possessions, but everything they owned was held in common. With great power the apostles gave their testimony to the resurrection of the Lord Jesus, and great grace was upon them all. There was not a needy person among them, for as many as owned lands or houses sold them and brought the proceeds of what was sold. They laid it at the apostles' feet, and it was distributed to each as any had need. (Acts 4:32–35)

The first breach in this idealized portrait is the troubling defection of Ananias and his wife Sapphira. I first learned of them when I was a youngster and enamored with the prose of Bernard Shaw. In his long preface to *Androcles and the Lion*, Shaw points out that the first miracle the apostles worked on their own "was to strike dead a wretched man and his wife who had defrauded them by holding back some money from the common stock." I remember being scandalized at this remark and then chagrined when, turning to the New Testament, I discovered that Shaw was right. That is exactly what happened, though a student of mine once argued that "it wasn't Peter who killed them; it was God"—as if that improved things.

With this story of Ananias and Sapphira we begin to read the long, checkered history of the *actual* religion—at least as the author imagined it—rather than its foundation documents. A development that might have been foreseen is the split between Jewish and Gentile Christians. Here is how Luke describes it:

> During this period, when disciples were growing in number, a grievance arose on the part of those who spoke Greek, against those who spoke the language of the Jews; they complained that their widows were being overlooked in the daily distribution. The Twelve called the whole company of disciples together and said, "It would not be fitting for us to neglect the word of God in order to assist in the distribution. Therefore, friends, pick seven men of the spirit and of wisdom, and we will appoint them for this duty; then we can devote ourselves to prayer and to the ministry of the word." This proposal proved acceptable to the whole company. They elected Stephen, a man full of faith and of the Holy Spirit, along with Philip, Prochorus, Nicanor, Timon, Parmenas, and Nicolas of Antioch, who had been a convert to Judaism, and presented them to the apostles, who prayed and laid hands on them. (Acts 6:1–6)

You may note that all of the new, so-called deacons (servers) have Greek names, which seems peculiar under the circumstances, and that the apostles are pictured as already withdrawing from public affairs in favor of some kind of preoccupation with the "word of God." Note also that they have "laid hands" on these deacons, an act which Luke thinks has already become the way to transmit spiritual authority; for it will quickly become clear that these newly appointed men are not at all simple quartermaster corps officials. The first two, Stephen and Philip, are—with Peter—the *heroes* of the first half of Acts. Stephen achieves fame by lecturing the Sanhedrin on what he takes to be a Jewish habit of rejecting the truth: "Our fathers would not accept his [Moses'] leadership but thrust him aside. . . ." And the present generation is doing the same: "How stubborn you are, heathen still at heart, and deaf to the truth! You always resist the Holy Spirit. You are just like your fathers!" Shaw, by the way, thought this speech so long, boring, and ungenerous that Stephen's subsequent stoning was "pardonable and human in comparison to the slaughter of poor Ananias and Sapphira." But it is clear that Stephen serves a theological purpose. On dying, Stephen paraphrases Jesus' cry from the cross (Luke 23:34) with, "Lord, do not hold this sin against them." Luke then summarizes what followed.

> This was the beginning of a time of violent persecution for the church in Jerusalem; and all except the apostles were scattered over the country districts of Judea and Samaria. Stephen was given burial by certain devout men, who made a great lamentation for him. Saul, meanwhile, was harrying the church; he entered house after house, seizing men and women and sending them to prison. (Acts 8:1–3)

With this last subtle but dramatic introduction of the hero of the second half of the book, we are nearing the end of that first Jewish-Christian church in Jerusalem, though for a while yet the city will continue to function as Christian headquarters. The deacon Philip is said to have carried the word from here northward into Samaria, where he works many cures and exorcisms amid great rejoicing. These Samaritan converts seem to be at first "halfway" Christians, people who have been baptized with water but not *with the Holy Spirit via the laying on of hands*. Peter and John will come up later to complete the job. The same curious distinction will appear later among the Ephesians converted by Apollos (see Acts 18:24ff.) Still later it will give rise to the sacrament of Confirmation, a laying on of hands, traditionally administered only by a bishop—a successor to the apostles. What is happening here in terms of both "clergy" and "laity" is the inevitable demise of that radical democracy which inspired the Q people and perhaps Jesus himself. Slowly but surely, ecclesiastical—even "salvational"—distinctions are arising. Apparently some people are admitted to the community (water) but don't qualify for full membership (spirit or fire). Some sorts of things no longer befit the apostles, and so on. On the horizon one sees cardinals and popes.

With the north secure, the "angel of the Lord" now tells Philip to turn south toward Gaza. On the way he comes across an Ethiopian eunuch, the treasurer of that kingdom, who just happens to be reading Isaiah as he journeys along in his carriage. I have always been stunned by this encounter. At which should I be more surprised: the chance appearance of this august and literate personage or the smoothness of the freeway south of Judea? What the man is reading aloud (which in fact *was* the way ancients read) is a passage we have seen to be fundamental to the understanding of Jesus as the "suffering" Messiah, Isaiah 53:7–8. Quickly converted and baptized, the Ethiopian eunuch passes out of history—apparently he never did receive the baptism of the Holy Spirit.

Setting aside for the moment Acts 9:1–30 (the first account of Paul's conversion, which forms another dovetail passage for part 2), let me complete the final activities of the Jerusalem church. While Philip has gone north and then south, Peter has journeyed westward toward the coast. At Lydda he cures a paralytic with the clearly Gentile name of Aeneas, after which a disciple who has apparently preceded him summons him to Joppa. This man has been concerned about the death of a girl, Tabitha (Greek *Dorcas*) whom Peter now raises back to life. Farther up the coast at Caesarea lives a centurion named Cornelius, one of those Godfearers I have spoken about, who has been told by an angel to send for Peter. The next day, while Cornelius's servants are still on the way to him, Peter is hungry and falls into a trance:

> He saw a rift in the sky, and a thing coming down that looked like a great sheet of sailcloth. It was slung by the four corners, and was being lowered to the ground. In it he saw creatures of every kind, whatever walks or crawls or flies. Then there came a voice which said to him, "Up, Peter, kill and eat." But Peter said, "No Lord, no; I have never eaten anything profane or unclean." The voice came again, a second time. "It is not for you to call profane what God counts clean." This happened three times, and then the thing was taken up into sky. (Acts 10:11–16)

Prepared by his vision for the full Gentile mission, Peter awakens and, guided by the Spirit, journeys to Caesarea, where he addresses the crowd. From a historical point-of-view, his speech may be the most important passage in Acts.

> Then Peter began to speak to them: "I truly understand that God shows no partiality, but in every nation anyone who fears him and does what is right is acceptable to him. You know the message he sent to the people of Israel ... how God anointed Jesus of Nazareth with the Holy Spirit and with power; how he went about doing good and healing all who were oppressed by the devil, for God was with him. We are witnesses to all that he did both in Judea and in Jerusalem. They put him to death by hanging him on a tree; but God raised him on the third day and allowed him to appear, not to all the people but to us who were chosen by God as witnesses, and who ate and drank with him after he rose from the dead. He commanded us to preach to the people and to testify that he is the one ordained by God as judge of the living and the dead. All the prophets testify about him that everyone who believes in him receives forgiveness of sins through his name.

> While Peter was still speaking, the Holy Spirit fell upon all who heard the word. The circumcised believers who had come with Peter were astounded that the gift of the Holy Spirit had been poured out even on the Gentiles, for they heard them speaking in tongues and extolling God. (Acts 10:34–47)

This last sentence is a recognition that *someone* who has handled this manuscript *did* understand speaking in tongues. But the overriding element in Peter's speech is its attempt to universalize the Christian cult. Gone is the problem of the judaizers, which, as we shall see, Paul had to struggle with forty years earlier. Gone also are the holiness laws Matthew was still championing. What we have here is a theological foundation statement for what by now is an accomplished fact: Gentile Christianity. After assuring himself that his companions have no objection, Peter now reverses the usual order and baptizes the new converts with water *after* they have received the Spirit. Yet when he gets back to Jerusalem, he has to answer for this non-Jewish outreach. According to Luke, he tells his associates in great detail of his food vision in Joppa; and they—unhesitatingly and unhistorically—say, "This means that God has granted life-giving repentance to the Gentiles also." The Great Church is on its way.

Word now comes of more Gentile conversions in Antioch on the Orontes, today a ruin covered in silt but then one of the great cities of the world. Founded by the Seleucid successors of Alexander, it was a sophisticated, cosmopolitan place. "It was in Antioch," Luke tells us, "that the disciples first got the name 'Christian.'" A man named Barnabas, apparently neither apostle nor deacon, is sent up from Jerusalem to investigate the conversions taking place there and is pleased with what he sees; he then in turn goes off to Tarsus in Cilicia for Paul. Paul's subsequent, fateful arrival in Antioch seems to symbolize the new course of the religion—particularly because it occurs at the same time as a martyrdom in Jerusalem, which represents the end of the *old* understanding. During Passover, Herod Agrippa I, king of Judea, executes the apostle James, the brother of John; and Peter is arrested, though he escapes. Acts part 1 ends as Herod is miraculously punished by being eaten by worms.

Summarizing all this would be a little like summarizing Wagner's *Ring*, and about as helpful. Acts part 1 is simply a romanticized tale of the geographical and ideological development of the Christian church. How much is historical? I would think very little. Obviously the author is far more interested in portraying a successful Gentile mission than he is in any sort of realism. His missionaries, Barnabas, Philip, and Peter, are barely distinguishable as characters. Clearly more important are the speeches Luke creates for them in which we have the faith, not of Mark, nor of the Q people, nor of

Matthew, but of the emerging Great Church. At the risk of some repetition let me at least try to summarize *that.*

Luke believes that Jesus' whole life was planned by God, including his being killed by some of the Jews of Jerusalem (who used the Romans as "innocent" instruments). He believes Jesus was raised from the dead three days later to spend forty days with the apostles, eating and drinking with them and giving them "ample proof" that he was alive. Bidding them preach his message to all men, Jesus then returned to heaven, and there he received the Holy Spirit once again—the same Spirit which would descend on the apostles themselves ten days later. It is this spirit which they themselves are to impart to believers by the laying on of hands. Finally, it is this spirit that has made it clear that there is no longer any necessity for observing Jewish law, for "God has no favorites." There are good men and women in all nations, baptized or not, and these, like the believers in Antioch, are welcome to become "Christians."

The second half of the book of Acts, including the dovetail passage which I skipped at 9:1–30, is devoted to the Gentile mission of Paul of Tarsus. At the outset it is important to note that Luke's account of Paul's character, life, and theology does not agree with that contained in Paul's own letters. So true is this statement that careful scholars write of "Luke's Paul" or "the Paul of Acts" as distinct from *Paul.*

How did such disharmonies come about? One attractive theory goes like this. Forty or fifty years before Luke wrote the book of Acts, Paul (Saul) had been proselytizing the Way. And decades before *any* of the Synoptic Gospels was composed, he had written marvelously compelling letters to several early Christian communities in modern Turkey and Greece. Some of these "churches" Paul had himself founded. By Luke's day, therefore, a body of oral and written tradition had grown about this Paul, including perhaps a travel diary or other such written source. But as far we can tell from Acts, his letters had not been widely circulated, but still reposed in the churches to which they had been sent. Luke did not know them, and there is no record of *anyone* reading them until the year 96 C.E. When he came to write the story of Paul's missionary activity, therefore, what Luke knew and described was the "traditional" early hero, the image of Paul preserved in the church's memory.

To understand this, imagine someone in the 1870s writing a life of Lincoln based on the popular stories told about the president—splitting rails, fighting in the Black Hawk War, defending an accused murderer with an almanac, marrying the wrong girl, etc.—without any recourse to what

Lincoln ever actually wrote or said. Imagine further that this "Life of Lincoln" is so popular that people begin to search for Lincoln memorabilia and discover authentic correspondence of the president dating from the 1860s. When these are published, they offer a portrait quite different from that of the folklore hero.

This apparently is what happened to Paul. In the 50s he wrote his own story in letters. In the 90s, Luke wrote a biography of him without recourse to these letters. But now came the switcheroo. The popularity of Luke's biography not only prompted people to publish Paul's earlier writings; it also motivated people to write *new* Pauline letters signed with the apostle's name but addressing the concerns of Christians living half a century later. We will later see *two* groups of such pseudo-Pauline letters, composed about twenty years apart. What is important for the moment is that where Paul and Luke narrate the same event, they often differ. Moreover, the speeches Luke creates for his character are often quite un-Pauline—being actually no different in style or content from those put into the mouths of his Stephen or his Peter.

With these warnings in mind, then, let us turn to the second half of Acts as if to a campaign biography or school-text life of a past hero, not expecting either accuracy or verisimilitude. In the passage which I temporarily skipped (Acts 9:1–30), Luke gives us his own third-person account of Paul's famous conversion, an experience that was of supreme importance to Gentile Christianity. Luke will later have Paul himself repeat the story twice more (and we will read Paul's own memoir of it in the following chapter), so there are three Lukan versions of this story, which vary only slightly: bystanders on the road to Damascus sometimes hear the voice but do not see the light and vice versa. Moreover, parts of this basic story are confirmed by Paul's own letters.

In outline it goes like this. Sometime in the 30s, Saul receives authority from the high priest in Jerusalem to arrest Christians in Damascus. While on the way there, he is knocked off his horse, sees a great light from heaven, and hears Jesus' voice asking why he is persecuting him. Temporarily blinded by the vision, Paul enters Damascus, where he lodges in the Street Called Straight. (It is still there, by the way, and was probably there when Abraham came through on his way to Canaan). In Damascus Paul is visited by a certain Ananias, who has likewise been given divine instructions. Ananias puts his hands on Paul, and Paul receives the Holy Spirit and his sight. There are troubling historical questions about this story. For instance, though Damascus undoubtedly harbored unorthodox Jews in this period, it stretches the imagination to think that a high priest in Jerusalem could empower Paul to arrest people living in a foreign country.

The rest of Acts part 2 is devoted to a detailed exposition of Paul's missionary work. After baptism in Damascus he begins preaching about Jesus in the synagogues, throwing the Jewish community there into confusion. Forced to escape, he returns to Jerusalem; but there the Jewish-Christians are afraid of him because of his past behavior, and the church "officials" finally send him to Tarsus for his own protection. Perhaps because of the persecution in which Stephen was killed, Jewish-Christians now begin to show up in Antioch; and Barnabas, who as we have seen has gone north to preach to this new mixed group, soon brings Paul from Tarsus. The two remain in Antioch for a year, during which time they take up a collection of money for their fellow Christians down in Jerusalem.

A bit later, Paul and Barnabas are directed by the Holy Spirit to go off on a missionary trek, which results in what has come to be called Paul's "First Journey." (There will be three of these journeys—whether actual or invented by Luke we do not know.) In any case, Barnabas and Paul now go down to the port city of Seleucia and from there set sail for Cyprus. Here they engage in what has become Paul's habitual practice, according to Luke: of first preaching in the local synagogue and then moving out to the Gentiles. Making their way through the island as far as Paphos, they find themselves opposed by a sorcerer named Elymas, who is in the retinue of the Roman governor. Paul miraculously (but temporarily) blinds this fellow, an act that converts the governor to Christianity.

From Paphos, Barnabas and Paul sail to Perga in Pamphylia on the Asian mainland, and then they go inland to Pisidian Antioch. Here Paul preaches a sermon in the synagogue that is of the same content and theme as Stephen's earlier speech in Jerusalem. Paul, however, meets with some initial success; but when large crowds begin to come to hear him, "the Jews . . . were filled with jealous resentment and contradicted what Paul had said, with violent abuse" (Acts 13:45). In fact, the "leading people" in town are so stirred up that Paul and Barnabas are expelled. At Iconium, farther inland still, a plot is laid to "maltreat and stone" them, but they escape to next-door Lystra, where they work miracles and are taken for Mercury and Jupiter, as I have already mentioned. Later, Jews from Pisidian Antioch and Iconium arrive, stone Paul, and leave him for dead, but his friends defend and revive him. This pattern will continue; it will generally be "the Jews," only sometimes in league with "Gentiles," who persecute Paul and his friends—never the Romans.

Paul and Barnabas now retrace their steps through these same towns (!) and sail home from Perga. In Antioch they find turmoil. People have come from Jerusalem who insist that Gentile converts to Christianity must be circumcised. Barnabas and Paul are therefore sent to see the "apostles and elders" in Jerusalem to try to straighten the matter out, a mission that results in a momentous event in the history of the early church, the so-called Council of Jerusalem. In Luke's version of this meeting, Peter takes the "liberal" side of the issue. He recalls that in the "early days" when God had decided that "from my lips the Gentiles were to hear and believe the message of the gospel," the Holy Spirit simply descended upon Gentile converts and no further "yoke" was laid on them. Why should more be asked of them now? James the brother of the Lord then authoritatively announces a compromise solution whereby Gentile converts will be bound only to abstain from fornication, from food that has been in contact with idols, from anything strangled, and from blood. A letter to this effect is then addressed to Antioch containing the curiously regal statement: "It is the decision of the Holy Spirit, and our decision, to lay no further burden upon you."

This account of the event is particularly fascinating to those professionally interested in the history of early Christianity, since Paul's letters flatly contradict it. In his Letter to the Galatians of forty years earlier, Paul had boasted that he had nothing to do with compromise and that "those reputed pillars of our society" down in Jerusalem only asked that he and his people take up a collection for them (Gal. 2:9)! Why the discrepancy?

I think Luke is probably relying on various and sometimes contradictory traditions and trying to honor them all. Note how Peter refers to the "early days"—though the reader has not experienced much elapsed time since the conversion of Cornelius—in which he was both head of the church and apostle to the Gentiles. Now he seems to have lost to James whatever leadership position he may have had, and to Paul the mission to the Gentiles. I suspect also that the compromise James sends out by letter, though unhistorical from the viewpoint of Paul, may represent an actual solution to the problem of the Jewish-Christian church in some *other* locale. In general, however, I think that these issues simply didn't much matter to Luke in 90 C.E., twenty years after the destruction of Jerusalem and its church. What is really important may be the simple "fact" that a council was held; for its occurrence answers the question, How does the church settle problems?

Paul's second journey is taken with Silas. The two of them start out overland from Antioch through Paul's home province of Cilicia, intending to visit the communities he has already established. When they reach Lystra, Paul picks up a disciple named Timothy whom he is said to have circumcised "in consideration of the Jews." Like the account of the council, this story sharply contrasts with Paul's own statement that he refused such a request in the case of another disciple named Titus (Gal. 2:3–4). Again I suspect that Luke has a memory of one way of solving an old problem and is unaware of Paul's opposition to it. Peculiarly, when Paul's little party tries to preach farther north toward the Black Sea, it is magically prevented from doing so.

> They traveled through the Phrygian and Galatian region, because they were prevented by the Holy Spirit from delivering the message in the province of Asia; and when they approached the Mysian border they tried to enter Bithynia; but the Spirit of Jesus would not allow them, so they skirted Mysia and reached the coast of Troas. (Acts 16:6–9)

What exactly the author means by the enigmatic "Spirit of Jesus" no one knows; but otherwise this is a typical supernatural act on behalf of the plot. Shut out of northeastern Turkey, the missionaries take a diagonal course to Troy, which lies on a coastal plain within striking distance of Europe and is—and *was*—the most illustrious ground of the "West." That a crossing over from here is part of a divine plan is confirmed by Paul's famous dream on that historic site. A Macedonian man appears at his bedside—the fashion in prophetic Greek dreams of this period—saying, "Cross over to Macedonia and help us." The text then continues, "As soon as he had seen his vision, we set about getting a passage" (Acts 16:9–10).

If you are a Christian, you may still thrill to these words, which symbolically, though not actually, represent the beginning of "Western Christianity." But if you are also a careful reader, you will have noticed that the point of view of the writing has suddenly shifted from third to first person plural. The reaction to Paul's vision, "*we* set about getting passage," is the first of the famous we-passages of Acts. From now on, these switches in point of view will occur frequently, especially at the beginning of sea voyages where the "we" appears and persists while the characters are at sea, only unobtrusively to disappear on land. No one has ever known what to make of this phenomenon. *Koinē* Greek, like English, allows for an authorial shift as in "Now that we have examined the use of . . ."; indeed, Plutarch writes this way frequently. But that is not the same thing. As suggested earlier, Luke may have had a travel diary written by some companion of Paul, but if so its author must have been remarkably uninterested in theology.

Now on Samothrace, Paul and Timothy sail to the mainland and visit in turn Neapolis and Philippi. At the latter Roman town, he converts a female Godfearer, Lydia, a dealer in purple dye, one of the first middle-class people he has won over. He also picks up an admiring slave girl who, through being possessed, provides a living for her owners by telling fortunes. This girl follows the missionaries about constantly shouting, "These men are servants of the Most High. . . ." "In exasperation," as Luke puts it, Paul casts out her devil to stop her mouth—which is a bad move since she now tells no more fortunes. Her owners in turn denounce the Christians as revolutionaries, with the result that they are thrown in jail. But help is on the way. In the middle of the night, God sends an earthquake, which unfastens the missionaries' bonds, so that when the jailer wakes up he thinks they have escaped. This fellow is about to commit suicide when Paul reassures him that they are all present. But typically, Paul is still aggrieved and embarrasses the frightened magistrates by insisting that they escort him out of town. There is no shortage of plot—or, I suspect, humor—in the Acts of the Apostles.

Paul's party now makes its way from Amphipolis to Thessalonica to Beroea and from there down to Athens, where he gives a memorable, stoic, quite un-Pauline speech.

> Athenians, I see how extremely religious you are in every way. For as I went through the city and looked carefully at the objects of your worship, I found among them an altar with the inscription, "To an unknown god." What therefore you worship as unknown, this I proclaim to you. The God who made the world and everything in it, he who is Lord of heaven and earth, does not live in shrines made by human hands. . . . From one ancestor he made all nations to inhabit the whole earth . . . so that they would search for God and perhaps grope for him and find him—though indeed he is not far from each one of us. For "In him we live and move and have our being"; as even some of your own poets have said, "For we too are his offspring."(Acts 17:22–29)

It is not that this sort of speech directly contradicts Paul's genuine doctrine; it is the fact that "Christ Jesus" not only doesn't appear in it but doesn't *need* to appear. In any case, though the Athenians are polite, only a few are converted. Paul now continues on to Corinth, where he meets a couple who will become great friends, Aquila and Priscilla, Jews originally from Pontus, and tentmakers like himself. Their importance lies in dating Paul's career; for this couple has "recently" been driven out of Rome by an anti-Semitic edict of Claudius dated to about 49 C.E. Moreover, when Paul gets into the usual trouble with the local synagogue, he appears before a proconsul named Gallio, whose term here can be dated to 51–53 C.E. Accompanied by these new friends, he now sails back to Antioch.

Paul's third journey takes him overland from Antioch to Ephesus again, where he makes his headquarters for some two years. During that time several instructive events occur. First of all, a Jewish Christian named Apollos shows up who baptizes "only with water in the manner of John," indicating that a doctrine of two baptisms was apparently still a reality though its details are now lost. Fortunately, Aquila and Priscilla have remained in Ephesus and now "take him in hand"; and after instructing him in the deeper lore, they see this missionary off across the Aegean to Greece, where we will later hear of him. I must say I feel a little sorry for Apollos. Like a good many early Christian zealots, like Aquila and Priscilla themselves, he has pretty much gone unhonored in the history of the faith. Sainthood, among other things, is a matter of luck.

Because of the obdurate nature of the Jewish community in Ephesus, Paul eventually retires from the synagogue and preaches in the lecture hall of Tyrannus, apparently with success of a certain type: "when handkerchiefs and scarves which had been in contact with his skin were carried to the sick, they were cured of their diseases, and the evil spirits came out of them" (Acts 19:11–12). There is also that wonderfully funny exorcism I mentioned earlier. When seven itinerant Jews try casting a devil out of a possessed man by saying, "I adjure you by Jesus whom Paul proclaims . . . ," the evil spirit responds, "Jesus I acknowledge, and I know about Paul, but who are you?" The possessed man then attacks all seven would-be exorcists with such fury that "they ran out of the house stripped and battered" (Acts 19:13–17).

But the most impressive anecdote from this period in Ephesus does not have Paul for its hero. To understand it you must know that the local deity was Artemis of the Ephesians, a renowned fertility goddess whose silver image with multiple breasts (or fruits) was recognized throughout the Mediterranean area. Naturally one of the largest "guilds" in the city was that of the silversmiths, and it was one of these craftsmen, Demetrius, who took it into his head that Paul's attack on "gods made with human hands" was bad for business and should be stopped. There followed a citywide uproar in which Paul and his friends were dragged to the theater (which is still there, by the way). Things are getting hot and dangerous when the town clerk steps forward. He quiets the unruly crowd and speaks:

"Men of Ephesus," he said, "all the world knows that our city of Ephesus is temple-warden of the great Diana and of that symbol of her which fell from heaven. Since these facts are beyond dispute, your proper course is to keep quiet and do nothing rash. These men whom you have brought here as culprits have committed no sacrilege and uttered no blasphemy against our goddess. If, therefore, Demetrius and his craftsmen have a case against anyone, assizes are held and there are such things as proconsuls; let the parties bring their charges and countercharges. If, on the other hand, you have some further question to raise, it will be dealt with in the statutory assembly. We certainly run the risk of being charged with riot for this day's work. There is no justification for it, and if the issue is raised we shall be unable to give any explanation of this uproar." With that he dismissed the assembly. (Acts 19:35–41)

I suppose the purpose of this scene is to show that nothing can really harm Paul as he follows out the plan of the Holy Spirit and that if the Romans remain true to their noble institutions they will see that Christians are no threat. Yet with the passage of time it is more and more the town clerk who captures the reader's attention and admiration. Oddly enough, the most civilized speech in the New Testament is delivered by an unnamed minor official of a pagan city who is at best neutral toward the Christian faith.

Paul now visits Macedonia again and Greece, returning by way of Philippi to the Troas where he preaches so far into evening that a young man named Eutychus ("Lucky") falls asleep and tumbles from an upper-story window. Paul raises him from the dead. But finally Paul is determined to return to Jerusalem. Sailing down the coast to Miletus, he meets with some Ephesian elders who have come down to meet him, and he bids them farewell, summarizing his mission and predicting his death. He then takes ship for Palestine, where, as soon as he lands, the disciples, "warned by the spirit," urge him not to continue on to Jerusalem. The celebrated prophet Agabus says the same thing. But convinced that he is following the will of God, Paul goes up to the capital to report to James. Since the Jewish-Christians are still disturbed by the notion of a Gentile gospel, Paul even goes through a purification ritual to satisfy them—and James.

The last part of Acts, from 21:27 to the end, is devoted to the apostle's adventures in Jerusalem and the resulting trials, followed by his voyage to Rome, where, "lodged privately with a soldier in charge of him," Paul disappears from history, still proclaiming "the Lord Jesus Christ quite openly and without hindrance." The whole account is filled with improbable events and coincidences; and yet there are tiny, circumstantial details difficult to dismiss as the products of invention. For readers of his letters, however, these concluding chapters present an almost unrecognizable "Paul." His personality and teaching are made into a caricature, particularly in the charges and countercharges of the several confusing trial scenes.

Let me summarize as briefly as I can this last adventure-packed "voyage." While Paul is in Jerusalem undergoing the purification rite James has insisted upon, he is recognized by some Jews from the province of Asia who then stir up the crowd, claiming that Paul has brought Gentiles into the Temple. There is another mob scene, and he is only saved from death by the intervention of a Roman detachment. On the steps of the barracks, Paul asks the centurion if he might address the crowd, and the officer agrees!

The ensuing speech is that second account of his conversion which I mentioned above. At first it is received sympathetically, but when Paul proclaims his mission to the Gentiles all hell breaks loose. He is pulled within the barracks and is about to be questioned (perhaps under torture) when he quietly asks the centurion, "Does the law allow you to flog a Roman citizen, and an unconvicted one at that?" (Luke's Paul is always very cool.) Apparently afraid he may have misused a Roman citizen, the official "frees" Paul, but makes him appear before the Sanhedrin.

In the assembly, Paul claims that he is a Pharisee who awaits the resurrection. He does this in order to split the assembly, setting the parties at loggerheads. The stratagem is effective; the meeting ends in an uproar, and the Romans withdraw Paul from the interview. That night Jesus appears to him in a vision, encouraging him and predicting that he will preach in Rome; but in the morning news arrives that "forty Jews" have taken an oath neither to eat nor drink until they have assassinated him. We never learn whether these conspirators die of thirst or not, for Paul's nephew tips off the authorities, who in turn arrange for a night escort to Caesarea: two hundred infantry accompanied by seventy cavalry and two hundred lightly armed men! And the commandant sends word with this army that he has no charge against the prisoner!

At Caesarea, the governor summons the high priest Ananias and some of the Jewish elders represented by the advocate Tertullus, who indicts Paul on the charge that he is a fomenter of discord among the Jews, a ringleader of the sect of the Nazarenes, one who has attempted to profane the Temple. Apart from perhaps the last, Paul is of course guilty as charged; but he defends himself by saying that he hasn't fomented discord *within the city*— and they can't prove otherwise. The governor, Felix, postpones his decision for a few days, allowing for a private interview between himself and his wife and Paul, the purpose of which, according to Luke, is to solicit a bribe.

Two years pass.

Felix has now been succeeded as governor by a man named Porcius Festus with whom the adamant forces in Jerusalem renew their charges. There is a second "trial" at Caesarea at which Paul makes his mysterious "appeal to Caesar." Without considering the logistics of the matter, Luke believes that any Roman citizen who uttered these words was automatically and irrevocably (cf. Acts 26:32) sent under guard to Rome, even when, as Festus admits, there is still no charge from which to appeal. While awaiting transport, Paul appears before King Agrippa II and his sister Bernice, who seem to have just dropped by for this purpose. Here Paul gives a Lukan speech which in "real life" would have startled his friends—not to mention Moses and the prophets.

> I assert nothing beyond what was foretold by the prophets and by Moses: that the Messiah must suffer and that he, the first to rise from the dead, would announce the dawn to Israel and to the Gentiles. (Acts 26:22–23)

Finally Paul is sent off to Rome accompanied by a centurion. Their thrilling sea voyage, narrated by "we," is first to Sidon, then along the northern coast of Cyprus to a port in Lycia where they transship for the long sail westward. Once past Crete and truly out to sea, Paul warns his shipmates of disaster, and of course a rousing storm ensues, magnificently enshrined in authentic *koinē* naval jargon. On the fourteenth evening they find themselves in danger of abandonment by the crew, but thanks to Paul they overcome this obstacle and eventually beach the ship on the island of Malta. Here he works a few miracles, ingratiates himself with the local magistrate and after three months continues his trip to Syracuse, Rhegium, and finally Puteoli, a port of Rome.

Surprisingly, Paul is met there by fellow *Christians;* and others welcome him on the Appian Way just outside the city. The archaeologist John Romer points out that graffiti in Ostia and Pompeii prove that Christians were in Rome at least by 79 C.E. (*Testament*, 192), and that a few were in Rome still earlier is confirmed by Paul's letter of the 50s. Yet, as usual, Paul seems more concerned with the Jewish community, going to the synagogue and converting "some." He then, as I have said, quotes Isaiah on the invincible blindness of Israel and the passing of the "hope" to the Gentiles—the same note struck by Stephen at the very beginning of this work—and in much the same style.

> How well the Holy Spirit spoke to your fathers through the prophet Isaiah when he said, "Go to this people and say: You may listen and listen, but you will never understand; you may look and look, but you will never see. For this people's mind has become dull; they have stopped their ears and closed their eyes. Otherwise, their eyes might see, their ears hear, and their mind understand, and then they might turn again, and I would heal them." Therefore take note that this salvation of God has been sent to the Gentiles; the Gentiles will listen. (Acts 28:25–28 [Revised English Bible])

You may recall that this passage from Isaiah was also quoted in Mark and, in a revised form, repeated by Matthew. The revisions were intended to suggest that if some people did not understand the Lord's preaching, it was their own fault, that it was not God who had dulled their minds but they themselves. Here Luke distorts Isaiah even further in this direction to show that the Jews *deliberately* rejected the good news; and therefore God had handed it over to the Gentiles. In this way, what was a historical fact of the early church, the disappearance of the Jewish-Christian community and the "triumph" of Gentile-Christians, is given an ancient prophetic sanction. These four uses of the same scriptural passage therefore provide an example of the entire developing Synoptic tradition and I shall end this discussion of Luke-Acts by simply quoting, from the Jerusalem Bible, the operative sentences of each.

> Isaiah: "Go and say to this people [of Judea and Israel], 'Hear and hear again, but do not understand; see and see again, but do not perceive.' Make the heart of this people gross, its ears dull; shut its eyes so that it will not see with its eyes, hear with its ears, understand with its heart, and be converted and healed." (Isa. 6:9–10)

> Mark: "The secret of the kingdom of God is given to you [the disciples], but to those who are outside everything comes in parables so that they may see and see again, but not perceive; may hear and hear again, but not understand; otherwise they might be converted and be forgiven." (Mark 4:11–12)

> Matthew: "The reason I talk to them in parables is that they look without seeing and listen without hearing or understanding. So in their case this prophecy of Isaiah is being fulfilled: 'You will listen and listen again, but not understand, see and see again, but not perceive. For the heart of this nation has grown coarse, their ears are dull of hearing, and they have shut their eyes, for fear they should see with their eyes, hear with their ears, understand with their heart, and be converted and be healed by me.' But happy are your [the disciples'] eyes because they see, your ears because they hear!" (Matt. 13:13–15)

> Luke: "For the heart of this nation has grown coarse; their ears are dull of hearing and they have shut their eyes, for fear they should see with their eyes, hear with their ears, understand with their heart, and be converted and be healed by me. Understand, then, that this salvation of God has been sent to the pagans; they will listen to it." (Acts 28:25–28)

With Paul's arrival in Rome, Luke's two-volume book come to its unsatisfactory conclusion; we learn no more of Paul's final end than of Peter's.

B y the end of Acts the Synoptic tradition has matured. To understand this is first of all to understand that Mark, Matthew, and Luke-Acts *do* form a tradition, a *developing* set of ideas and feelings about the story of Jesus and its relation to Judaism. I emphasize the word developing because as far back as we wish to go in these documents and in the speculation about them, we will never come upon a "beginning." We are never confident that we are hearing Jesus' own words; always we deal with interpretations. A recognition of this fact is a condition of our reading these documents sensibly.

You may recall that the earliest materials in this tradition are Q and the Gospel of Mark. The first may have been complied as early as 50 C.E., the second dates from about 66 or 70. The Q people believed in the soon-to-be Second Coming of the Lord—at least in the final form of their sayings—and they took fervor from the belief that many good things would come to those who would see it. It was the source of their hope: "better times are coming," as the Civil War song has it. Meanwhile, poverty—indeed austerity—had its own joys. According to Mark, Jesus' immediate followers, the eyewitnesses of his ministry, fail to understand him and in the end betray him. But by some postresurrection miracle, perhaps too well known or too sacred to be discussed, we readers of Mark—we foreign, Gentile believers—have already received the Risen Lord and now await his coming in the sky.

What did Matthew believe when fifteen to twenty years later he rewrote a combination of Mark and Q? Well, for one thing, he understood and sympathized with the Jewishness of the story and therefore retold it so that this element of the tradition was preserved and made prominent. Moreover, he believed that the *parousia* of the Lord would not be soon, but long delayed. Indeed, Matthew's Gospel can be read as a kind of narrative answer to Mark—as well as an answer to those first Gentile converts whom we are to meet in the next chapter, the disciples of Paul. They were not wrong, says Matthew, but only less perfect than his own Jewish-oriented community. Nor were those early apostles in Jerusalem wrong; nor did they completely misunderstand the message of Jesus, the Messiah. To be sure they were human and fallible, and they rightly wished to preserve their heritage, but in the end those "fathers of the church" also realized that Judaism needed to be reformed into a new universal religion, superior to that being worked out by the rabbis at Jamnia. Much of Matthew's view has persisted in Christian theology: his vague ethic, his insistence on the roots of the church in Judaism, his operatic last judgment, his ecclesiology.

What will become the "mood" of the church's theology, however, is derived from Luke: the Hellenistic mission religion. Luke still considers the age of Judaism heroic; but now, safely relegated to the first of three time dispensations, it need no longer be an object of concern. So too, as a matter of fact, is what will later be called the "Jesus of History," the *biographical* Jesus whose ministry we have just finished reading about. For Luke, as for many Christian thinkers, what is of supreme importance is that Holy Spirit which descended upon the church at Pentecost and remains with it through all the waiting time—whether one imagines him as the "risen Lord" or the third person of a coming Trinity.

Even such a brief summary tends to exaggerate the diversity of the Synoptic tradition. Though each evangelist downplays some of its elements and emphasizes others, depending on the interests of his time and his place, these Gospels are less "redactional" than many scholars believe. This is to say that they are less controlled by the author's theme and more inclusive of variant traditions than the commentaries suggest. Many of the differences among them are striking only because we read them *against their fellows* in the wholly artificial context of an anthology.

How did this qualified unity come about? Perhaps the best way to think about this Synoptic unity is provided by Burton Mack, who speaks of the creation of a Christian epic—one that would seize upon Jewish scriptures and make them its own—at least in their Septuagint form. Many Christians seem never to have reflected on this fact, taking their "two-book" religion for granted and being careless of how this interpretation might look to their Jewish neighbors. But it is very clear that though they vary in their use of proof texts, all the evangelists are in the business of making a grand prose epic which combines the literature and beliefs of both faiths. In Luke, the story begins at the creation and extends to the end of time. Nor was the underlying problem of there being two ways of reading the Jewish scriptures ever ignored. Indeed, beginning with Justin Martyr in the second century, the early fathers were consumed with making a case for the Christian reading of that ancient body of writing—not always unmixed with outright anti-Semitism. Eventually and despite obvious difficulties, they were able to read nearly every line as a forecast of Jesus Christ. Here is Mack's ironic comment:

> The predictions were hiding here and there amidst a voluminous literature. The Christian exegete had to find them, match them up to details of the gospel story, and argue for reading them as a prediction of Jesus instead of belonging to the stories of Israel. And since they were predictions, their hidden "meanings" could possibly have been known about. Thus the predictions had lain dormant (in the scriptures!) until Jesus came and his followers discovered that the predictions had been made. Like Alice in Wonderland, the modern reader will find this line of reasoning curiouser and curiouser, for the prediction finally does not predict at all. (*Who Wrote the New Testament,* 269)

Given the delay of the *parousia,* what theological good news did this Jewish-Christian epic finally contain? Well, by the time of the writing of the

Synoptic Gospels, Christians were apparently focused almost exclusively on reaching "the kingdom"; *when* had little meaning for them. Meanwhile, they wanted to live transcendently, that is, on some level vaguely superior to the way in which they had lived as pagans or Jews. It was of these people that I asked at the beginning of this chapter, What did they expect from the new religion, apart from the cultic feeling of belonging and solidarity and the joy that comes from secret knowledge? I think now it is possible to answer that question, not only for Luke-Acts but for the Synoptic tradition in general. They simply wanted *better times*.

One sees this in their curious lack of mystical fervor. In the Synoptics we almost never hear of "the joy of being in Christ," which characterizes Paul's notion of the indwelling spirit. Moreover, their authors seem to have had little interest in the *process* of their own conversion. Though they were intent on recommending belief and trust in the Lord and hope in the coming kingdom, they had practically no interest in the act of faith itself. The Synoptics are careless of humankind and unconcerned with what might make Jesus' kingdom (ambiguous as it is) desirable to us. Neither psychological inquiry nor existential anxiety plays a role in these writings. The Synoptic Gospels contain no "anthropology," as modern theologians confusingly call a religious analysis of the human condition—the kind of thing you find in Job or the Psalms.

From the surface way the writers look upon their world there follows an odd "materialism." Pagan civilization is not condemned, only the fact that its profits go to the wrong people. So true is this, that in our own day Latin American thinkers have been able to create a plausible revolutionary theology out of these same texts. More importantly, despite their omniscient point-of-view, these writers see very little into the human heart. Surprisingly, they get further into the mind of the Lord than into anyone else's—Peter's, say, or Judas's. Nearly all their other characters are stick figures with names, or walk-ons with one-liners or a single good speech to deliver: Martha or Zacchaeus, or the Good Thief, or the centurion, "*Domine, non sum dignus.*" There is therefore a Dickensian quality to the Synoptic Gospels; life and death and even the hereafter are simply things that *happen* to people, and people are those to whom what happens, happens. What anyone *thinks* of all this we never learn. Peter hears the cock crow, he sees what he has done, he weeps.

Let me put it another way. No one in these Gospels seriously and sympathetically and intelligently objects to Jesus and his story, except—in the Garden of Gethsemane—Jesus himself! His opponents not only don't have a legal charge against him, they don't have a motive for one. As Luke presents them, the scribes and Pharisees are simply bad men. Their enmity is taken for granted; it is not even deliberately mysterious. In fact, there is very little mystery of *any* sort in these writings. Mystery is walking on water or multiplying loaves of bread, rather than the heart of darkness.

William James believed that all religion exhibits three essential elements: (1) a sense that something is wrong with us, (2) a belief that we can be saved from that wrongness by a higher power, and (3) a notion that whatever is "not wrong" in us, the higher power has "more of the same." The Synoptic Gospels all but ignore the first and third elements, to dwell almost completely on the act of being saved itself. They ignore what is wrong with humans and how it came to be and are unconcerned with what may be God-like in them, dwelling instead on the mechanical act of being saved by a higher power and admission to the kingdom. The result is that the great banquet in the sky is something offered to us *beyond* what we are normally capable of or expect—not a change in our being. The *kingdom* is something "added on"—better times.

And that finally is the trouble with the Synoptics when they are read sensibly. We cannot get back onto their simple, mechanical stage. Nobody in these stories is as complex as we assume we are today; nobody has a "desire for oblivion," as Philip Larkin phrased it; nobody thinks the world absurd; no one is willing to reign in hell rather than serve in heaven; no railroad passenger condemns God for the evil he sees all about him and, like Ivan Karamazov, "respectfully returns his ticket." No one in Matthew, Mark, or Luke has a subconscious—the foolish demons won't do—nor does anyone feel determined by genetic content and/or social environment. No one in these Gospels, even in the broad-minded ambience of the book of Acts, understands a relation like *and/or*. For all this, we must turn either to modern thought or to the letters of the apostle Paul.

CHAPTER 4

The Theology of Paul

One of my favorite books about Paul is a nearly unknown little volume by William Burnet Wright, *Cities of Paul: Beacons of the Past Rekindled for the Present*. Published at Boston's Riverside Press in 1905 by Houghton Mifflin, it is a handsome, green, well-bound text, the size of a modern paperback with generous margins of heavy, pleasantly aged paper. In his preface, Wright acknowledges that the same diseases that "infested all, and ruined most," of the cities he is about to describe are not strangers to the modern world. He believed that turn-of-the-century America was also guilty of contempt for the disadvantaged and municipal corruption and even greed—that "taint of the spirit which degraded Greek athletics is said to have touched our own universities." Yet Wright believes things are on the mend: "the corrupters are hard pressed" by young men who are taking up the cause of reform. It is for these "Christian heroes" that he has composed his work, so that in "hours of discouragement" they may ponder the example of the intrepid apostle.

Cities of Paul sets a high standard, one I'm afraid I will not reach. It compares Paul to Montefiore or Disraeli, "than whom no Jews were prouder of their Hebrew lineage and no Englishmen more loyal to their British birth." Wright's Paul is a reputable, even aristocratic Roman citizen with links to authority going back a generation in his hometown of Tarsus, to when Cicero governed the province; his thirty or more references to athletics and his many metaphors drawn from things military demonstrate gentility. Indeed, Wright's Paul is the kind of early Christian Evelyn Waugh might have invented: well connected, suave, abreast of all that is truly worthwhile in late classical culture, but underneath a firebrand of zealous evangelism.

I particularly admire Wright's style. Here he is describing Paul's hometown of Tarsus on the Cydnus River in Cilicia. Intent on setting his hero in a grand historical context, he develops a three-part rhetorical formula beginning with Alexander the Great, the "kinglet" who conquered Paul's birthplace.

> Three hundred and thirty-two years before the birth of Christ Persia was the one conspicuous nation in the world . . . [though] those living at that time may have heard rumors of military preparations in the north of Greece. Compared with the kinglet who was making them, the Persian monarch appeared as the Russian Czar . . . [but] had the kinglet been asked whither he was going, the reply might have been, "To Tarsus, for the conquest of the World!"

Wright then moves up to the time of the Roman civil wars, when Antony and Cleopatra met in this same city.

> Forty-one years before the birth of Christ, you might have seen in the harbor of Egyptian Alexandria a vessel loading with purple and gold and pearls and perfumes. Had you asked its owner, "Whither shall it bear you?" the reply . . . spoken in a voice of such alluring sweetness that to resist its enchantment seemed beyond the power of mortal man might have been, "I am going to Tarsus to conquer the world!" And a little later the Cilicians saw a gilded barge gliding up the Cydnus, propelled by sails of purple silk and oars of silver.

Finally, he reaches the time of Paul's birth.

> Had you been alive when Christ was born, you might have seen a little boy playing in a garden at Tarsus. . . . Had you asked him whither he was going, he could not have told you, but we can reply. "He was going *from* Tarsus to conquer the world!"

Cities of Paul is not just a lot of fun; it is a fine example of the simplicity with which it was once possible to think about the Apostle to the Gentiles. Like most of his generation, Wright first assumed that Paul was *his sort* and then that he operated in the world described by the Synoptic Gospels. But as we have seen, the earliest Gospel was written nearly forty years after Paul's conversion and its writer was unaware of his existence; and Luke's biography of Paul, which we have just read, dates from thirty years later still and is largely a fiction meant to illustrate that the church had a heroic past. By the time Acts was composed, Christians had made peace with their Jewish roots—largely by severing them, and the Gentile faith could be taught even on the Athenian Areopagus. It was there, in fact, that Paul is imagined preaching just the sort of doctrine Wright considered his own: open, no nonsense, rational, and manly.

The Letters

When we read Paul himself, however, we discover someone wholly unlike a nineteenth-century hero. Nor are we left in doubt concerning his personality. Paul's prose is as prickly and fresh as—well, as if you had just torn your hand on fence wire this morning. He dictates furiously, often angrily, abruptly forgetting his place so badly that the scribe can't resolve his sentences. He makes questionable jokes about his enemies and uses the most specious logic to force a point. He is a strange, mystical fellow, and (according to legend) looked it: bowlegged with a balding head and eyebrows that grew straight across his nose. Certainly he was a city person. When he tries to use a metaphor based on grafting fruit trees (Rom. 11:17–19), he makes a fool of himself.

But Paul can speak for himself.

> I must make it clear to you, my friends, that the gospel you heard me preach is not of human origin. I did not take it over from anyone; no one taught it to me; I received it through a revelation of Jesus Christ.
>
> You have heard what my manner of life was when I was a practicing Jew; how savagely I persecuted the church of God and tried to destroy it; and how in the practice of our national religion I outstripped most of my Jewish contemporaries by my boundless devotion to the traditions of my ancestors. But then in his good pleasure God, who from my birth had set me apart, and who had called me through his grace, chose to reveal his Son in and through me, in order that I might proclaim him among the Gentiles. Immediately, without consulting a single person, without going up to Jerusalem to see those who were apostles before me, I went off to Arabia, and afterwards returned to Damascus.
>
> Three years later I did go up to Jerusalem to get to know Cephas, and stayed two weeks with him. I saw none of the other apostles except James, the Lord's brother. What I write is plain truth; God knows I am not lying. (Gal. 1:11–20)

I cannot overemphasize the importance of this passage. Note the uncompromising independence of what Paul calls his "gospel." He has received his good news directly, in a revelation from the risen Christ: "I did not take it from anyone; no one taught it to me." This is the language of mysticism, as he makes clear in 2 Corinthians:

> I am obliged to boast. It does no good; but I shall go on to tell of visions and revelations granted by the Lord. I know a Christian man who fourteen years ago (whether in the body or out of it I do not know—God knows) was caught up as far as the third heaven. And I know that this same man (whether in the

body or out of it, I do not know—God knows) was caught up into paradise, and heard words so secret that human lips may not reveal them. (12:1–4)

Yet as we shall see, it is a revelation strangely limited. If Paul knew anything at all about the historical Jesus—his life or preaching or career, his passion or death or resurrection (apart from their occurrence)—he refused to mention it. This is all the more startling because his letters are the first messages we have from the new faith. The first documents of the New Testament to be composed, they come to us out of the blue opacity of the Hellenistic world, real letters sent to a few tiny religious communities he had founded and to one larger Christian community he had only heard about: Rome. Yet odd as it may seem today, from the beginning these letters were the core of Christian scripture. The first man we know of to try to put together a "canon," Marcion (ca. 140), chose Paul's letters along with Luke's Gospel and tried to demote all the other writings.

Yet despite their importance, they remain letters—not public documents like the Gospels, which were meant to be read by large numbers. These epistles are private communications on which we, in a sense, eavesdrop in a way unintended by their author. We have come upon his correspondence with people who are strangers to us who were born and bred far from Jerusalem, long after the crucifixion; yet we read his letters as if they were a statement of faith.

I should not exaggerate. Paul's letters are never *completely* involved in local and fleeting concerns; and clearly the longer texts like Romans are also meant for a wide audience. Nevertheless, whatever theology they contain—and they contain a lot—generally arises ad hoc and in the process of giving specific advice. Fortunately also, they are some of the most interesting, entertaining letters ever written.

Modern scholarship is fairly agreed that only seven of Paul's *authentic* letters have survived, though he alludes to others and they may someday turn up. These are 1 Thessalonians, Galatians, 1 and 2 Corinthians, Philippians, Romans, and Philemon. Though written in the 50s, they may not have been collected and published until shortly after 90 C.E. The writer of *1 Clement* (ca. 96) knows them, as does Ignatius, who wrote his own epistles about ten years later. The other epistles traditionally thought to be Paul's, as has been pointed out above, are pseudonymous, either in whole or in part, and date from the 90s to well into the next century. No one knows the exact order in which the authentic letters were written; however, the sequence I have listed them in may be fairly close.

Our problem is to read these letters as their recipients of those years would have read them, not as they were read by late-nineteenth-century religious writers like Wright—regardless of the naïve charm of his style. To do this we must dismiss from our minds what we already know about the new religion, even its "traditional" use of language. For example, the word *gospel* in Paul simply means the revealed "good news"; it will not refer to a literary document until Mark uses it in that way about 70 C.E.

L et us begin with *1 Thessalonians*. Here we have the first gasp, so to speak, of the new cult of Christianity as it appears in Europe. The year is 51. The town is at the northwest corner of the Aegean Sea, on the famous Egnation road, an ancient Roman highway that ran straight across the top of modern Greece, having Thessalonica at its midpoint with Mount Olympus to its southeast. This was the road with which the Romans connected the Adriatic with the Hellespont. Wright recalls that Cicero had been here in Thessalonica a generation or two earlier, writing complaining letters to Atticus; and he draws the contrast between the author of *Concerning the Gods* and the small group of Thessalonian believers Paul writes to. The letters which the politically defeated Cicero wrote from Thessalonica are filled with the thought of suicide; indeed, he laments that he has not already killed himself. Paul's people, on the contrary, wouldn't have dreamt of doing away with themselves; they were awaiting the coming of the Lord, the rapture. They had hope. Cicero did not.

That hope in some future and *final* goodness had come to them and to other Greek Christians through the newly formed small assemblies Paul had established around the Aegean. Rudolf Bultmann called them "eschatological communities"; that is, groups of people waiting for the "last day" (*eschaton*.) By the 50s there must have been many in Macedonia and Thessaly, in Boeotia and Ionia—some founded by "apostles" now forgotten or by others like Apollos, who are only names to us. In reading Mark and Q we learned about such communities by inference. But now in Paul we have direct evidence. Like the later Christians, these people were convinced that their present state in the world was bad and that worse was to follow: an undefined and swift "wrath to come." But they believed that Jesus, who himself had been raised from the dead, was the guarantor that they and those who had already died would be bodily raised into some sort of new life. We should note the "simplicity" or, if you like, the un-Jewishness of this central belief. Here there is no allusion to Daniel, no proof text, no appeal to anything but Jesus and the fact that he was raised from the dead: *as he, so you.*

In 1 Thessalonians, Paul's church exhibits those sociological characteristics of apocalyptic belief I have earlier described. The "perceived relative deprivation" is here, though we lack details and must make do with passing references: "the message meant grave suffering for you . . . we do not curry favor with men. . . ." Esoteric knowledge has certainly been brought to the community by a seer, and the group clearly believes in an end-time in which they, unlike their neighbors, will triumph.

Who were these people? In the book of Acts, Paul habitually begins his preaching by visiting the local synagogue and attempting to convert his fellow Jews. But the evidence of 1 Thessalonians is otherwise. In Greece, at least, he apparently first gathered congregations of pagans—former idol worshipers, as he calls them. Though they were not at all from the lowest ranks of society, they were not the elite. In fact, Paul's converts seem to have been quite ordinary Hellenistic folk who, were they not Christians, would have believed in one or another of the mystery religions—or several at once—initiates into the rites of Demeter at Eleusis perhaps, or devotees of the parallel rituals of Orpheus or Attis or Osiris, depending on where they lived. Each of these pagan religions honored a god who died and was reborn and thereby offered the hope of immortality. Though it sometimes shocks modern Jews, parallel beliefs were current at this time in some synagogues of the Diaspora, and there are Jewish parallels to Paul's apocalyptic doctrine. In *2 Esdras,* for instance, a largely Jewish apocalypse from about 100 C.E., the seer experiences a revelation on the same pattern: the righteous will find eternal peace after an apocalyptic end-time. *2 Esdras* even contains a rare recognition of the arrogance of such belief. The archangel Uriel says to Esdras (Ezra), "You are completely at a loss to understand this world; can you expect to understand the way of the Most High?"

"Yes, my Lord!" says Esdras.

This answer typifies the Hellenistic religious world which surrounds and influences early Christianity. People like Esdras simply *must* have an answer to the fundamental questions of life. As Esdras says, "Better never to have come into existence than be born into a world of evil and suffering we cannot explain!" This Hellenistic demand for a revelation is quite different from classical Greek thought. The famous statement of Socrates, "The unexamined life is not worth living," means that the philosopher is content with inquiry; Paul and Esdras—even though they are both nobodies, students of no famous teacher, members of no philosophic school—both demand and expect answers. Such men and their readers have the intellectual arrogance of the uneducated. To illustrate this, Bernard Shaw once imagined a conversation something like this:

One fellow asks another, "Do you know anything about poetry?"

"No, of course not!"

"Science?"

"Hardly anything; mystery to me."

"Philosophy?"

"Never had the time."

"Does God exist?"

"Of course!"

"Isn't it odd," says Shaw, "that the fellow who knows nothing about poetry, science, or philosophy, knows the answer to the question that has baffled all the poets, scientists, and philosophers."

What is perhaps more important than this sad proof of human pride, is the fact that the Jewish apocalyptist Esdras and the Christian Paul—though providing different answers to the problem of human mortality—see the cosmos in the same way and use much the same language. In 1 Corinthians 15:51ff., Paul addresses the people with this promise:

> Listen! I will unfold a mystery: we shall not all die, but we shall all be changed in a flash, in the twinkling of an eye, at the last trumpet-call. For the trumpet will sound, and the dead will rise imperishable, and we shall be changed. This perishable body must be clothed with the imperishable, and what is mortal with immortality. And when this perishable body has been clothed with the imperishable and our mortality has been clothed with immortality, then the saying of scripture will come true: "Death is swallowed up; victory is won! O Death where is your victory? O Death, where is your sting?"

Similarly, in *2 Esdras,* the archangel says,

> It is for this reason that the Most High has made not one world but two . . . when the Most High has given final sentence for a man to die, the spirit leaves the body to return to the One who gave it, and first of all to adore the glory of the Most High. But as for those who have rejected the ways of the Most High and despised his law, and who hate all that fear God, their spirits enter no settled abode, but roam thenceforward in torment, grief, and sorrow. . . . The present world is not the end, and the glory of God does not stay in it continually. That is why the strong have prayed for the weak. But the day of judgment will be the end of the present world and the beginning of the eternal world to come, a world in which corruption will be over, all excess abolished, and unbelief uprooted, in which justice will be full-grown, and truth will have risen like the sun. (6:50, 78–80, 112–15)

Both men live in the same two-tiered moral universe. They never question it, nor, one suspects, do their readers. True justice and happiness are available to people only elsewhere ("over Jordan," as the old spirituals have it) and then only for the righteous. For the rest there is the "furnace of hell" in Esdras, but not in Paul. In most apocalyptic writing, the coming of the end in which "elsewhere" is revealed and the two sorts of people sorted out will be signaled by a great panic and an increase in wickedness: Rome will become a trackless desert, the sun will shine at night, the stars will change their course, etc. But in this regard, 1 Thessalonians is different; here there is only the *fact* of the end and the salvation of the elect.

Common to both apocalyptic writers, however, is an idea that the Jewish author expresses as "this aging world." Both Esdras and Paul assume they live in a cosmos growing ever more feeble as it nears the end, where only sin increases. Paul expresses the idea in Romans: "For the created universe . . . was made the victim of frustration, not by its own choice, but because of him who made it so" (Rom. 8:19–20). Something is *wrong* with the world as well as with us.

Implicit in both writers also is what will later be called "dispensational-ism," the idea that God has divided time into periods or "dispensations," each of which has a preordained structure of happiness or sadness, war or peace. The idea seems to date from Israel's postcaptivity period when the so-called Deuteronomic theology, which explained the sufferings of Israel as punishment for a kind of national failure to keep the covenant, no longer satisfied. Then arose the notion that Yahweh had arranged periods of prosperity or suffering for Israel *irrespective* of the nation's behavior: defeat and suffering were not necessarily caused by sin but were dependent on the vast historical scheme of the Almighty. The people at Qumran kept copies of such dispensational apocalypses, and these ideas continued among Jews into the time of Paul and beyond.

As the writer of 2 *Esdras* clearly perceived, this dispensational view demanded a new notion. If suffering in this life can be unconnected to morality—if it is random—there must be *another* life in which national and individual justice is finally accomplished. Paul accepts this view of the universe. But unlike most other apocalyptic writers he is convinced that only God knows the details of the end. In 1 Thessalonians he writes, "About dates and time, my friends, we need not write to you, for you know perfectly well that the Day of the Lord comes like a thief in the night. While they are talking of peace and security, all at once calamity is upon them, sudden as the pangs that come upon a woman with child; and there will be no escape" (5:1–3).

A more dramatic difference between Paul and his fellow apocalyptists is, of course, his incorporation into this scheme of the Messiah, characterized as a suffering redeemer—a figure hinted at in "Deutero-Isaiah" and now identified as Jesus of Nazareth. Belief in Jesus' death, resurrection, and return provides the hope that characterizes the "waiting time." By reason of the revelation given to him by the Lord, Paul can also answer the question,

How should we conduct ourselves *until* Jesus comes? His answers are contained in the so-called parenetic (from *parenesis*), or advisory, sections of his letters, usually toward the end. These detailed prescriptions of how to live are sometimes called "household codes" and are very similar to pagan advice of the same period, reflecting both what we would today call "morality" and "manners," as we saw in the Synoptics. But in matters of human behavior, Paul's letters are a good bit more specific than *any* of the Gospels. The parenetic section of Galatians (5:15–23), for instance, is so notoriously comprehensive that Browning's rascally monk in "Soliloquy of the Spanish Cloister" used it as a snare. He believes that if he gives it to Brother Lawrence at the point of death, his fraternal enemy will necessarily remember breaking one of these commandments, fall into despair, and be damned:

> There's a great text in Galatians,
>   Once you trip on it, entails
> Twenty-nine distinct damnations,
>   One sure, if another fails:
> If I trip him just a-dying,
>   Sure of heaven as sure can be,
> Spin him round and send him flying
>   Off to hell, a Manichee?

The parenetic section of 1 Thessalonians seems to imply that the ideal Christian in that community lived a life-style not much different from that of the Amish of today or of some other quietist sect—which, of course, is what the founders of these sects aimed at. The Thessalonians are quietly to mind their own business, all must work with their hands, and they should pray constantly. Though the "end" may be in the future, the community is to live as if it were already saved. Yet it is still the concept of the "end" that motivates this behavior. To appreciate the force of this, we might try to imagine the first reading of 1 Thessalonians—leaning a little on Acts. The disciples are assembled, perhaps in an arched room above a shop, one large window looking down on the narrow street below, cots flung about the table for the meal of bread and wine and figs. These are the people who took Paul in after his first, disastrous experience in forming a western congregation at Philippi; he has been gone for some months now, but Timothy's recent visit is fresh in everyone's mind. As people pass the letter back and forth, they talk excitedly, recalling the things he did when he was with them: his preaching, maybe a miracle or two; his temper and pride; his messages "from the Lord"; perhaps his occasional periods of deep despondency. If we add further details from Acts, we may even hear talk of the near riot the Philippians started, or of the peace bond Jason had to put up when he took the letter writer into his home for safety.

But what the congregation is chiefly concerned about, and what Paul is writing to them about, is the delay of the *parousia*. It has been nearly twenty years now since the crucifixion, and these people are naturally concerned about their promised salvation, particularly the status of Christian friends and relatives who have died. Will they also be saved? The question is not so naïve as it may seem. Though Paul's people are Greeks, they do not think in terms of classical fifth-century philosophic distinctions of body and soul, material and immaterial. They share what today we would call a "Jewish" anthropology in which the human being is one entity, alive or dead; it is this body-soul that will rise at the coming of the Lord. Peculiar questions therefore abound. How can decayed bodies rise in the air? Would anyone welcome such levitations? Indeed, Paul will later be forced (1 Cor. 15:35ff.) to invent a "spiritual body" to counter the natural processes of decay. For now he is content to tell the docile Thessalonians not to worry; their dead relatives will rise first, and then the living will join them in the air to meet the Lord. Jerry Falwell likes to tell the story of the fellow who asked his preacher *why* the dead rise first. The answer: "'Cause they got six feet farther to go!"

One can imagine similar theological queries among Paul's first converts; for, as he tells us, few of them were wise or powerful or wellborn. Yet, as I have said, these earliest Christians in Thessalonica or Ephesus were not simply the marginal poor. If Wayne Meeks at Yale is correct—and he is the expert on the social milieu of Paul's epistles—they represented a sort of cross-section of the society. Our most complete portrait of them is provided by two mosaics made out of fragments of letters, which were probably written across the Aegean at Ephesus, where for some time Paul had been in the religion business. These are now called *1* and *2 Corinthians*. William Wright has two chapters on the city of Corinth, both concerned with its "fleshly" nature in Paul's day. If the city's titular god was Aphrodite, says Wright, its secondary deity was Mammon. In tracing out the emergence of these two dominant themes, he recreates the city's decay from its prominent place in the classical world as the site of the Isthmian games.

Before 146 [B.C.E.] Athens had died, Sparta had died, Thebes had died; that is, if death is the flight of the spirit from the body. Each of these cities left a legacy of splendid deeds. The body of Corinth, like the others, still lingered. If accumulating money and using it so as to make the whole earth a pander to guilty passions while piety and patriotism steadily decay be prosperity, she was prosperous. If to fester with a moral leprosy so conspicuous that when any man in any nation between Spain and the Euphrates becomes eminent as a cheat or debaucher his neighbors say "He was Corinthianized," be *living*, Corinth lived on, growing richer every year; making herself a coffin of gold studded with jewels, and thinking it a throne.

A harsh judgment. I suspect its only purpose is to form a contrast to Paul's famous peroration on true love: "Though I speak with the tongues of angels . . ." (1 Cor. 13:1–13). In fact, Hellenistic Corinth was probably a model of moral rectitude compared to, say, modern day New York. Certainly the Christian community there was no hotbed of greed and lust. Nevertheless, Paul has heard accounts of disturbing events: factions within the group and one irregular sexual union. He means to correct the situation; and in the process of admonishing these early believers, he tells us a good deal about them. First of all, the Corinthians were a noisy lot. Though Paul repeatedly tells them they "live in Christ" and he in them, I don't suppose a stranger would have noticed that, in the hubbub of their morning potluck picnics (1 Cor. 14:23ff.). According to Paul they all talked at once, a few a little tipsy with wine, some quite drunk on the ecstatic talk alone. The well-heeled were there with their fancy food and expensive baskets; so too the envious poor. Some, he says, are making "wise speeches," others healing; some working miracles, others prophesying; some distinguishing spirits, while still others interpret the gibberish that the tongue-speakers utter. This last—you will recall that Luke was hazy about the matter—is a scandal to unbelievers: "If the whole congregation is assembled and all are using the strange tongues of ecstasy, and some uninstructed persons or unbelievers should enter, will they not think you are mad?" The other gifts of the spirit can be almost as bad. "Of the prophets, two or three may speak, while the rest exercise their judgment upon what is said. If someone else present receives a revelation, let the first speaker stop. You can all prophesy, one at a time. . . . It is for prophets to control prophetic inspiration, for the God who inspires them is not a God of disorder but of peace" (1 Cor. 14:29–33). Paul is painfully aware that unchecked ecstatic experiences are dangerous. Suitably regulated, on the other hand, these flights probably aided the survival of the cult until it developed into a mainline church. The pattern will be repeated: from backwoods enthusiasts to respectable members of the First Methodist; from picking up snakes to singing in the choir of the United Baptists, Northern Branch; from an apartment house in Corinth to the Vatican. Along with attempting to tone down all this evangelical fun, Paul gives the Corinthians some very sophisticated advice. My favorite admonition is directed at a member of the congregation who has been invited to dine by an unbeliever: "eat whatever is put before you without raising questions of conscience. But if somebody says to you, 'This food has been offered in sacrifice,' then, out of consideration for him, and for conscience' sake, do not eat it—not your conscience, I mean, but the other man's" (1 Cor. 10:27–29). I don't recall ever hearing anyone preach on this sound text, but perhaps memory fails me.

As we have noticed in connection with Luke, Paul's account of the Communion Service in the Corinthian correspondence is one of the very few elements in his letters which has close links to the Synoptic Jesus. In 1 Corinthians 10:15 we read "When we bless the cup of blessing, is it not a means of sharing in the blood of Christ? When we break the bread, is it not a means of sharing in the body of Christ?" And in 11:23–25:

> For the tradition which I handed on to you came to me from the Lord himself: that the Lord Jesus, on the night of his arrest, took bread, and after giving thanks to God, broke it and said, "This is my body, which is for you, do this as a memorial of me." In the same way, he took the cup after supper, and said, "This cup is the new covenant sealed by my blood. Whenever you drink it, do this as a memorial of me."

How old this is, how important! Compared to this, the written texts we are now reading have always been only tangential to the Christian religion. The Eucharist is at its center. In the first pages of *The Shape of the Liturgy*, the great Anglican liturgist Gregory Dix says that the Eucharist is "what the church fundamentally is, a corporate 'holy priesthood to offer up spiritual sacrifices acceptable to God through Jesus Christ [1 Peter 2:5].'" As early as 96 C.E., before some of the New Testament had even been composed, let alone brought together, Clement of Rome seems to be writing about this liturgical action and that it had been established by the Lord. Fifteen years later Ignatius refers to the obligation to attend the bishop's Sunday Eucharist. And indeed the essential "shape" of the Eucharist, as Dix called it, has been remarkably stable down the centuries. The same is less true for the language of this liturgy. I have already spoken of my childhood search for the "proper" Latin formula for this magical act, as we thought of it in our devotional Catholicism. Yet the still current liturgical phrase "lift up your hearts" is known from before the year 200.

It is the *meaning* of the ritual that has changed the most. Before the Reformation the significance of the Eucharist was vague. Different theologians held different theories, and it is not at all clear what ordinary people thought. But Luther forced the Council of Trent into definition, with Aristotelian realism as the result. At the consecration, though the "accidents" remained the same—the look, taste, smell, and so on of bread and wine—the underlying Aristotelian *substance* of the offerings was said to change into the body and blood of the Lord. This change was called *transubstantiation;* and we heirs of Trent at Holy Angels parish in the 1930s believed in it and knew the word! Some would even have died for it. This was typical of our Catholicism; we were used to accepting opaque or even contradictory propositions and proclaiming them like a flag. "I am eating the body of Jesus Christ"; "God is three persons in one"; and so on. A few such gnomic statements are also found in Paul's writing; but most of the mysteries we held dear in those days were arrived at by later councils of the church which tried to think through the notions the apostle had tossed off to a secretary in the middle of a heated letter.

Since liturgical actions have nearly always been independent of their explanations, artists have often been better at picturing the reality of belief than theologians. With regard to the Eucharist, I think no one has gone beyond the ruminations of Joyce's Leopold Bloom as he watches the women of the sodality take communion in All Hallows Church, Dublin, June 14, 1904:

> The priest went along among them, murmuring, holding the thing in his hands. He stopped at each, took out a communion, shook a drop or two (are they in water?) off it and put it neatly into her mouth. Her hat and head sank. Then the next one: a small old woman. The priest bent down to put it into her mouth, murmuring all the time. Latin. The next one. Shut your eyes and open your mouth. What? *Corpus.* Body. Corpse. Good idea the Latin. Stupifies them first. Hospice for the dying. They don't seem to chew it; only swallow it down. Rum idea; eating bits of corpse why the cannibals cotton to it. . . .
>
> They were about him here and there, with heads still bowed in their crimson halters, waiting for it to melt in their stomachs. Something like those mazzoth: it's that sort of bread: unleavened shewbread. Look at them. Now I bet it makes them feel happy. Lollipop. It does. Yes, bread of angels it's called. There's a big idea behind it, kind of kingdom of God is within you feel. First communicants. Hokypoky penny a lump. Then feel all like one smart family party, same in the theatre, all in the same swim. They do. I'm sure of that. Not so lonely. In our confraternity. Then come out a bit spreeish. Let off steam. Thing is if you really believe in it. ("Calypso," *Ulysses*)

What precise meaning the Eucharist had for that earlier peripatetic Jew Paul of Tarsus is so far lost to history. Like the Dublin women, he may in fact have celebrated it without a great deal of analysis. On the other hand, his language of dying and rising with the Lord suggests that he understood the ritual in a mystery cult context. Though no proof is available, this is the interpretation attributed to him by A. N. Wilson and other popular writers:

> Paul does not commend Jesus to his followers as an admirable moral teacher, nor as a storyteller, nor as a famed healer and miracle-worker. He commends

him in purely mythological terms. Jesus is the Messiah; Jesus is the rock in the desert from which the people of Israel drank pure water; Jesus, like Mithra, God of the morning, can be drunk from an uplifted cup of blood; Jesus the dying demigod who comes to life again, is to conquer death itself. (*Jesus: A Life*, 21).

In what is now 2 Corinthians, Paul turns to the theological question that is never far from his mind: What is the relation of the new faith to the old? Here he asks it in terms of the scriptures and answers it with surprising help of allegory. It turns out that the ancient Jewish documents were really Christian all along; but people had failed to recognize this truth: "But to this very day, every time the law of Moses is read, a veil lies over the minds of the hearers" (2 Cor. 3:15). Unless, of course, the hearers happen to be Christians for whom "there is no veil." "With this masterful move," says Burton Mack, "Paul made it possible for Christians to acquire the books of Moses without having to read them the way they were read in the synagogues" (*Who Wrote the New Testament*, 136).

Though something of the theology of Pauline Christians is therefore observable in the Corinthian correspondence, it is *Galatians* and Romans that contain Paul's most profound thought. The first is an early letter of uncertain date directed vaguely to people living in south central Turkey, perhaps the communities Paul himself had established at places like Derbe and Lystra in his missionary work north of Antioch. At the beginning of this chapter we read what he said in this letter about his early life. The occasion for his writing, however, is that he has learned of Christians who have come up from Jerusalem and refused to associate with their new, uncircumcised brothers; they would not eat with people who did not respect the dietary laws. Paul takes a strong line against these "judaizers" who hold to a Jewish-oriented, legalistic interpretation of the "Way." He says that in this matter he even opposed Peter and stood up against those "so-called pillars of our society," in Jerusalem—the apostles, and particularly perhaps James the brother of the Lord, who was called "The Just." This passage is the earliest preserved reference to the "Jerusalem church," that is, the Christian "institution" in that city which survived the crucifixion. Apparently James (the brother of the Lord) and Cephas (Peter) and John still were practicing some parts of the Jewish holiness code. Unfortunately, we know little else, since the accounts of this conference in Acts are heavily romanticized and contradictory.

In taking this Gentile stance, Paul was the voice of the future—as is clear from the book of Acts—but it was always a troubled voice. As the product of a beloved religious tradition in which he no longer believed, Paul felt compelled to reject Judaism yet somehow to affirm it. Though he considered it now outmoded, Judaism had been in some way very good to him; clearly he loved—loves—being a Jew and must find a way to fit the old religion into his new belief. It is as if a lapsed Catholic had taken up crystal gazing or sitting in odd positions or eating mushrooms or joined the Episcopal church and then felt compelled to establish some continuity with the Vatican. Paul can never therefore *completely* abandon his tradition; he is in fact obsessed by it, returning to the question again and again; and his "final" view of the matter is found only in the late (perhaps 58 C.E.) *Letter to the Romans.* As the capital of the empire, Rome was perhaps even then beginning to look like the coming center of the new religion; and the letter nominally addressed to its citizens has all the aspects of a summary exposition of the faith.

B efore we turn to that letter, let us pause briefly to consider the enigmatic city to which it was written and into which, finally, its author will disappear. Since William Wright unaccountably gives us no picture of this last of Paul's cities, let me describe for you the giant pitiless monster then growing like a cancer on the banks of the Hudson—I mean, of course, the Tiber. (This is a typical Roman device. Cicero once said in court, "Now this lady's lover—I mean her brother—was seen that night....")

From the sky, the city lay within its seven hills in a great circle of flat-roofed sameness. Since there was no industry as we know it, only trading, an urban sprawl of warehouses stretched out in all directions as far as the eye could see. Streets in the center of town were such a hopeless, narrow tangle that all cart traffic was prohibited in daylight hours. In addition to fifteen hundred private homes, there were perhaps thirty-five thousand apartment houses, limited by law to a height of 65.4 feet—above which, as wisdom had shown, they collapsed. The typical flat had no fireplace, no running water, no toilet facilities, and was connected to no furnace. Most of these needs were met by public facilities. Just as in New York City, however, you put the garbage out on the curb. By the year 58 C.E., the town that dated itself from the eighth century B.C.E. had nearly 1.5 million citizens, two-thirds of whom were in some way subsidized by the government, with 150,000 completely dependent on welfare. People who had jobs worked a six-hour day, but often at nominal and unproductive tasks. One hundred and sixty days of the year were given over to the games; for since the "mob" was the major internal threat to peace, it was constantly bought off by "bread and circuses."

It is for the people of this city—at least its Christians—that Paul tries to argue out the "Jewish" question from scratch, beginning with the query that sooner or later dawns on every member of this two-book religion. Do Jews have an advantage over the rest of humanity? Are they any better off? The answer is yes. In their national religion, the Jews had possessed—Paul had possessed—the "oracles of God." But this wisdom was only a temporary device for regulating life until the Christ should appear; he would expiate that sin that all people are heir to, Jew or Gentile. Paul describes his new situation in an odd metaphor, comparing the new Jewish-Christian to a woman who has been faithful to her husband (the law) during his lifetime, but at his death is free to marry again. "So you, my friends, have died to the law by becoming identified with the body of Christ, and accordingly you have found another husband" (Rom. 7:4).

But that is only his first attempt to solve the dilemma. In chapter 9 Paul touchingly confesses his grief over his fellow countrymen, who are now bereft of the "truth" and of whom only a remnant will be saved. By chapter 11, he is announcing, "I am an Israelite myself of the stock of Abraham, of the tribe of Benjamin." Then he ponders the question, "When they [the Jews] stumbled, was their fall final?" He answers, as we know he must, "May it not be so!" Finally, in v. 25, he announces what he calls a "divine secret": the hardening of the hearts of Israel will last "only until the Gentiles have become admitted in full strength; once that has happened, the whole of Israel will be saved. . . ."

Whew! He made it. Paul has come a long way from that anger with which he denounced the Galatian judaizers for demanding circumcision: "Those agitators had better go the whole way," he wrote, "and make eunuchs of themselves!" Sadly, later Christians will rarely follow him in this rapprochement; more often they will believe that not only Jews and pagans are to go unsaved, but even whole categories of Christians who are not among the "elect" will be damned. Using principles drawn from this same Epistle to the Romans, John Calvin came to that clear, hard perception of the kingdom of God that would so influence Europe and America. Since God transcends all finite causality, puny human struggles, even struggles to believe, cannot affect him, and salvation must therefore be a completely free gift: some receive it, others don't. Though it may be possible to tell who has salvation and who hasn't, it is *never* possible *to earn* it. To hold such an impious view would be to constrain God.

Though never really absent from Christian orthodoxy, this sort of predestination has become increasingly foreign to modern people. That all humans are depraved and can never merit heaven, but that God deems that some will reach that goal while others will not (through no respective merit or fault of their own), increasingly sounds like a bad joke. Visiting a friend's class in intellectual history the other day, I watched his sophomores shudder in disbelief that anyone could ever have held such an idea, even as they sat there in what is still the Ecclesiastical Society of Farmington, Connecticut.

In addition to this theory of election, Paul's Letter to the Romans also contains the great principle of Pauline Christianity: salvation by faith alone. Today we are so familiar with this idea we don't realize how new it once was. In classical Judaism, only covenant loyalty was important, not faith—*everybody* had faith. The problem was how to *obey* Yahweh and the Torah—there was no question of his existence or the truth of the law. But in Galatians, Paul said that "belief" in Jesus Christ was the completion of the law and rendered loyalty to the law and the law itself defunct. The law had been "a temporary measure pending the arrival of the issue [Christ] to whom the promise was made" (Gal. 3:10). This was the first announcement of Paul's fundamental theology. In Romans, it receives its final form.

The argument begins in human freedom. Paul uses the metaphor of a minor heir and his tutor to explain his former relationship with Judaism and the law. When he came of age (became a Christian), he was no longer under tutelage but was set "free" from that religion and its law. This notion gave all sorts of trouble to the early Christians. Almost immediately there arose antinomians in Corinth who thought they could do anything. (The same thing will happen among the Anabaptists at Münster during the Reformation.) Paul therefore wrote to the Corinthians that they *could* do anything, but insisted that there were things they *shouldn't* do. "Anyone can see," he had written in Galatians, "the kind of behavior that belongs to the lower nature: fornication, impurity, and indecency; idolatry and sorcery; quarrels, a contentious temper, envy, fits of rage, selfish ambition, dissensions, party intrigues, and jealousies; drinking bouts, orgies, and the like"—a traditional list. No one who lives on a higher spiritual plane would indulge in these evil behaviors.

Nor does Paul mean that Christianity is the religion of free individuals as opposed to slaves or that believers freely *choose* to believe in Christ. On the contrary, faith is a *gift* of God. Paul means that the gift of faith *makes* one free, which is to say that it causes one to rise above all human states of either liberty or subjugation. One who receives Christ Jesus rises above even his own desire not to be constrained. He is now free from the boundaries of inherited belief, free to follow the promptings of Christ who, if one believes, "dwells in that person." Modern readers, especially English-language readers, do not always appreciate the importance of the concept of freedom in Paul's theology. Perhaps because we are used to being politically free, we take for granted the notion of freedom itself. To understand the full meaning of what he is saying it is perhaps better to read Romans through sixteenth-century European eyes.

In the village into which Martin Luther was born there was only one path to the kind of transcendence Paul had in mind: the church. Its ministers could indelibly mark each soul in baptism and confirmation and—so at least the populace often believed—they could *save* that soul from slavery to the devil. The church did that by providing holy "works"—masses, pilgrimages, and indulgences. It was this last which Luther initially attacked, but his criticism eventually destroyed a whole obediential-sacramental system, at least for northern Europeans and for the new Americans.

Once it was gone, however, Luther repeated Paul's experience. He suddenly found himself free to choose Christ—no strings attached, not to believe in him, but to *identify with him.* In hindsight, it looks as if Europeans were just waiting for this liberation. In the fall of 1517 all of Wittenberg was living out its days and dying under a rigid but sacred economy as old as Constantine and as certain as the ten heavenly spheres. Four years later it was all gone. Laws so old no one could trace their origins were cast aside; priests and nuns married—frequently each other; meat was eaten on the wrong days; consecrated wine was handed around at mass; the mass itself was read in German by men in street clothes. Soon married himself, Luther expressed only mild, ironic surprise at the change. "One wakes up in the morning and finds a pair of pigtails on the pillow." But the change was fundamental. Luther's was the authentic Pauline experience of freedom.

So profoundly did that same experience affect Paul that he began to look back, pondering why, in all the time he had lived as an observant Jew, the law had never made him free in this sense. The reason, he says—turning his self-revelation into an attack on the reader—is that "you hated it in your heart." We hate the law because it never expresses our inmost nature. The law never accounts for the changing, and the perverse in us; it is always ideal and always the same.

I think Paul is dead right about this. Haven't we always known it in our hearts? Haven't we always been aware of our love of evil and self? Haven't we always known the foolishness of all those optimistic, rational Athenians, right down to and including St. Thomas and Thomas Jefferson, who would believe that humans are naturally directed toward the rational good. Even when on occasion we manage to desire the correct thing, we fail to accomplish it: "The good which I want to do, I fail to do," says Paul, "but what I do is the wrong which is against my will" (Rom. 7:19).

The renewed perception of this moral fact in the sixteenth century—

along with the rediscovery of freedom—put an end to the harmonization of Christianity and Greek philosophy that St. Thomas and the scholastics had effected. Indeed, it nearly put an end to Catholicism itself. "None take a natural delight in the law," says Luther, nor can they be argued into it. For Paul and Luther, even the *desire* for the good is unnatural for fallen humans; the desire for righteousness and righteousness itself are gifts of God. What we have here is both the privatization of religion and the end of theology. Looked at from the point of view of this world, each person is defined by his or her own volition, free to choose the divine—or not to choose it. But looked at from the point of view of God—who enjoys that same freedom— each of us is predestined.

Christology

With Romans, the surviving authentic writings of Paul come to an end. As we have seen, these are the earliest documents in the anthology that will come to be called the New Testament. Historically, as I have said, they are its irreplaceable core; for the Gospels come later, not just in regard to their time of composition but in their acceptance as sacred. Unlike the Gospels, however, Paul's letters are not at all concerned with Jesus' life or personality. Paul writes: "With us therefore worldly standards have ceased to count in our estimate of anyone; even if once they counted in our understanding of Christ, they do so no longer" (2 Cor. 5:16). Apart from local matters in the churches, Paul is solely concerned with the *risen* Christ and truths about him; that is, he is solely concerned with theology.

Despite their specificity, therefore, these letters state the fundamental principles of Christianity, then and now. They can be reduced to three: (1) an idea of Jesus as a Godlike figure, (2) a death and rebirth plot in which this Godlike figure functions as the deity of a mystery religion, (3) a concept of "faith" that relates the believer to this character and plot and provides him with "salvation" and "righteousness." Let me consider these elements in order.

Among the fragments of traditional prayers, hymns, and belief statements embedded in Paul's letters, we find two that affirm some sort of divinity for Jesus. In 1 Corinthians we find:

> For us there is one God, the Father, from whom are all things and for whom we exist, and one Lord, Jesus Christ, through whom are all things and through whom we exist. (1 Cor. 8:6)

In Philippians, he seems to expand the idea:

> Let your bearing towards one another arise out of your life in Christ Jesus. For the divine nature was his from the first; yet he did not think to snatch at equality with God, but made himself nothing, assuming the nature of a slave. Bearing the human likeness, revealed in human shape, he humbled himself, and in obedience accepted even death—death on the cross. Therefore God raised him to the heights and bestowed on him the name above all names, that at the name of Jesus every knee should bow—in heaven, on earth, and in the depths—and every tongue confess, "Jesus Christ is Lord," to the glory of God the Father. (Phil. 2:5–11)

In the first quotation we are confronted with the fact that not twenty years after Jesus was executed, there is a tradition in which the universe was created *through* him. Clearly this Jesus is not simply a wandering preacher who announces the "end." Jesus is not simply an Orpheus-like fertility Lord who dies and is reborn into the crops of the field; he is something mind-blowing, something different and "higher." We and the universe are said to exist *because* of him, who himself came directly from God. The second quotation attempts to describe the relation between this exalted Being and the Almighty. Unfortunately Paul's language is every bit as mysterious in Greek as it is in English. What did he mean by "divine nature" and "snatch at equality with God"? We don't know. But the kneeling in Heaven and Earth is clear enough: though perhaps not fully God, Jesus is surely more than angelic.

Yet this exalted view is rare in Paul and expresses the limit of his thought. Generally in reading Paul's letters, one *is* presented with that figure the Greeks were more comfortable with, but we find strange: divinity as human, a godlike figure conceived not so much on the model of Zeus or even Apollo, but Hercules. In thinking of Jesus in this way Paul recognizes that whatever else Jesus may be he is certainly "Lord"—in the half-human sense of a fertility god. And the duality of this human and divine combination never seems to trouble Paul as much as it troubles the later Gospel writers, Matthew, Luke, and—as we shall see—John. You may recall their nagging worry over just what sort of creature the risen Christ was. Jesus was first and indubitably a man, but after the resurrection he was also seen to be ... what? It is as if these writers were aware of the range of possibilities from ghost to angel to a being who nearly had "equality with God" through whom all things had been created; but they could no more decide *which* than we can. Consequently, falling back on his humanity, they compose those curious scenes in which the risen Jesus protests that he is not a ghost and proves it by eating something—a low Christology.

That "Greeks" should be comfortable with such "primitive" notions often comes as a surprise to today's undergraduate, whose idea of a Greek is either a fifth-century metaphysician or Euclid. But by New Testament times the classical age was long gone; and belief in the old thinkers and the *old gods* had long been replaced by "new thought." From the stoics, most Hellenistic people had become convinced that though the universe was ordered and rational, the human race was not. Humans were slaves to sense perception, bodily desire, and endless forces beyond their control. In the soul, however—that immaterial best part of the person—one had a share of the divine order; and therefore various arcane powers (demons, angels, gods etc.) could or would act in one's behalf. Yet even with such help, justice and ultimate joy were not attainable in the present life, but only, as I have said, elsewhere. True success in life therefore depended on gaining divine help from these supernatural powers (see Helmut Koester, *Introduction to the New Testament*, 1:141–204).

That it is difficult to appreciate how strongly Hellenistic people felt about these vague assumptions about life and afterlife and their attendant rituals in no way negates this ancient feeling; Christianity itself makes the same vague promise. It persists even when mythic narrative is reduced to pantheism. In the *Gospel of Thomas*, for instance, Jesus says, "from me all come forth, and to me all attained. Split a piece of wood; I am there. Lift up the stone, and you will find me there" (v. 77). At the end of "Song of Myself" Walt Whitman writes:

> I bequeath myself to the dirt to grow from the grass I love,
> If you want me again look for me under your boot-soles.
>
> You will hardly know who I am or what I mean,
> But I shall be good health to you nevertheless,
> And filter and fibre your blood.
>
> Failing to fetch me at first keep encouraged,
> Missing me one place search another,
> I stop some where waiting for you.

As to the logic of all this, perhaps we should simply listen to Sir James Frazer in *The Golden Bough* as he discusses the Greek belief in the immortality conferred by the myth of Persephone:

> The reasoning that satisfied Saint Paul and has brought comfort to untold thousands of sorrowing Christians, standing by the deathbed or the open grave of their loved ones, was good enough to pass muster with ancient pagans, when they too bowed their heads under the burden of grief, and, with

the taper of life burning low in the socket, looked forward into the darkness of the unknown.

In any case, it is this "reasoning" that is at the heart of Paul's first principle, that Jesus was a Godlike figure. In its highest form, this idea is ambitious in the extreme. At the ultimate *parousia*, Paul believed, even the material world will be saved; the cosmos itself will return to its first, ideal state! You may recall the lines from Romans that I quoted earlier:

> For the creation waits with eager longing for the revealing of the children of God; for the creation was subjected to futility, not of its own will but by the will of the one who subjected it, in hope that the creation itself will be set free from its bondage to decay and will obtain the freedom of the glory of the children of God. (Rom. 8:19–21)

The second element of Paul's theology is the "plot" of Jesus' time on earth: the Godlike Lord dies and rises again, a story familiar in the myths of Hellenistic deities. Again this is not the thinking of fifth-century Hellenistic philosophers, but the assumption of the Hellenistic period that, as Jesus will say in John, "a grain of wheat remains a solitary grain unless it falls into the ground and dies; but if it dies, it bears a rich harvest." Nor was this fertility notion limited to the uneducated; the sophisticated, brutal Greek politician Demetrius and the well-educated Roman emperor Claudius were alike determined to become initiates of Demeter at Eleusis. In fact, during Paul's lifetime, the annual September wheat festival at Eleusis was still as sacred as in the old days when Alcibiades was exiled from Athens on suspicion that he had mockingly revealed its sacred rites. In Paul's day, Persephone's disappearance in winter and her return to the Eleusian grain-growing valley in spring were still taken as the pattern of humanity's own possible immortality, and people beheld it in fear and trembling. So widespread was the idea, in fact, that it was recognized to be independent of any particular myth of resurrection. The drama of the stories of Demeter and Kore (Persephone) at Eleusis was also observed of Astarte and Adonis in Damascus, of Cybele and Attis in Phrygia, of Isis and Osiris at Thebes, and all of these in Rome. Knowledge of the death–rebirth cycle was the gnosis that gave dignity to life.

In seeing this same pattern in the life of Jesus, Paul writes the first "apology," or explanation for the salvific death and resurrection of the Lord which is both the cause and symbol of our own near-term resurrection. If we return to 1 Corinthians we find this stated explicitly:

> For if the dead are not raised, it follows that Christ was not raised; and if Christ was not raised, your faith has nothing to it and you are still in your old

state of sin. It follows also that those who have died within Christ's fellowship are utterly lost. If it is for this life only that Christ has given us hope, we of all men are most to be pitied.

But the truth is, Christ was raised to life—the firstfruits of the harvest of the dead. For since it was a man who brought death into the world, a man also brought resurrection of the dead. As in Adam all die, so in Christ all will be brought to life; but each in proper order: Christ the firstfruits, and afterwards, at his coming, those who belong to Christ. Then comes the end, when he delivers up the kingdom to God the Father, after deposing every sovereignty, authority, and power. (1 Cor. 15:16–19)

It is important to note that Paul believes Jesus was raised from the dead *corporeally*. To persistent objections that the body decays and that in any case it is an awkward material thing to bring into the heavens, Paul invents, as I have said, a body that is not a body, a "spiritual body" in fact—and hang the contradiction. The passages in 1 Corinthians 15 in which he manages this are some of the most tortuous he ever wrote. But *corporeal* resurrection, whatever it meant to his hearers, seems to have had little meaning for Paul himself, other than as a kind of guarantee that Jesus really did accomplish this feat. He has no interest in the physical details: there is no empty tomb in Paul, no Galilean or Jerusalem tradition of observable phenomena, only the *fact* of the risen Lord. To be sure, he claims that Jesus' "body" has been seen by Peter and the Twelve and James and five hundred others, of whom some are still alive; and, in fact, that he has seen it himself. But that's enough. For Paul, Jesus Christ has now passed into some other, spiritual mode—the mode he came from—and is *no longer* corporeal at all; for in his new life, Christ lives in us and we in him.

The result is that we are also rehabilitated, not only in the long run, but at the moment we believe. As we have seen, the scholarly term for this immediate salvation is "vertical eschatology" as opposed to "horizontal eschatology" (sainthood at the apocalypse). The Synoptics are generally interested only in the last; Paul is devoted to both. For him, Christ's resurrection initiated a new mode of existence in which the believer *already* lives on a new plain. In some mysterious way the Christian inhabits a parallel, perfected universe where the temperature is as stable as Miami's and the lion lies down with lamb. This is why Paul thinks his readers should be full of joy (*chara*). They have been made saints.

For centuries beliefs like those I've just summarized were taken literally by Christians, hardly even examined. It was the way we were. But that day is over. Even the most conservative churches are today faced with giving some more understandable meaning to this death–rebirth plot. That such a rethinking is inevitable and that it will inevitably be mixed with ecclesiastical politics and worry about "scandalizing the faithful" are clear to anyone who picks up a contemporary work of Christian theology. Here, for instance, is the first sentence *only* of Richard McBrien's treatment of the resurrection in his magisterial *Catholicism*. "The resurrection has been understood poorly. We refer here not only to the question of facticity (whether it was a bodily, historical happening) but to the question of its place and significance in the whole Christian event" (p. 428).

If you are my age, your heart sinks reading that. From that first sentence you know it's no go. Though we were brought up to consider the fact of Christ's rising from the dead to be the ultimate confirmation of the faith, McBrien now calls this belief a "narrow view." It is indeed. Paul understands it as the knife edge on which lie all his hopes. "If Christ is not risen we of all men are most to be pitied." But that haunting remark in itself is of no more use to us than the simple belief of millions and millions of Eastern Christians who have greeted each other on so many successive Easters with "Christ is risen. Christ is indeed risen." Nevertheless, you sympathize with McBrien. He is a loyal American Catholic intellectual, his book an honest attempt to come to grips with all sorts of traditional doctrine, not only biblical. McBrien and the rest of the theologians who take a more "enlightened" view of the New Testament must somehow come to terms with the resurrection as a part of *contemporary* faith. But is that possible? Is it possible for a contemporary Christian to hold that the earliest church mistakenly thought Jesus had risen from the dead and unfortunately passed this notion on? Is it possible for the contemporary Christian to hold that Jesus was mistakenly and after the fact taken to be the risen Christ? I don't object to these enlightened notions, you understand; they are conclusions toward which my whole book points. But I am as puzzled as anyone else as to how Christians are able to adjust to them. And I *do* object to the overly careful language McBrien and others use in dealing with these matters—*nuancing* they call it—as if *no* mistake had been made about Jesus, as if *nobody* ever lied. Would Paul talk this way?

The third element in Paul's theology is his notion of faith: A Godlike Lord dies and rises again, so that we who *believe* in him are saved. When we come to examine this faith, the engine, as it were, which makes the system run, we find what has truly lasted in the Pauline message. You will recall that at the end of the discussion of the Synoptic tradition I said that what the modern reader missed in these accounts was the psychology of humanity itself and that this omission would be redressed by Paul. This is precisely the role of Pauline *faith*, for by that word Paul does not mean "intellectual assent" or some simple acknowledgment of the resurrection. As we have seen, he does not mean "choosing to believe." He means an act of the will, a dedication of the self and the community which results in life lived on a higher plane in a state Paul calls *righteousness*.

This act of the will is not something limited that one can do for oneself. As we have seen, the natural human condition stands outside the possibility of righteousness; it is only by the saving God that a person is ever brought into right relationship to the universe and its creator. This idea is difficult to understand. Why should God have created such a lame creature in the first place? And what would be a *right* relation to God or the universe? The idea seems contrary to the relativity in which we live. Perhaps, as a character in Thomas Mann says, "Theology cannot be modern"; to ask for a "right relation to God and his Cosmos" inevitably returns us to the Gothic towers of Wittenberg and from there, back in time, to a house-church in Thessalonica.

And even if one regards such a request as rational, why would God—who is conceived as perfectly just—grant this "right relation" to some and not to others? And why should possession of an unmerited gift allow one to reap benefits denied to others? Both Paul and Luther were aware of these difficulties. For the enduring paradox of both reformers is that for all their protestations about the "plain truth" and what is obviously and objectively true, both realized that the real devils, the ones that matter, are within—not those tame Synoptic demons, of course, but our real diabolism, the pain of being human. The paradoxes of just and unjust, free or slave, right or wrong are fundamental categories in our experience—each pair occurring simultaneously. I am determined by my genes and by sociological forces; but I sometimes have an overwhelming sense of freedom of choice. I know roughly what justice might be; but I am confident it will never be general on earth—and hopefully I will never meet with it. I recognize the good, the heroic, the noble; but rarely if ever do I achieve them: "What I do is not what I want to do but what I detest," says Paul.

The human condition of being without faith that Paul describes is a kind of illness, a joyless, selfish insecurity and lack of courage that results in evil. Since the Renaissance, secular thought has tried to deal with this human sickness through biology or economics or psychiatry—but, it must be admitted, unsuccessfully. Yet religion often has helped; faith as described by Paul has often been a successful way of dealing with very real evil. As William James knew, people show a surprising unanimity in their insistence on faith, almost without regard for its object. For Paul as for Luther, Abraham is the great example of such saving faith. Of his obedience to God's command to kill his son, Paul quotes Genesis 15:6, "Abraham put his faith in God, and that faith was counted to him as righteousness." For Paul, the Christian lives like Abraham, not by example or by admonition, as in the Synoptic Gospels, but by reliance on Christ. Luther agreed, "It is not enough or in any sense Christian to preach the works, life, and words of Christ as historical facts, as if the knowledge of these would suffice for the conduct of life; yet this is the fashion among those who must today be regarded as our best preachers."

In the nineteenth century, Søren Kierkegaard took up the same theme in *Fear and Trembling*—in fact, the same example. Kierkegaard begins by saying he cannot understand Abraham; then he adds, "in a certain sense there is nothing I can learn from him but astonishment." What he means, I think, is that there is nothing *rational* (nothing to learn) in Abraham's trust in Yahweh, a god who can demand that he kill his own son. In order to obey God, Abraham *suspends* rationality; for all abstract moral truth stands in opposition to the killing of Isaac. What is significant here is that Abraham's faith was irrational, just as Paul's was "foolishness to the Greeks." Indeed, Kierkegaard can be read as a reworking of Pauline existentialism. But why is God irrational? Well, let us suppose the contrary—as we used to say in high school geometry. Suppose God is rational: he cannot square a circle, he knows that a part cannot be greater than its whole and so on. Are not these principles of reason then *above* God, who must obey them? Or are they somehow identical with God? The first is impossible by definition; nothing is above God. And if the second is true, God becomes something like Paul's "law"; except that in modern terms he would not be the Torah, but perhaps the sum of the rules of physics and mathematics plus the probabilities of the less exact sciences. Or more simply, "the way things are." God is what is.

European philosophers from St. Thomas to Hegel had understood God precisely in this legal, scientific way: the sum of rationality, the Truth, so that by the nineteenth century Yahweh had become a Euclidean hypothesis. But for Kierkegaard as for Paul, God is an individual, personal existent who is beyond reason. His God, and Paul's, loves and desires and even plays favorites. At least from our point-of-view, he enters into a relationship not with humanity, never with humanity, but with *me*. There is a terrible wisdom in each recurrence of this ancient idea. Abraham and Paul and Luther and Kierkegaard—all who make this discovery think they have rescued their private experience, their gnosis, from the confining deities of Ur or the Torah or Roman Catholicism or from Hegel or from Logic. With *his* notion of this faith, Paul solved the problems of the foolishness of religious belief.

With *his* perception, Luther produced the great inward revolution of freedom that Germans revere to this day. With *his*, Kierkegaard finally freed moral philosophy from a kind of deadly human engineering.

The difference is that in Paul this leap to faith which transcends reason depends on the resurrection of Christ Jesus. It is the Easter faith. In the twentieth century, however, the theology of the Easter faith has been turned upside down. Where Paul thought Jesus' resurrection validated his own hope for eternal life, Kierkegaard and Karl Rahner and all the existential theologians who descend from them think that it is our own *hope* for a resurrection that validates the risen Lord. This is to say that Christians of our time begin with themselves and their own hopes and fears and then go to the New Testament to find stories that give them value. Indeed, I don't think modern people *can* think of the resurrection narrative in any but a subjective way. As Hume showed, we cannot accept the miraculous even if we want to.

More often than not, then, modern people convert Jesus' resurrection into a "proof" of whatever they already subjectively believe. When I, as a modern, read the story of Jesus' death and resurrection, therefore, I read it not as a fact—history knows no such fact—but as an expression of my own desire for something more than this life. It is this subjective truth which then guarantees the validity of Jesus' death and resurrection. In short, we have taken refuge in the hoary old argument from desire. In fact, of course, as modern persons we may not desire to live forever; but we would at least like *to count*. We don't want to be mere stuff, piled up like cordwood outside a gas chamber somewhere in Poland.

But the argument is the same. Because we desire to triumph over time and mortality and stuffness, our theologians tell us, we have only two choices: either to recognize our desire as a "transcendental necessity to believe in our own value and thus triumph over the flux of time, or reject that desire as foolishness." Karl Rahner, for instance, believes in a "triumph over the flux of time" because, as he wrote, "time becomes madness if it cannot reach fulfillment" (*Foundations*, 271). I *don't* believe in such a triumph, and I think time is madness in any case.

Paul *does* believe in it. This leap of faith came to Paul—as it comes to most people—as a solution to the unsatisfactory nature of human life. It solved for him the dilemma of his own insignificance and sinfulness: "I do not even acknowledge my own actions as mine, for what I do is not what I want to do but what I detest. . . . The good which I want to do I fail to do; but what I do is the wrong which is against my will." Faith in Christ Jesus— *sensible* or not—resolved all that.

For the message about the cross is foolishness to those who are perishing, but to us who are being saved it is the power of God. For it is written, "I will destroy the wisdom of the wise, and the discernment of the discerning I will thwart." Where is the one who is wise? Where is the scribe? Where is the debater of this age? Has not God made foolish the wisdom of the world? For since, in the wisdom of God, the world did not know God through wisdom, God decided, through the foolishness of our proclamation, to save those who believe. For Jews demand signs and Greeks desire wisdom, but we proclaim Christ crucified, a stumbling block to Jews and foolishness to Gentiles, but to those who are called, both Jews and Greeks, Christ the power of God and the wisdom of God. (1 Cor 1:18–24)

My aim in this chapter has been to illustrate how Paul's thought persists into modern philosophy and theology. In so doing I have confined myself to its fundamentals and have left unaddressed Paul's peculiar views regarding the pleasures of marriage, the condescension involved in the Pauline Privilege—if anybody still knows the term—the status of women in religion, his animadversions against homosexuality and so on. I do not think that Paul's notions about these matters are wiser than anyone else's, then or now. Nor am I much impressed with the rest of his *parenesis*. Paul's ethics are those of an apocalyptic community of the first century—and a peculiar one at that. Though he has instances of acute practical wisdom, his moral opinions are often so odd and dated as to be dangerous. Should we always obey the secular law on the premise that all authority is from God? Surely not. Should we fear all political parties? Should slaves remain in their status? Must we *all* work with our hands? Should we be on guard against sorcery? Is it forbidden to file a lawsuit against a fellow Christian? People who complain about cafeteria Christianity don't realize that Christianity, especially in its ethics, has *always* been selective.

Unfortunately, these historically particular views of Paul get in the way of what is permanently valuable in his writing. J. Christiaan Beker voices the dismay of many Christians:

We are genuinely perplexed today why Paul's gospel—once the glorious centerpiece of the Reformation with its revolutionary and liberating message—has become so alien to us and evokes so much hostility, especially because of its many culturally determined pronouncements concerning, for example, the status of women, slavery, marriage, sex, or homosexuality. (*Heirs of Paul*, 29)

Once we abstract from such views, Paul becomes once again significant. His intuition that human beings on their own are never righteous is correct.

Objectively true moral values are simply not available to us; nothing ever comes tagged—behaviors or people. Despite Thomas Jefferson, there are no inalienable rights, and no particular behavior can be shown to be Good or Evil. As far as reason can see, we *are* simply stuff, conglomerates of carbon molecules. Under these circumstances, it is rationally absurd, as Kierkegaard saw, to think that humans are of any more value than the grasses of the field. In the face of that absurdity, Paul asserts that only a grace from elsewhere, not a law or a tradition, can prompt us to make a leap to the Good. This existential idea (perhaps we should say this *psychological insight*)—which quite reverses scholastic and rationalistic philosophy— may be true or false; but it lies deep in the heart of every modern man or woman.

CHAPTER 5

The Theology of John

My earliest memories of John's Gospel are from Holy Angels Church and School, Gary, Indiana. By the time I reached the seventh or eighth grade, I was already a learned little fellow in glasses, who was beginning to condescend to his parents and brothers as well as to the millhands and open-hearth workers who made up the parish and swallowed whole the odd miracles and trumpeting anathemas Father Sullivan found in the Synoptics, on the one hand, and in Paul, on the other. Poor Sisters Emily and Esther were perhaps merely deluded—in the fashion of women, I reasoned—but Father Sullivan and his assistant, Father Elliot, were without excuse.

But as I grew older, there was one exception to the alternating amusement and disdain with which I had come to view the beliefs of our parish. In those unreformed, Tridentine, Latin days, the Roman mass came to its conclusion with a reading of the first fourteen lines of John, a custom, I later learned, that had begun in the eleventh or twelfth century and was codified in the sixteenth. Now even Father Sullivan couldn't ruin *this* majestic and philosophic definition of Jesus as the *Word*, the "reason" for creation itself. Though the rest of the New Testament could be lovely or frighteningly demanding by turns, it was obviously intended for the *hoi polloi*. John was for *intellectuals*.

> In the beginning was the Word:
> the Word was with God
> and the Word was God.

I suppose by then I was in high school and someone had explained to me the multiple meanings of the Greek word *logos* or had talked to me about Plato and his shadowy, doubt-filled cave. In any case I had come to believe that John's highfalutin material was in some way *real* Catholic theology and was therefore almost certainly intended for *me*. As I recall, I had no grasp of the immense preexistent claims made by this famous passage; what I liked was its highfalutin quality, the majesty and sweep of the ancient poem and the bold imitation of the first lines of Genesis.

Though this specific language of the Prologue does not appear again in John's Gospel, its high Christology and gnostic view of the world certainly do. Indeed, the entire work is astonishingly unlike anything we have read so far. Here is the spiritualized, Godlike Jesus of Paul, all right, but consistently conceived within an impressive cosmology which demands of him neither sacrificial death nor apocalyptic return. And the whole is preached in a sophisticated mixture of artificial dialogue and wonder-worker history without parallel in literature. So different is this Gospel, in fact, that some warning of what is *not* to be found in John is necessary; otherwise readers—even "sensible readers"—will mentally supply a "filler" of foreign, Synoptic anecdotes as they go along.

I have already mentioned the two most important of these missing ideas, namely, the sacrificial death and the apocalypse. But additionally, Jesus is never a wandering Synoptic holy man in John; and there are no stories about people who think he is "beside himself," no exorcisms, no attempts to free up the late Jewish holiness code, no ethic of daily life. There are not even any parables in John, nor any foundation story for the Eucharist, and the crucifixion itself is a matter of triumph and glory rather than defeat. Instead of an apocalypse and Second Coming there is the promise of a new spiritual figure to come called the "Comforter," or *Paraclete*.

Indeed, John's omissions are so many that most New Testament introductions provide a list. Following Stephen Harris's *New Testament: A Student's Introduction,* one notes that John's Gospel has no infancy story or genealogy and no tale of a virgin birth; Jesus is not baptized—in fact, the ritual itself is a puzzle to John. There is no "temptation dialogue," no Satan and his three offers (this is a Q story, and John doesn't know Q). In John, Jesus does not preach for one year only, ending in a single visit to Jerusalem; he preaches for at least three years and visits Jerusalem often. John's Gospel presents and comments on only seven miracles, of which only the feeding story followed by the walking on water has a parallel in the Synoptics. Moreover, John usually calls these miracles *erga* (works) or *sēmeia* (signs) not *dynamai* (powerful acts) as in the Synoptics; and the miracles he describes, turning water into wine, for instance, are often significant only in what they point to, either liturgically or metaphysically, rather than in any good they do.

L et me ask you to pause here before we go on. How much of what you consider essential to the Christian story have the previous two paragraphs eliminated? Would you even recognize the faith without some of what John has omitted? Devout readers used to apologize for these lacunae by insisting that the fourth evangelist came to Gospel writing late and didn't want to repeat matters already rehashed in the Synoptics—which of course he had read. But this will not do. First of all, John is not a "late" work, even in its final form. Second, it is clearly independent of the Synoptics. Third, it is difficult to accept the third-century tradition that this Gospel was the work of a single man, the apostle who appears in the Synoptics as John son of Zebedee. This belief can be traced no further back than Irenaeus, ca. 180 C.E.; after it left his hands it came to include the notion that John lived in Ephesus, into the time of Trajan, where he continued to be the guardian of the Blessed Virgin. Moreover, contrary to common belief, John is never even mentioned in the Gospel, and in the absence of tradition we would never connect the author of the Fourth Gospel with any particular apostle. It is true that a "beloved apostle" appears in the last two chapters of the work, but all we know about *him* is that in some vague way he is superior to Peter and that our author or authors believe that it is *his* "witness" that underlies the Gospel (19:28–34). Who he was remains a mystery. There is even a theory that the Beloved Disciple was always only a fiction invented to claim apostolic authority—without risk of proof or disproof.

Like modern critics, several early fathers discounted the story that the apostle John was the author of the Fourth Gospel; indeed, some refused to accept the Gospel itself. (They were called the *alogoi* from their rejection of its *logos* theology.) In fact, it was not generally accepted as canonical until sometime in the fourth century, and critics long maintained—as did my own professors in college—that it was a literary product of the late second century, when its sort of Gnosticism was current. John's Gospel was supposed to be a kind of theologically inspired poem on the life of Jesus. In our own day, however, any number of texts have been discovered to push "gnostic" thought of the type represented in John back at least to the last two centuries before the Christian era. Moreover, in 1935 a papyrus fragment found in Cairo some fifteen years earlier was identified as a fragment of John and was dated by its handwriting to about 130 C.E. The upshot is that there is no reason to suppose that John is much later than Matthew or Luke. None of this solves the question of authorship, however; and the multiple author/redactor view, with a history of composition from 70 to 90, still seems to be the best explanation for the peculiarities of the text.

What is more important is that both the composition and content of the work presuppose a tradition quite different from that of the Synoptics, one in which a god takes human form, goes through a kind of pantomime of human life, and "dies" in what looks like a cruel execution but is actually the means by which he can return to the empyrean. This plot is fleshed out in an appropriate manner. Here Jesus speaks grandly and mysteriously: "whoever drinks the water that I shall give will never again be thirsty" and "I am the bread which came down from heaven . . . the bread of life" and "whoever eats my flesh and drinks my blood" and "before Abraham was born I am." In making these pronouncements, he sometimes even uses what is called the *ego eimi* ("I am") formula, a grammatical flourish unclear in English translation. In *koinē* Greek, using the unnecessary pronoun *ego* in saying "I am" had something of the aura of Queen Victoria saying, "We are not amused." In this Gospel also, Jesus gives long, rambling discourses in a vocabulary that would be almost wholly unintelligible to us if its meaning had not been preserved by the early church. He speaks in a kind of code of the *word*, the *water of life*, the *vine*, and so on. The speeches in which this language occurs are often triggered by a secondary character's artificial leading question or misunderstanding, a pattern the author likes so much that he sometimes incorporates what he assumes will be the reader's question. In a famous scene, a secondary character named Nicodemus does not know what it means to be "born again," and Jesus has to tell him—somewhat sarcastically. Here Nicodemus obviously speaks for us; it is *we* who do not understand and are taught. Turning to action rather than speech, we discover that a surprising amount of what happens to John's Jesus is explicitly said to fulfill "proof texts" found in one late biblical book: Deutero-Zechariah. These include the manner of Jesus' entry into Jerusalem, the thirty pieces of silver given to Judas, the dispersal of the disciples at the Lord's arrest—like scattered sheep—the parade of people who pass by the cross looking at Jesus' pierced side, the cleansing of the Temple, and finally that business of the "living water" already mentioned.

The text itself is full of difficulties—disorganized to such an extent that it does not really make good continued sense. In fact, a scholar once seriously proposed that the "original" manuscript had been written on loose leaves of papyrus which were subsequently dropped and scrambled, and that no one has ever been able to sort them out correctly. This Humpty-Dumpty theory may sound silly until you learn the details of the problem. Chapters 5 and 6 are simply out of order. In chapter 5 Jesus leaves Galilee for Jerusalem; but in chapter 6, without remark, he is back in Galilee. Good sense is restored when they are reversed. Other problems are not so easily solved. In 7:21, Jesus says he has performed only one work (miracle) so far—which is not the case. In 12:36 he is said to have gone into hiding, but eight verses later he is speaking again. Having apparently concluded his Passover discourse at the end of chapter 14, Jesus says, "Come let us go!" But at the beginning of chapter 15 he is still talking and continues talking for three more chapters! In 13:36, Peter asks Jesus where he is going; but in 16:5 Jesus complains that *no one* asks him where he's going. So odd is the sequencing of this text that the much-loved but inauthentic story of the woman taken in adultery could later simply be inserted at 8:1–11 without difficulty.

The most common way to explain all this is to posit various stages of composition and a succession of inaccurate editors. Such a theory not only attempts to account for these *aporia,* or difficulties, but to provide a kind of window into the development of John's form of Christianity. The hope is that when correctly isolated along "seams," as they are called—breaks in the text marked by missing or confused transitions or shifts in terminology and/or theology—the separate parts of the construction will reveal particular, time-bound understandings of Jesus and his preaching. The whole of John might then be read as a record of the development of Christianity at least in one community.

Though such an inquiry into the genesis of John's Gospel is peripheral to our reading, some knowledge of this scholarship is necessary for understanding the final Gospel. The first version of John may have been written in Judea as early as 70 C.E. and not later than 90 C.E. Based on orally transmitted material and independent of the Synoptic tradition—though it had several anecdotes in common with it—this early text emphasized miracles and the simple belief they inspired in people. Apparently it contained the seven signs and the transitions between them, all of which occur before 12:42; then it skipped over the Farewell Discourse to the crucifixion story (18:1ff.) and concluded with the "first ending" at 20:31. Missing were the Prologue, the Nicodemus interview, and the highest flights of the preaching material. Missing also was the second ending, or appendix, of chapter 21.

This first Book of Signs, as it is called, would have reflected a low Christology comparable to that of the Synoptics. But about 90 C.E., it was rewritten into a second edition, influenced by the liturgical practices and theology of Jewish-Christians then being expelled from the Judean synagogues. This second edition therefore exhibited an increased hostility to Jesus' enemies, "the Jews"—an expression that has always puzzled people since practically everyone in the Gospel story *is* a Jew, including Jesus himself. It can be shown, however, that this expression was used by the second editor to refer only to the Jews of Jerusalem and Judea who were in power during the 30s and actively opposed Jesus. Unfortunately, later readers did not understand this, and the usage has significantly contributed to Christian anti-Semitism.

The second edition seems also to have added or reinterpreted both miraculous and nonmiraculous events to give them symbolic value. The scene with Nicodemus already mentioned is an example, but the same thing is observable in John's anecdote of the Samaritan woman and his expanded story of the loaves and fishes. Each of these sequences is made to focus on theology rather than miracle. A third and final version or editing is said to have produced some of the duplicate material and to have attempted to emphasize the theological nature of the entire account, with the addition of the Logos Hymn as prologue, much of the Farewell Address, and the second ending—but there is no proof of this. In fact, there is no *external* evidence that the Gospel ever existed without its present material and in its present chaotic form, except for "the woman taken in adultery," which occurs only in late manuscripts and then in different locations—sometimes even in different Gospels. Yet the general theory of John's composition, apart from specific details, seems sound.

As is to be expected with pieced-together documents, the final version of the Fourth Gospel is full of editorial remarks, *glosses* as they are called. Some are similar to those in the other Gospels: translations of Semitic terms or notes calling attention to the fulfillment of a proof text. Others are dramatically interpretative. Indeed, these Johannine glosses shape the narrative into a long argument for a peculiar conception of who Jesus was. In 5:18ff., for example, the editor concludes a story of Jesus curing the sick on the Sabbath with: "This made the Jews all the more determined to kill him, because not only was he breaking the Sabbath but, by calling God his own Father, he was claiming equality with God." In 6:6, when Jesus has asked a disciple where they will buy bread to feed the multitude, the editor writes, "He said this to test him; Jesus himself knew what he meant to do." In 7:21, after Jesus says that Moses gave them the law of circumcision, the editor corrects him, "not that it originated with Moses, but with the patriarchs." In 12:33, after Jesus has talked of being "lifted up," we have the explanation, "This he said to indicate the kind of death he was to die." There are a dozen or so more such glosses. In reading John sensibly, one is curiously aided by such glosses through which the final (or nearly final) editor makes very explicit his purpose and to some degree his method. In the last lines of what is now the penultimate chapter of the Gospel—but what surely was once its conclusion—we have, for instance:

> There were indeed many other signs that Jesus performed in the presence of his disciples, which are not recorded in this book. Those written here have been recorded in order that you may come to believe [or continue to believe]

that Jesus is the Christ, the Son of God, and that through this faith you may have life by his name. (20:30–31)

With this in mind, it is clear that the last author-editors arranged a text that begins with a Prologue (1:1–18), continues with an expanded Book of Signs (1:19–12:50), and is followed by the so-called Book of Glory (13:1–20:31). Finally, someone attached an Appendix (chapter 21).

Let us begin our reading where the author begins, with that mind-boggling poem about the word, the *logos*. I print it here as you will find it in many modern texts, with its editorial interruptions in italicized prose. As is readily apparent, these are glosses concerned with the relation between Jesus and John the Baptist.

> In the beginning was the Word:
> the Word was with God
> and the Word was God.
> He was with God in the beginning.
> Through him all things came to be,
> not one thing had its being but through him.
> All that came to be had life in him
> and that life was the life of men,
> a light that shines in the dark,
> a light that darkness could not overpower.

A man came, sent by God; his name was John. He came as a witness, as a witness to speak for the light, so that everyone might believe through him. (He was not the light, only a witness to speak for the light.) The Word was the true light that enlightens all men; and he was coming into the world.

> He was in the world
> that had its being through him,
> and the world did not know him.
> He came to his own domain
> and his own people did not accept him.
> But to all who did accept him
> he gave the power to become children of God,
> to all who believe in the name of him
> who were born not of human stock
> or urge of the flesh
> or will of man
> but of God himself.
> The Word was made flesh,
> he lived among us,

and we saw his glory,
the glory that is his as the only Son of the Father,
full of grace and truth.

John bore witness to him and proclaimed: "This is the man of whom I said,
'He comes after me, but ranks ahead of me; before I was born, he already
was.'"

From his full store we have all received: Grace from Grace;
For the law was given through Moses,
But grace and truth came through Jesus Christ.
No one has ever seen God;
God's only son, he who is nearest to the father's heart,
Has made him known.

This, I thought as a youngster, was the real thing. But the youthful snobbery which caused me to reject the low Christology of the Synoptics in favor of John's metaphysics is an illustration of a general rule I have already mentioned: every Christian is a "Cafeteria Christian," and always has been. What we like we retain; what we do not like or cannot believe, we leave aside. I liked the highfalutin—though eventually it would prove too much for me; for in these famous lines lies a conception of Jesus so grand as to be unimaginable. I call your attention especially to v. 3: "and without Him nothing was made." An itinerant preacher who was actually a being through whom all space and time was created (an idea we have also found buried in Paul's rhetoric) was too large for my eighth-grade grasp. And when I *did* understand it, I could not believe it.

But I also liked this poem's dramatic light-and-dark imagery, even though our missal gave us the puzzling translation: "and the darkness did not comprehend it" for *et tenebrae eam non comprehenderunt.* The original reads: *kai hē skotia auto ou katelaben,* that is, "the darkness did not overpower it." I also liked John's insistence that despite all this Jesus was still a human being. In those days when the priest read "and the word was made flesh," we all genuflected, as if somehow Jesus was not simply one with the Father but was more important than the Father precisely because he had become human. At Holy Angels, of course, Jesus *was* more important than God, more important than anyone except, perhaps, the BVM. That's how we thought in those days—though we would never have admitted it—and again that's pretty much how Christians have always thought. It is the reason why whoever produced the final version of this poem had to add all those warnings about the inferior status of John the Baptist. Christian readers might also make some sort of idol of *him.*

It was therefore only gradually that I came to ask, "What view of the world can elevate a Jesus of Nazareth to a being through whom the world itself was created?" And only in college did I learn that the particular view which made such a leap possible was called "Gnosticism," a widespread Hellenistic attitude that saw the whole cosmos in terms of two principles: good (immaterial) and bad (material.) Gnostics believed that certain forms of immaterial "knowing" (*gnosis*) are solutions to the disappointments of this lower plane of material existence. Like modern-day existentialism, with which it has much in common, Gnosticism was primarily an attitude toward life; but like all such attitudes, it implied a metaphysics. Hellenistic Gnosticism held that sacred knowledge was truth in its substantive, Platonic sense of a higher being. As in Plato's philosophy also, Truth actually resided in the higher of two realms, a different *world*, perfect and eternal. Since humans live in an imperfect, material, and time-bound realm, getting to that higher world was the aim of philosophy and religion.

As one might imagine, different gnostic sects had different means of achieving this. But common to all was a low estimate of the value of truth gained from unaided human reason. In fact some sort of cleansing ritual like baptism was often needed to cast off such inferior thinking and enter into a higher knowledge and level of existence; passwords or "acts of knowledge" also performed this function. Pagan gnostics sometimes posited a continuous creation that began with the highest deity, the Ineffable, and descended through passive mind (*Noos*) to Active Mind (*Logos*) through "the Anointed One" (*Christos*) and Wisdom (*Sophia*) down to the first admixture of matter in the evil ruler of this world, Ialdabaoth (Yahweh, in anti-Semitic areas) and continuing downward to the least speck of common clay. Tales were told of how a wandering *Sophia* fell into the netherworld and was rescued by *Christos*. Christians of the second century never cease warning us against such mythic tales.

But it is not necessary to go to these late pagan mythologies to encounter the gnostic attitude toward the world. The same sensibility appears in the "wisdom books" of the Hebrew Scripture. It is also found in the documents of the people who lived at Qumran and in the "Jewish-Christian" intertestamental literature: you may recall that in discussing the "little apocalypse" in the Gospel of Mark I cited a passage from the apocryphal, intertestamental 2 *Esdras*, which begins "The Most High has made not one world but two. . . ."

From that other world came "Wisdom" as portrayed in the book of Proverbs, a book that unashamedly combines the most practical social advice with breathtaking visions.

I am wisdom, I bestow shrewdness
and show the way to knowledge and discretion . . .
The Lord created me the first of his works
long ago, before all else that he made.
I was formed in earliest times
at the beginning, before the earth itself. . . .
For whoever finds me finds life
and wins favor with the Lord,
but whoever fails to find me deprives himself,
and all who hate me are in love with death. (Prov. 8:12ff.)

Here is the same conception made more "spiritual" as it had evolved in Judaism by 180 B.C.E. in the apocryphal *Ecclesiasticus* or *Wisdom of Jesus, Son of Sirach.*

I am the word spoken by the Most High;
it was I who covered the earth like a mist . . .
Before time began he created me,
and until the end of time I shall endure . . .
Come to me, all you who desire me,
and eat your fill of my fruit . . .
Whoever feeds from me will hunger for more;
whoever drinks from me will thirst for more. . . . (Ecclus. 24:1ff.)

This sort of thinking was a common element in late Judaism and early Christianity. Whether it was part of the *earliest* Christianity or not is hotly debated, though Paul's notions of the 50s seem to be formed on a similar pattern. Clearly, John's Gospel is quite comfortable with such an outlook, though here and there he must insist that Jesus is also truly human. As in the Synoptics, he provides scenes in which the risen Christ eats food.

But the inevitable tension between the two Christologies, *high* in Paul and John, *low* in the Synoptics, will bedevil Christians from the time of the writing of the New Testament to well beyond the Council of Nicaea and down to today. Accordingly, the Gnostic elements in John were often represented by Christian scholars as the result of fighting fire with fire, as if the author were trying to find as much common ground as he could with his opponents. But the truth seems to be that the Johannine school itself simply believed in a Gnostic form of Christianity.

The Book of Signs

In its final form, the first half of the Gospel of John steadily mounts in tension from the Logos Hymn to the Last Supper, with the passage of time marked by references to recurrent Jewish festivals. Interspersed among the seven original signs are the imposing theological discourses characteristic of this Gospel. As in Mark, there is no infancy story; the narrative begins with John's baptizing at the Jordan River, where Jesus appears and gathers his first disciples. But the whole event is here imagined as a four-day experience. On the first day, "the Jews" (those misnamed Jerusalem opponents I have spoken about) come out into the wilderness to ask what the Baptist thinks he's doing. For an answer, the author places *directly* into John the Baptist's own mouth that proof text from the Septuagint Deutero-Isaiah which in all the Gospels explains his mission: "I am a voice crying in the wilderness, 'Make straight the way for the Lord.'" On the second day, John sees a man approaching and has a vision of a spirit descending upon him and naming him "God's Chosen One." He immediately declares to those around him that *this* is the man he had predicted—the one who will baptize in the spirit rather than with water. Jesus is "the Lamb of God who takes away the sins of the world," says John, adding in confirmation of the Prologue, "before I was born, he already was." On the third day, when Jesus again passes by, two of John's disciples defect to him, calling him "Rabbi," a name the author translates for us as "Teacher." One of these first disciples, Andrew, now goes off to his brother, Simon, telling him, "We have found the Messiah." Again the author stops to tell us that this is the "Hebrew" for the Greek *christos*. When Andrew brings his brother to the Lord, Jesus gives him an Aramaic nickname, "Cephas," which the author explains means "Peter, or 'the Rock,'" a pun on the Greek *petros*. On the fourth day, Jesus adds two more disciples, Philip and Nathanael, the latter unknown to the Synoptics. All of these men are Galileans, and it is toward Galilee that the little party now journeys. As they go, Jesus promises that once there they will see "in very truth . . . God's angels ascending and descending upon the Son of Man."

This whole opening section obviously makes use of a tradition different from, but parallel to, the story told in the three Synoptics. In this view of events there is an increased uneasiness about Jesus' relation to John the Baptist and to baptism itself. We notice this first in the glosses set into the Logos Hymn. We find it again in 3:22, where the author says that Jesus "remained there [Judea] with his disciples and baptized," only to change his mind a dozen verses later "although, in fact, it was his disciples who were baptizing, not Jesus himself." The reason for this double-talk has never been recovered, but the author may have come to believe that to be baptized was somehow beneath Jesus, as do the Synoptic evangelists. But the writer is also concerned about Jesus baptizing *others*, so much so that, having mentioned it, he then denies it ever occurred. Curiously enough, Paul doesn't care to admit very many baptisms either (see 1 Cor. 1:13–17). Perhaps all the early Christian writers were a bit wary of this ritual because of similar cleansing rites performed in pagan cults of the day; such parallels bothered Justin Martyr, and they caused the anti-Christian Celsus to rejoice. The whole matter remains puzzling. In any case, it is obvious that the author wants to make explicit Jesus' superiority to John the Baptist—as in the Prologue. Indeed, he piles up titles for him: Lord, Lamb of God (only implicit in the Synoptics, but explicit in Paul in 1 Cor. 5:7), God's Chosen One, Teacher, Messiah ("the one of whom Moses wrote about in the law"), and finally Son of Man. In using this last expression, the author is aware of the judging figure from the book of Daniel, but provides us with no similar apocalypse. Instead, he connects the title Son of Man with that vision of angels moving up and down a heavenly ladder which God once gave to Jacob.

Two days later, Jesus works his first "sign." It is the end of the first week of his recorded ministry and we are at a wedding feast at a town nine miles north of Nazareth. Present are Jesus, the new disciples, and his mother. She tells him the wine has run out; he says he's not ready to work miracles. She relies on his good nature and, presto, there appear twenty or thirty gallons of a better vintage than the guests had already gotten drunk on. (Both the amount of the wine and the drunkenness of the guests are disguised in English texts.) This magical performance is an example of John's use of signs: that which is pointed to by the miracle is more important than the triviality of the miracle itself. But what *is* being pointed to? Is the new wine better in the sense that Jesus' doctrine is better than traditional Judaism? Is this wine a reference to an already established Eucharist? We don't know. All we know we learn from the author's gloss: "This deed at Cana-in-Galilee is the first of the signs by which Jesus revealed his glory and led his disciples to believe in him."

If we go on to ask whether Jesus' presence at a marriage symbolizes his "bridegroom role" of the Synoptic parable or makes marriage a "sacrament," as Catholics used to argue, we encounter a whole literature of speculation; for it has always seemed to later Christians that John has tailored this and other signs to serve as foundation stories for the sacraments of the Great Church. But the question is vexed, particularly since the Reformation, and complicated by the ambiguity of the text itself. As we have seen, John is nervous about "Baptism" in the sense of an actual ritual of water, though throughout the Gospel there is plenty of sacerdotal language about baptism as a spiritual event. In like fashion, whether or not the wine at Cana alludes to the wine of communion, there is a wealth of eucharistic imagery elsewhere in the Gospel—even though John's Last Supper doesn't contain a "Eucharist"! To make matters worse, this Gospel preserves another cleansing ritual, "foot-washing," which is still retained as a papal Lenten ceremony (and recently encouraged in other contexts) though it has never been made into a Roman Catholic sacrament.

In any case, the tiny group of Galileans—augmented by Jesus' brothers—now makes its way down to Capernaum on the lake. From there he goes up to Jerusalem for Passover, apparently for the first time. Once in the city, Jesus makes a whip and drives the money changers and buyers and sellers of sacrificial animals out of the Temple, the "cleansing of the temple" which the Synoptic writers place late in the ministry. As we have seen, however, these poor retailers were quite legitimate and necessary; what John and the Synoptics record must be a distortion of what was originally some sort of symbolic act—if it is not fiction. This is suggested by the dialogue John provides between Jesus and "the Jews," with a gloss (italicized) suggesting that the Jerusalem Temple is now no longer the Holy Place and that it has been replaced by the body of Jesus and by extension, perhaps, the body of the believer.

> "Destroy this temple," Jesus replied, "and in three days I will raise it again." They said, "It has taken forty-six years to build this temple. Are you going to raise it again in three days?" *But the temple he was speaking of was his body. After his resurrection his disciples recalled what he had said, and they believed the scripture and the words that Jesus had spoken.* (John 2:19–22)

As I have said, this sort of theological gloss is peculiar to John's Gospel, where the relationship between the author and his text is quite different from that in the Synoptics. The author of the Fourth Gospel writes without the slightest pretense of belonging to the generation of the disciples, viewing the story of Jesus quite consciously from the perspective of a later time and authoritatively interpreting what has been handed down to him.

While in Jerusalem, Jesus has made converts because of his signs, but we are told that he does not trust these new disciples, "for he himself could tell what was in people" (2:23–25). But one night an important man, a Pharisee and member of the Sanhedrin, comes to speak with him. Their ensuing dialogue contains Jesus' first formal discourse in the Gospel (3:1–21). It is here, as noted above, that he says, "Very truly, I tell you, no one can see the kingdom of God without being born from above." When Nicodemus points out that this is physically impossible, Jesus says that one must be "born of water and spirit," asking somewhat sarcastically, "You a teacher of Israel and ignorant of such things?" He then begins a speech the like of which we have not yet read—but one that will become so familiar that it will eventually appear on bumper stickers.

> In very truth I tell you, we speak of what we know, and testify to what we have seen, and yet you all reject our testimony. If you disbelieve me when I talk to you about things on earth, how are you to believe if I should talk about the things of heaven?
>
> No one ever went up into heaven except the one who came down from heaven, the Son of Man whose home is in heaven. The Son of Man must be lifted up as the serpent was lifted up by Moses in the wilderness, so that everyone who has faith in him may in him possess eternal life.
>
> God loved the world so much that he gave his only Son, that everyone who has faith in him may not die but have eternal life. It was not to judge the world that God sent his Son into the world, but that through him the world might be saved. (3:11–17)

This passage is important to evangelical Protestantism, particularly in America; indeed the last two sentences will become the password that our home-brewed Gnosticism demands for salvation. For a certain kind of believer, these words elicit a confident hope in the nonjudgmental gift of eternal life and validate the conversion experience of being "born again" or "making a decision for Christ," as Billy Graham likes to call it. But that is to look far ahead indeed.

Turning back to the first-century narrative, we find that Jesus' conversions in the city have made him even less welcome to the Pharisees, and he decides to leave Judea and return to Galilee. Passing through Samaria, that foreign and heterodox land where the inhabitants accept only the Pentateuch and pray at their own temple in Gerizim, he becomes involved in an episode that parallels the interview with Nicodemus. Jesus talks to a Samaritan woman of dubious repute and asks her to draw a cup of a water for him from the well—shocking his disciples. ("Jews do not share drinking vessels with Samaritans," says the ever-alert editor.) But the water the text speaks of, like the *birth* in the Nicodemus interview, is symbolic. It is the "living water" which functions throughout the Gospel as a metaphor for eternal life. Moreover, the well at which the two are seated is Jacob's Well, associated in the reader's mind with that night at Beth-el millennia ago when Jacob saw that vision of the "ladder, which rested on the ground with its top reaching to the heavens and angels of God were going up and down on it." This, of course, is the very Galilean vision Jesus has promised to show his disciples at the beginning of the Gospel, but which, in fact, he never does reveal to them in this Gospel. The writer may also have in mind Jacob's acknowledgment upon awakening from that dream: "Truly the Lord is in this place, and I did not know it." Third, and more important, the writer wishes to suggest something else, something on a grander scale. When the woman points out that she and her ancestors worship in Samaria and not in Jerusalem as "you Jews" demand, Jesus replies:

> "But the time approaches, indeed it is already here, when those who are real worshipers will worship the Father in spirit and in truth. Such are the worshipers whom the Father wants. God is spirit, and those who worship him must worship in spirit and in truth." The woman answered, "I know that Messiah (that is the Christ) is coming. When he comes he will tell us everything." Jesus said to her, "I am he, I who am speaking to you now." (4:23–26)

Having remained in Samaria for two days, Jesus goes on to Galilee. By now, his neighbors have returned from the holy days in Jerusalem where they have seen his signs, and all the townspeople have heard of him. Arriving at Cana again, he meets a Herodian officer whose son lies near death down in Capernaum. Jesus reassures him that the child is cured; and sure enough, servants returning from the lake bring news that the child has recovered—the same story, obviously, which appears in the Synoptics as the "centurion's servant" cure. Lest it seem a somewhat questionable miracle, the author adds:

> They said, "Yesterday at one o'clock in the afternoon the fever left him." The father noted that this was the exact time when Jesus had said to him, "Your son will live," and he and all his household became believers. (4:52–53)

The author-editor now remarks that this "was the second sign which Jesus performed after coming from Judea into Galilee," an accounting that does not agree with the surrounding text. This sort of carelessness, if that's what it is, continues into the next section, chapter 5, which begins, "Sometime later, Jesus went up to Jerusalem for one of the Jewish festivals." But there is something more. Can you hear in that sentence how far the author of this Gospel has come from Judaism? "One of the Jewish festivals"! In its chilly, vague offhandedness it forecasts in miniature the tragic history of the two faiths.

At Jerusalem's Pool of Bethsaida (originally a site of pagan curing) Jesus cures a man on the Sabbath as his third sign, and the author-editor comments:

> It was works of this kind done on the Sabbath that stirred the Jews to persecute Jesus. He defended himself by saying, "My Father has never yet ceased his work, and I am working too." This made the Jews still more determined

to kill him, because he was not only breaking the Sabbath, but, by calling God his own Father, he claimed equality with God. (5:16–18)

As I pointed out earlier, chapter 6 opens abruptly and incongruously with Jesus on the opposite shore of the Sea of Galilee, and it is once again near Passover. It is here on the eastern, or pagan, side of the lake that he performs the same miracle of loaves and fishes as in the Synoptics (the "five thousand" version), which is counted as his fourth sign. Then he follows it—again as in the Synoptics—by walking on water, the fifth sign. These connected stories represent another brief conjunction between the Fourth Gospel and the Synoptic tradition, a fact that has inspired an immense commentary. What lies behind this matter is the whole puzzle I have referred to earlier as the study of "Christian origins." To try to elucidate the relation between the Synoptics and John is to ask, How and where and in what form did these traditions first become memorialized and what were the steps by which they came to be written down? Good progress has been made in this field, but as yet no one can say how this particular unit of stories—though hardly anything else—came to appear both in John and in the Synoptics.

Meanwhile Jesus has come back across the lake; and in the morning, when the people discover that he is gone, they too cross back to Capernaum to find him. He then speaks to them as if taking up the thread of the previous day's sign:

I am the bread of life. Your ancestors ate the manna in the wilderness, and they died. This is the bread that comes down from heaven, so that one may eat of it and not die. I am the living bread that came down from heaven. Whoever eats of this bread will live forever; and the bread that I will give for the life of the world is my flesh. (6:48–51)

Are these disjointed remarks foundation statements about the Eucharist? And were they written back into the Gospel by the early church for that very reason, as many scholars believe? It is important in considering such claims to remember Paul's foundation story in 1 Corinthians 11:23ff., which suggests that, though John may have created this language about the Eucharist, the Eucharist itself had long been celebrated. So old is this ritual, in fact, that it is difficult to imagine anyone but Jesus himself creating it.

In chapter 7, we surprisingly find a kind of expansion of the difficulties Jesus has had with his family—difficulties we only briefly heard about in the Synoptics. I say "surprisingly" because every once in a while John's Gospel suddenly presents us with one of these unidealized scenes that contrasts strongly with its usual manner of telling the Jesus story. Here, for instance, is a bit of a gritty dialogue right out of *Elmer Gantry. Jesus'* brothers are speaking—please note the gloss.

"You should leave here and go into Judea, so that your disciples may see the great things you are doing. No one can hope for recognition if he works in obscurity. If you can really do such things as these, show yourself to the world." For even his brothers had no faith in him. (7.3–5)

When Jesus finally arrives in Jerusalem for the second time, he begins to teach in the Temple, where he astonishes "the Jews" with his learning. In describing this situation, our author gives us a portrait of the people of the city, which, like the scene with his brothers, strikes some readers as realistic and perhaps historically accurate (7:25–31). The author tells us that everyone was wondering why, if the authorities wanted to kill Jesus, they allowed him to speak in public. "Can it be that our rulers have decided that this is the Messiah?" Most of the people think that the birthplace of the Messiah must be Bethlehem. Some, however, believe that no one is to know where the Messiah comes from. All know Jesus is from Nazareth! He himself points to his signs; and in turn the people ask themselves, "When the Messiah comes, is it likely that he will perform more signs than this man?" In the end, the city remains divided in its beliefs; some think he is a prophet, some the Messiah. The situation is so tense that the Temple police are afraid to arrest him, saying, "No one ever spoke as this man speaks"—a remark Albrecht Dürer will later apply in precisely the same sense to Martin Luther.

This portrait of the people of Jerusalem ends with a colloquy in which Nicodemus defends Jesus against the Pharisees. In the traditional text, this scene in the Temple offices was followed by the anecdote of the "Woman taken in Adultery"; but when that section is removed, as in modern New Testaments, we have, "Once again Jesus addressed the people . . . ," and his discourse continues. Finally, in chapter 9 we have the sixth sign, the very difficult curing of the man blind from birth, in which the author seems to revert to the primitive style of Mark. Jesus spits on the ground and, making a paste with the spittle, spreads it on the man's eyes. And when the disciples pose the fundamental problem of evil, "Why was this man born blind?" Jesus replies, "He was born blind so that God's power might be displayed in curing him." A good friend of mine who is now in his eighties has been blind since the age of nine—as a result of a handgun accident. When he hears this passage (and he has heard it often) he is simply dismayed with the Gospel and, I'm afraid, with Jesus himself. It does not help to explain to him that if he will read on in the anecdote he will find that this curing is only meant as a sign representative of divine illumination. I'm afraid my friend necessarily reads this story rather literally, and I am at a loss to tell him how he might construe it sympathetically. I tell him John is simply a writer like any other writer, whose taste and judgment sometime err, and that he clearly never anticipated that a real blind man might actually read this speech.

One explanation for this lapse is that the author had a kind of contempt for individual people, that he thought God—like evolution—was careful of the human species but careless of the person. Yet in the following passages only a few verses farther on, John has Jesus formulate one of the most beloved and tender images of Christendom:

> It was winter, and the Festival of the Dedication [Hanukkah] was being held in Jerusalem. Jesus was walking in the temple precincts, in Solomon's Portico. The Jews gathered round him and asked; "How long must you keep us in suspense? If you are the Messiah say so plainly." "I have told you," said Jesus, "but you do not believe. My deeds done in my father's name are my credentials, but because you are not sheep of my flock you do not believe. My own sheep listen to my voice; I know them and they follow me. I give them eternal life and they will never perish; no one will snatch them from my care. My father who has given them to me is greater than all, and no one can snatch them out of the Father's care. The Father and I are one." (10:22–30)

Everything is here: the insistence of the first version of the Book of Signs on the "deeds" or miracles to substantiate the Messiah claim, yet Jesus' typical waffling over this very question ("I have told you . . ."), the concept of "my own sheep" (the Christians) for whom there is eternal life, and finally the high Christology of "the Father and I are one." Here too is more evidence that the tragic split between Judaism and Christianity has already occurred, "because you are not sheep of my flock. . . ."

The entire series of signs finally comes to a conclusion in the raising of Lazarus, the seventh. Found only in John, this miracle uses names and people and events that appear also in the Synoptics, but uses them in a very different way. Lazarus is not the beggar of the after-death vision in Luke 10:19ff.; he is instead a friend of the Lord and brother to two sisters: Mary, who will anoint Jesus with oil, and Martha—perhaps the same women mentioned in Luke 10:38–42. The sign consists of the resurrection of Lazarus, who has died just outside of Jerusalem in Bethany and has been entombed; four days later Jesus raises him from the dead. In the laconic telling of this miracle, as in the curing of the blind man, the author seems again to disdain the individual human being. We never hear anything *about* Lazarus or learn why *he* in particular should be raised; he is simply a stick figure who emerges from the tomb in spooky wrappings to demonstrate the power of the Lord and to present a foretaste of Jesus' resurrection—and to hell with anything else. Indeed this anecdote has all the all-too-obvious trappings of a *sermonic* illustration. "I know that he will rise again at the resurrection on the last day" says Martha," teaching the reader a little theology. And Jesus replies, "I am the resurrection and the life. Those who believe in me, even though they die, will live, and everyone who lives and believes in me will never die." (11:24–26). This is altogether too neat—whatever one thinks of it as religious dogma.

It is significant that apart from the unique first and last signs, the Book of Signs shares the miracle material of the Synoptic tradition. Presumably these stories came to John in oral form, however, for the changes—child/servant, Herodian officer/centurion in sign 2—are precisely the kind of variation characteristic of orally remembered material. You might prove this to yourself at the next family gathering by listening very carefully when people tell beloved in-house stories. In any case, many people in Jerusalem are now said to believe in Jesus. But some, apparently disaffected, run off to tell the Pharisees; and the Jewish authorities now plot to kill Jesus, arguing in a very unclear way that he is a threat to their relations with Rome. Caiaphas, the high priest, is quoted as saying to his fellow conspirators, "You know nothing whatever; you do not use your judgment; it is more to your interest that one man should die for the people, than that the whole nation should be destroyed" (11:49–50). Whereupon our author writes a kind of *supreme* gloss, interpreting (or creating) even *this* speech as pre-arranged divine irony:

> He did not say this of his own accord, but as the High Priest in office that year, he was prophesying that Jesus would die for the nation—would die not for the nation alone but to gather together the scattered children of God. (11:50–52)

Jesus now retreats to an unidentified border town (it is called Ephraim) to reappear in Jerusalem six days before the Passover; but again he has been spending his nights in the suburb of Bethany, where people are now arriving to see Lazarus as well as Jesus himself (the authorities therefore decide to kill *Lazarus* as well as Jesus; see John 12:10–11). And it is in Bethany that Mary performs the anointing for burial, which is given other settings in the Synoptics; the next day Jesus enters Jerusalem on a donkey to hosannas and the waving of palm leaves. So famous has he become that a group of *Gentiles* want to see him; but after a final pronouncement, which includes the notion that the coming crucifixion is a "lifting up" and a "glorification," he goes "away from them into hiding." Finally, in a passage reminiscent of our interpretation of Mark's Gospel, Jesus asserts that his preaching has been a kind of failure which will only bring forth fruit in a later generation. Note that this speech contains the same quotation from Isaiah that we looked at earlier in four different versions; this time it is in its deterministic form (John is not bothered by determinism) and contains the direct claim that Isaiah "saw" Jesus' glory and spoke about him.

> In spite of the many signs which Jesus had performed in their presence they [the Jews of Jerusalem] would not believe him, for the prophet Isaiah's utterance had to be fulfilled: "Lord, who has believed what we reported, and to whom has the power of the Lord been revealed?" So it was that they could not believe, for there is another saying of Isaiah's, "He has blinded their eyes and dulled their minds, lest they should see with their eyes, and perceive with their minds, and turn to me to heal them." Isaiah said this because he saw his glory and spoke about him.
>
> For all that, even among those in authority a number believed in him, but would not acknowledge him on account of the Pharisees for fear of being banned from the synagogue. For they valued human reputation rather than honor which comes from God. (12:37–43)

Thus ends the re-edited and expanded Book of Signs. As far as we know, the banning from the synagogue occurred sometime after 80 C.E. when the *birkat ha-minim*, or "benediction of the heretics," actually a curse, was introduced to Jewish communities, supposedly as a curse on the Nazarenes. It may be this event which lies behind the Gospel's attack on "the Jews."

The Book of Glory

The so-called Book of Glory which follows is made up of a Farewell Discourse (13:1 to 17:26) and the death and resurrection narrative (18:1–20:31). The first is supposedly delivered at the Last Supper, which differs from the same event in the Synoptics. In John there are no mysterious directions for finding an upper room; we are simply there. Nor is the meal a Passover *seder;* it is eaten on the Day of Preparation, the day preceding to the first day of Passover. (This change solves a lot of problems about the trials and the crucifixion that would not ordinarily have occurred during the high holy days.) Nor is there any Eucharist. Too long to have actually been delivered, the Farewell Speech itself can be divided in various ways on the basis of subject matter and form (it ends with a long prayer). But none that I have seen makes much sense of what is in fact a pasted together mélange of ecstatic remarks. What is significant is not its structure, but the worldview it assumes. In the introduction I pointed out that the New Testament contains a whole series of ideas that are held by the reader to be untrue everywhere but in its pages. The Farewell Speech is a case in point. For five chapters (13–17) it assumes a universe at odds with the one you ordinarily inhabit. To read it sensibly, therefore, demands that you make a conscious effort to entertain its odd Hellenistic cosmology. Religious people sometimes avoid this sort of thing, preferring simply to repeat a ritual or a prayer or a Gospel passage without actually thinking about it, but with ancient documents like those of the New Testament such a practice is fatal to understanding.

The "universe" of this discourse is, of course, both very familiar and very strange. Let me describe it as I would for someone who has never heard of the Christian religion. As in 2 *Esdras,* God has created two levels of existence: the material one below, called here the "world," and the immaterial realm above. Because he loves the material inhabitants of the lower, inferior "world," God has made it possible for them to be raised up and live forever in his immaterial realm. To accomplish this, he uses beings from the upper level: the "Son" is one such being, and the Paraclete, or "Comforter," is another. The earthly activities of these beings have been prefigured in Jewish scripture, which, as John interprets it, discloses that God's "Son"— whatever that relation might mean—will come down into this world in the person of Jesus of Nazareth and go through a series of predetermined actions ending in his and his Father's "glorification," John's surprising term for Jesus' execution. The Lord's coming death is a triumph rather than a tragedy, because it ushers in a new heavenly friend to humanity: the Paraclete. In accomplishing this plot, the Son will have caused a small group of people to have "faith in him" and in what he says, producing in them some sort of union with the divine and enabling the lower being to live like the upper being.

> In a little while the world will see me no longer, but you will see me; because I live, you too will live. (14:19)

With this Gnostic-like "raising up" and returning, Jesus will not only give eternal life to his followers but will teach them to love each other and himself; there are no other ethical injunctions in John, and even the injunction to love is surprisingly described as a "new" covenant:

> I give you a new commandment: love one another; as I have loved you, so you are to love one another. If there is this love among you, then all will know that you are my disciples. (13:34–35)

In this sort of universe the relations among mortals and immortals are understandably complex; for one thing, they can "dwell" in each other—as in Paul. In this indwelling, the Father, the Son, the faithful believer, and even the Paraclete or Spirit of Truth, though not actually the *same* being, seem at least to be transparent to each other—though I would not like to be pressed on what *that* means either. Jesus can "live" in both the Father and in his disciples; and the Father likewise can have these various dwellings.

> I am not myself the source of the words I speak to you: it is the Father who dwells in me doing his work.... I am in my Father, and you in me and I in you. (14:10)

After his death, Jesus will prepare a "place" on the immaterial level in which the faithful can live eternally, but the "indwelling" of the spirit begins at the moment humans first "believe." This is to say that John has both a vertical and a horizontal eschatology. But it is the vertical that is important to him. In the conversion experience, believers become strangers to the world, which is said—peculiarly enough—to hate Jesus and his disciples, even though he is its sovereign and even though it was created through him. So foreign to the world do the faithful become, in fact, that their unbelieving Jewish brothers throw them out of the synagogues and beat them.

In *The Origins of Christian Morality*, Wayne Meeks sums up the situation as follows:

> Though the world grows darker and more sinister as the story progresses, the positive side of the Johannine ambivalence is not entirely submerged. The world is not evil *ab ovo*. It was created through the Logos who has now "become flesh." He is the world's light and its savior (4:42; 12:47); he gives it life (6:33), for God loves it (3:16). Yet what hope this Gospel holds out for the world is paradoxical at best. (p. 59)

Though this whole view is rather close to that assumed by Paul—but without an apocalypse—John's radical dualism is different. It is as if John, attempting to make philosophical and substantive ideas that in Paul were largely metaphorical, had been led into Gnostic metaphyscs. The results are puzzling. What sort of eternal life will the disciples have? Why is the Lord's death both necessary and glorious? How is it that the world is both good *and* bad, hateful *and* lovely? (I don't mean, of course, that it isn't; I mean *why* is it that way?) What happens to all those people who haven't heard of the Word? If all of history has been scripted, including the story of Jesus, what merit can be ascribed to any one of its characters? A problem for the future is: If God and the Paraclete and Jesus all continue to dwell in individual Christians, will these Christians continue to unfold *new* truths?

I do not ask these questions in order to answer them—though over the years the church will try to do just that. I ask them to show that the text itself assumes that such inquiries are beside the point, or never even imagines their being asked. Perhaps John thinks that if you are the sort of person who asks such things, you are not the sort of person who should be reading his Gospel. Indeed, a good bit of modern thinking about this Gospel is governed by this very notion, that in its final form it was composed for the members of a particular community, Christians already set in its Gnostic-like theology and already thrown out of the synagogues (see John 9:22 and 16:2). The idea is that this Gospel was intended to strengthen these people in their beliefs as they confronted specific Jewish opponents, and to encourage them to leave "the world " and remain in the community—a theme that will be underlined in an epistle from the same group, 1 John.

All well and good, perhaps, but if one is not a member of that ancient community, what is one to make of the text? The great scholar Rudolf Bultmann made the very "emptiness" of Jesus' revelation in John the core of its existential meaning. Its rejection of all statable theology put humanity itself "into question." In this understanding, John—somewhat like Paul—is simply asserting the possibility of a transcendent life for human beings. Another way of stating it is that despite all its involved "lore" John's language says simply, "Set your troubled hearts at rest"—the opening verse of chapter 14. Jesus' disclosure of a divine plan involving a whole operatic, Hellenistic set of "worlds" and "beings" is a kind of gigantic, unreal stage set, the Lord's mythological way of offering a final reassurance to the loving disciples he is leaving: "Set your troubled hearts at rest."

I remember a meeting of the Theosophical Society in San Antonio in the 1950s. I was in the army then at nearby Fort Sam Houston and it must have been a long time before payday, for we decided to attend—three young, grinning enlisted men, among twenty-five or thirty old people, some of whom were clearly ailing. In front of us at the podium was a fellow with wavy silver hair in a powder blue suit. His talk made reference to Madame Blavatsky and Annie Besant and was full of the sort of thing heard in the Farewell Discourse, though the man did not speak of *himself* as the means of salvation as Jesus did. This theosophical speaker believed in certain "presences," ethereal Gnostic creatures of the heavens, unchanged substantially since the first century. He spoke of them in a confidential, secretive way, punctuated with gestures "to the beyond" and muffled reassurances to his listeners. "We know, we know, good friends, don't we?" he would say, while all around us the old and the sick breathed back, not only acquiescence, but joy. I was sardonic about such stuff then; I am much less so today. Age and sickness must find their Comforter or Paraclete wherever they can. But having set myself the task of reading John's Gospel sensibly, I must also recognize that the speeches it gives to Jesus, details apart, often reduce to the same comfort as the theosophy preached to those old people that day in Texas.

How did such discourses ever originate and how did they come to be pieced together into this Gospel? Stevan L. Davies (p. 178) has pointed to the notion contained in the last lines quoted above: "I am in my father, and you in me, and I in you." If the Divine Spirit is always in the people, ongoing prophecy and "Jesus speech" are only to be expected. When a Christian talks, it is the Spirit who is talking: Pat Robertson receives what he calls a "word of knowledge" from God right before our eyes on his *700 Club*, and turning to the camera he repeats it for *us* right there in our living rooms. In at least one early Christian community, then, there must have developed the habit of "Jesus speech," a kind of open-ended talk that resembled jazz, endless variations on a mystical theme.

L et us now complete our reading. Though John's crucifixion story is very close to the account given in the Synoptics, it has its own peculiarities. At the very beginning, when the police come to arrest Jesus, an editorial remark tells us, "Jesus, knowing all that was coming upon him, went out to them." And when the police ask if he is Jesus of Nazareth and he answers royally, "I am," John adds, "they drew back and fell to the ground." Meeks sees this as the ironic "climax" of the book: "The moment of Jesus' helplessness before the posse that has come to arrest him is transmuted into an epiphany, as his captors fall to the ground at his simple pronouncement" (*Origins*, 59).

At the subsequent inquiry, John's Jesus behaves quite differently from the Jesus of the Synoptics. He affirms, "I have said nothing in secret" (18:4–7, 20), for instance. And while John's Pilate is even more "innocent" than he is in the other Gospels—"From that moment Pilate tried hard to release him . . ."—"the Jews" are even more culpable (19:12). A friend of mine who conducts a chorus that performs Bach's *St. John's Passion* is regularly visited backstage by Jews protesting the anti-Semitism of the piece. He once asked me what to tell these people, but didn't think any scholarly talk about the restricted meaning of "the Jews" in the second redaction of John would be of much help. There are other oddities. John's Mary returns to the narrative in the scene at the foot of the cross with "the disciple whom Jesus loved"; and there are Jesus' peculiar last words, "It is accomplished," with the liturgical flow of water and blood from a lance in the side. In their various ways, these unique elements seem to symbolize and bring to a conclusion the major themes of the narrative; and they will decisively influence the liturgy of the Great Church.

The resurrection story and what seems to be the "first conclusion" of the gospel is the burden of chapter 20. On Easter morning, Mary of Magdala notices that the stone has been moved from the grave and reports this fact to Peter and "the other disciple" (probably to be identified with "the one whom Jesus loved.") These two run to the tomb and the other disciple wins the race. When this disciple sees the empty wrappings of the corpse, we are told that he *believes*. Perhaps to excuse what seems a surprisingly late conversion for one who has been with Jesus all along, the editor adds "until then they had not understood the scriptures, which showed that he must rise from the dead" (20:9).

The men now leave, but Mary of Magdala, weeping, sees two angels in the tomb and, turning, confronts a man she takes to be the gardener, but who turns out to be Jesus himself. Jesus says to her, "Do not cling to me, for I have not yet ascended to the Father," perhaps meaning that he is ghostlike and cannot be embraced; later, and in this same state, Jesus will walk through a wall into the room where the disciples are cowering out of fear of "the Jews." In describing these first postdeath appearances, the editor seems to think of Jesus as temporarily spectral and inferior to that resurrected reality he will later demonstrate by eating food. Famously, the disciple named Thomas is not present at this first appearance of the Lord. When he hears about it, he says that until he touches the Lord's wounds he will not believe. A week later, Jesus miraculously comes to them again and shows Thomas his wounds. In so doing he draws for us readers the moral that the entire Gospel has been aiming at: "Because you have seen me you have found faith. Happy are they who find faith without seeing me" (20:10–29). John's Gospel then comes to its first conclusion, with the following:

> There were indeed many other signs that Jesus performed in the presence of his disciples, which are not recorded in this book. Those written here have been recorded in order that you may believe [or "continue to believe"] that Jesus is the Christ, the Son of God, and that through this faith you may have life by his name. (20:30–31)

At some very early point in time, however, a curious appendix (chapter 21) was added, which records *another* appearance of the Lord—in Galilee rather than Jerusalem. (You may recall that Luke also included both the Jerusalem and the Galilean traditions.) This appendix, like the rest of the Gospel, is full of problems. We are on the Sea of Galilee, where the disciples have returned to their fishing, laboring all night with no success. Suddenly they see the resurrected Jesus on the beach with a fire already kindled and fish cooking on it; he calls to them to cast out their nets once again to starboard. While they are drawing up a net full of fish, Simon plunges into the water in his hurry to see the Lord. "They were only about a hundred yards from land," says the editor. On the beach, the net proves to contain 153 large fish (no one knows what this peculiarly exact number means—if anything) providing breakfast. Afterwards, Jesus holds a mysterious colloquy with Peter in which he asks him three times whether he loves him. Each time Peter answers yes, Jesus tells him to feed his lambs and sheep. Then he adds, "When you are old you will stretch out your arms, and a stranger will bind you fast, and carry you where you have no wish to go." With the aesthetic distance that is typical of this Gospel, the editor then explains, "He said this to indicate the manner of death by which Peter was to glorify God."

Finally Jesus says to the disciples, "Follow me." When Peter sees the disciple whom Jesus loved coming along, he asks, "What will happen to him?" Jesus replies, "If it should be my will that he stay until I come, what is it to you? Follow me." The editor then writes, "That saying of Jesus became current among his followers, and was taken to mean that this disciple would not die. But in fact Jesus did not say he would not die." In these final lines we have another tiny window on the life of the early church: a memorialized saying about one of the heroes of the faith has given rise to a "false" story that he didn't die; the editor is trying to "correct" it. But the writer continues, "It is this same disciple who vouches for what has been written here. He it is who wrote it and we know that his testimony is true." Does the word *it* refer to chapter 21 only? Or the entire Gospel? And who are *we*? No one has good answers to these questions. John's Gospel now concludes with a "second ending," whose use of pronouns only complicates matters further:

> There is much else that Jesus did. If it were all to be recorded in detail, I suppose the world could not hold the books that would be written. [Is the "I" here the same as the "we" in the previous paragraph?]

(I would ask the reader to keep in mind this editorial confusion of pronouns along with the mysterious Beloved Disciple when we come to the Letters of John.)

So serious are the various problems of the Fourth Gospel that we may tend to forget its major difficulty: the Johannine conception of Jesus. For John, Jesus is both a divine being—perhaps not God himself but very close to it—and a man. He is the being through whom the universe was made *and* an itinerant preacher with dirty feet in sandals. Difficult as this combination is, John holds on to it, as does Paul, as will the early church. Perhaps it was easier for them. To ancient Greeks whose heroes and heroines imperceptibly shaded into gods, such an idea would have been commonplace. Even to these late Hellenistic people, there may not have been any very great dichotomy between the divine and the human. The difference was in the shading. Pagans typically blended the two in favor of the human, producing thereby a limited notion of the divine—as Zeus, the henpecked husband, for instance. Christians, on the other hand, of the type represented by John's Gospel, undervalued the human element in the combination to produce the Godlike being of the Farewell Discourse. In the long run, neither of these ancient "shadings" of the divine-human has proved tenable. In either case, humanity and divinity inevitably split apart. The historical Jesus of Nazareth becomes a puppet; and the Christ of faith turns out to be just another name for God.

But here a voice from my past says, "Of course it's unintelligible; it's a mystery of faith." Ah, but what then do we proclaim, when we assert this mystery of the God who is human? Perhaps the doctrine is our flag, which we honor, salute, and on occasion die for. Perhaps it means—can mean—nothing in itself; it only identifies us like our names: "We are the people who believe Jesus is Lord; you are the people who believe. . . ." Perhaps all our supernatural beliefs are like this. When we say the creed—even when we die for it—we declare who *we* are, not who Jesus was. Consider the matter yourself. Here is that creed as originally passed in 325—heavily influenced by Johannine and Pauline Christianity (I will not try to change the familiar, exclusive language):

I believe in one God the Father Almighty, maker of heaven and earth and of all things visible and invisible.

And in one Lord Jesus Christ, the only begotten Son of God, begotten of the Father, as only begotten, that is, from the substance of the Father before all ages. God of God; light of light; true God of true God. Begotten, not made, of the same substance as the Father, by whom all things were made both in heaven and earth. Who for us men, for our salvation, came down from heaven and became incarnate and was made man. He suffered and was buried. On the third day he rose again and ascended into heaven. And he shall come again to judge the living and the dead.

But those who say "Once he was not, or he was not before his generation, or he came to be out of nothing, or who assert that he, the Son of God, is of a different hypostasis, or ousia, or that he is a creature, or changeable or mutable," the Catholic and Apostolic Church anathematizes them.

By the time this creed was written, all of Christendom had come to agree with John that anyone, perhaps in the twinkling of an eye, could be "born again" and suddenly live on some other plane or as some other, better creature—a god perhaps. The late American cartoonist Abner Dean, who always drew his characters naked, once made a picture of this eschatology. Across a stage arrayed as for a high school graduation marches a row of unclothed men and women. When each person reaches the podium, he or she is struck on the top of the head by a sort of school superintendent who stands on a stepladder and wields a giant mallet. The superintendent is also naked, but wears earphones whose wires run straight up, out of the top of the picture frame. As each graduate is struck, a giant tulip springs from his or her head, and, smiling, he/she files out stage right.

To consider the truth or falsity of such a concept goes beyond the goal I have set for myself in this book: reading the New Testament sensibly. For the latter it would appear sufficient to elucidate John's cosmos and plot and accept his metaphysics—for the moment and "for the sake of the tale." Our belief or unbelief would not necessarily be involved. Unfortunately, perhaps, John's narrative is designed to force the issue. That is the purpose of all those clarifying glosses. That is the reason for creating a Jesus who debates and lectures those curiously passive listeners: Nicodemus, the Samaritan woman, doubting Thomas himself—*our* representatives. As we read the Fourth Gospel, we realize—sooner or later—that the author is trying to argue us into something.

This is not true of the others evangelists. When we read Mark, we read a tale that assumes a superiority to the apostles. In reading Matthew and Luke, *we* assume the tenets of the two different communities that produced them—otherwise, what are we to make of their disparate genealogies and infancy tales? But John, and Paul—though on the surface only preaching to the choir—are in fact producing an argument. Put directly, this Gospel asks you to affirm or deny: There is another, more perfect realm of existence available to humans to which the *logos*, a divine being, Jesus Christ, who existed before creation, is the only way—through love. Everything in the Gospel ends in this. Its plot is simply a script that has been written out before the creation of the world. Jesus and Peter and the others stumble through their roles like singers in Italian opera, trying to feel the grand emotions that would properly go with their lines. That the play is improbable from the beginning is clear if you return to v. 3, "and through him all things were made" and try to imagine Jesus of Nazareth present at what? The Big Bang sixteen billion years ago? Can we really think of Jesus helping God create the universe at time zero and then, after more than a billion years, being born to Mary in the reign of Augustus and dying in the reign of Tiberius and now being here *in* me in the form of the Paraclete as I read this document in 90 or 1990 C.E.? On this sort of reflection, the initial Wagnerian conception of the Jesus story seems sharply to decline from the formation of the cosmos to what Pilate understood as a quarrel between two sets of first-century Jews, to a mere feeling within *me*. Given all that initial grandeur, the end result seems hardly worth the effort.

The same is true, of course, for the book of Genesis. Consequently, since the days of the near contemporary of Jesus, Philo, until the present, educated people of both faiths have always tried to rid their religion of historical dependency. To do this is to read Sacred Scripture as an allegory of the eternal present. God becomes indistinguishable from the *first cause* conceived of as *justice*; Jesus is love conceived of as *mercy*; the Holy Spirit represents intelligence conceived of as *religious wisdom*. St. Augustine and St. Thomas both made attempts in this direction, trying to read both Old and New Testaments sensibly. They went further; they conceived of wisdom as inhering in all truth, Aristotle or Plato as well as Moses; love as everywhere present in creation itself—a kind of gravity; and God's causality as a pure relation of existential dependence without space or time. All such conceptions logically depend on the last—timeless causality.

But I personally have never been sure that this idea has any meaning at all or that it is even a successful metaphor. Always when I try to think of a nontemporal, nonspatial causality, I find myself losing *thought* itself. Augustine had the same experience, memorably described in chapter 11 of his *Confessions*. The problem continues into modern theology, where Paul Tillich is reduced to speaking subjectively of God as "the ground of my being," or my "ultimate concern."

It is obviously not my intention here to decide such matters. What I wish to observe is that contemporary Christians, especially those attached to a high Christology, are *driven* to allegorizing the "primitive" New Testament cosmology of writers like Paul and John. But the result is curiously unsatisfying. Having discovered that our *own* cosmology—including our mathematics, physics, and philosophy—is merely a projection of ourselves, we are like Alice, staring into the looking glass of the universe. And we don't like it. Here is Allen Tate's portrait of the situation:

> Love for herself who, as an earthly twain,
> Pouted to join her two in a sweet one;
> No more the second lips to kiss in vain
> The first she broke, plunged through the glass alone—

Alone to the weight of impassivity,
Incest of spirit, theorem of desire,
Without will as chalky cliffs by the sea,
Empty as the bodiless flesh of fire:

All space that heaven is a dayless night,
A nightless day driven by perfect lust
For vacancy, in which her bored eyesight
Stares at the drowsy cubes of human dust.

—We too back to the world shall never pass
Through the shattered door, a dumb shade-harried crowd
Being all infinite, function depth and mass
Without figure, a mathematical shroud

Hurled at the air—blesséd without sin!
O God of our flesh, return us to Your wrath
Let us be evil could we enter in
Your grace, and falter on the stony path!

CHAPTER 6

Later Canonical Writings

Looking Backward

We have now read what has always been considered the core of the New Testament. Though most Christians insist that the whole book is in some way the word of God, they generally pay more attention to the first half of the anthology than the second. This is unfortunate. Considered as sacred literature, the Gospels and Acts—and preeminently the authentic letters of Paul—are far more powerful and intellectually inspiring than what follows them; but considered as historical windows into the early church, the back of the book is often more enlightening.

The reading of these materials brings new demands, however, and new literary conventions. With one exception, these documents have traditionally been called "epistles," or letters; but that term is misleading. Most are disguised tracts, sermons, or position papers; and again with one exception, they are misassigned, each actually being the pseudonymous production of some unknown writer of the period 90 to 140 C.E. As you might expect, the place of such documents in the canonical New Testament was hard won. As late as the fourth century, some churches did not accept one or the other of the following: Revelation, Hebrews, James, Jude, 2 Peter, and 3 John. At the same time, early Christians often accepted as inspired other works that in the long run did not become canonical.

Of the fifteen documents to be considered, most look forward to the foundation of that Great Church which will inherit the Roman Empire, beginning about the year 314. Three, however, look back to Christianity's Jewish roots and attempt to preserve a fading attitude and spirit. Two of these backward-looking documents, though disguised as letters, are really apocalypses: the pseudonymous 2 Thessalonians, written as if by Paul, and the book called Revelation by John of Patmos. I have previously remarked on the popularity of apocalyptic writing during the first century of the Common Era, citing *2 Esdras* from the apocryphal works to illustrate that both Christians and Jews wrote apocalypses. Indeed, the surviving texts are sometimes ambiguous with regard to their affiliation, their authors being more intent on finding seers from the past who will proclaim their views. Several, for instance, make use of the figure of Enoch from Genesis 5:21ff., not because Enoch was a Hebrew but because he did not die—he "was seen no more because God had taken him away." Often what is attributed to the seer is repeated several times with varied imagery and set within a rudimentary plot; alternatively, it may be presented as a list of oracles, testaments, and similitudes, or, in the case of *2 Thessalonians,* as an apocalyptic vision folded into an imitation Pauline letter.

How did such a complex document come about? Sometime in the 90s when Paul's letters were first widely circulating—perhaps because of the fame given to Paul by the popularity of Acts—certain Christians deliberately lengthened out or partially rewrote existing letters or composed from scratch new letters which they then ascribed to Paul. In the case of 2 Thessalonians, the specific occasion for the forgery is evident from the text itself, which assumes that its readers know of a previous letter circulated over Paul's name. This earlier forgery apparently expressed the view that Jesus has already returned, the *parousia* has already occurred. This earlier heretical letter has not survived—at least it has not come to light—but 2 Thessalonians is an attempt to refute it, also in the name of Paul.

The writer begins by denying the authenticity of the previous letter: "do not be alarmed by any prophetic utterance, any pronouncement, or any letter purporting to come from us, alleging that the day of the Lord is already here." He then refutes the notion that the second coming has already occurred by describing a series of events that must occur *before* that sacred day—despite Paul's own statement in the authentic 1 Thessalonians that that day will come unsignaled, "like a thief in the night." Now to describe events immediately prior to a Second Coming is also, obviously, to write an apocalypse:

> For that day will not come unless the rebellion comes first and the lawless one is revealed, the one destined for destruction. He opposes and exalts himself above every so-called god or object of worship so that he takes his seat in the temple of God, declaring himself to be God. . . . For the mystery of lawlessness is already at work, but only until the one who now restrains it is removed. And then the lawless one will be revealed, whom the Lord Jesus will destroy with the breath of his mouth, annihilating him by the manifestation of his coming. The coming of the lawless one is apparent in the working of Satan,

who uses all power, signs, lying wonders, and every kind of wicked deception for those who are perishing, becaues they refused to love the truth and so be saved. (2 Thess. 2:3–10)

This is the voice of Hellenistic Jewish-Christian apocalyptic, shot through with a sharp division between good and evil (the friends of God and his enemies) and filled with a shocking desire for vengeance, an element evident both here and in other late Christian writings: "It is surely just that God should balance the account by sending trouble to those who trouble you, and relief to you who are troubled, and to us as well, when our Lord Jesus Christ is revealed from heaven with his mighty angels in blazing fire" (2 Thess. 1:6–7).

Through the historical window such writings provide, we see the beginnings of the church's concern for orthodoxy. By the 90s it is important that one profess right doctrine. Unfortunately, the "wrong doctrines" have generally not survived, but most of them seem quite mild. This particular "heresy," for instance, probably differed little from the "vertical eschatology" we have seen in Paul and John. Remember John's repeated phrase, "the time is coming and is now"? Indeed, we may have already met these "heretics" in the later editors and readers of John's Gospel who also thought that Jesus had returned in the guise of the Paraclete, or Comforter. This return was "spiritualized," of course, a descent of the Spirit on the community of the faithful and into the life of each of its members; but its effect was to affirm that Christ having come back, nothing more was to be expected. Deplorable, of course, but this letter in refutation of the idea is such an inept forgery—about a third is cribbed from 1 Thessalonians—that the readers' shock gives way to amusement as they come to the complimentary close: "This greeting is in my own handwriting; all genuine letters of mine bear the same signature—Paul."

Much longer and more inventive is the great apocalypse of the period, *Revelation*. It too is disguised as a letter—a very long one—with salutation and close; and it too is a cry for vengeance. Despite the fact that Revelation has given its Greek title to the entire literary genre, it differs from all other apocalypses of the period in having a living author. Four different passages in the text refer to "John," apparently a contemporary seer living off the coast of Ionia on the island of Patmos. Perhaps he was a Roman prisoner, perhaps not; but certainly his visions are directly concerned with the Roman cult of emperor worship and its enforcement under Domitian. This subject matter, quite apart from obvious stylistic differences, tells us he is not the John of the Gospel or the letters, but we know little else about him except that his Greek was not polished and that perhaps he still thought in a Semitic language.

As is true of many apocalypses, the purpose of Revelation is to strengthen readers who may be persecuted for their faith. There is no secret about this. Even where John chooses to write about Roman villainy in code, he makes sure to give us the key—again like nearly all writers of apocalypses. Where we have difficulty understanding him is not in these passages but in those in which he piles up multiple or contradictory images of what moderns are used to thinking about in abstraction: war, death, suffering, pure evil, gentleness, despair, and so on. Symbolized as fanciful beasts (who talk and marry) or hordes of insects or brimstone from heaven, these emotion-laden symbols are often posed against each other statically and repetitiously rather than being moved through an intelligible plot. Often they have a peculiarly "floating" pictorial quality very much like Chagall's airborne angels and horses: and, as in that painter's work, their very variety puts a connected allegory out of the question—though that has rarely stopped fools from trying to find one. Also frequently misinterpreted in Revelation are the passages which, by the 90s, have become liturgical. Embedded in the text, for instance, are doxologies, "To the One seated on the throne and to the Lamb, / be all praise, honor, glory and power, / for ever and ever"; and there also hymns: "Holy, holy holy." Ritualized phrases preserved in Aramaic such as *amen* and *hallelujah*, and woes (curses) in series also appear. It is often hard to keep in mind that John is not inventing these churchly phrases but borrowing them from an established liturgy.

A further difficulty can arise out of the author's use of numerology. Like other Jews of his day, John thinks some numbers are better than others: *seven* is the number of "completeness," for instance, as is its half, whether represented by three and a half days or weeks or months or years (forty-two months)—or "weeks that *stand* for years" as modern millenarians like to believe. The numbers *four* and *twelve* are sacred, as are their multiples, like 144,000. Revelation also makes use of a system, common to both Aramaic and Greek, by which letters stand for numbers and vice versa—most notably in the coded name 666. Finally, readers should note that a great deal of the language and symbolism of Revelation is based on Daniel, Isaiah, Ezekiel, and other Hebrew writings. Especially prominent are symbols borrowed from chapters 1–8 of the minor prophet Zechariah: the variously colored, disaster-laden horses, the horns of power, the measuring of Jerusalem, lampstands and bowls, the appearance of the Adversary, Satan, and so on. In Zechariah, the "Messiah" is similarly called the The Branch, and is identified with the Persian governor, Zerubbabel, who was in fact a descendant of

David, though the title "Branch" is derived from Jeremiah 23:5. In quoting from Revelation in what follows I italicize these borrowings.

For most of Christian history Revelation has been difficult to read because of the unfamiliarity of its pictorial effects. But today—for good or ill—we have multimedia stage presentations that actually approximate the literary effects intended. Having seen rock-and-roll extravaganzas and virtual reality electronic imagery, today's students can at last "produce" Revelation in their imaginations. Conceive of a huge proscenium arch stage with a small podium to one side in the orchestra under a spotlight; John will narrate from a lectern in this small area. Across the rear of this stage extends heaven, with God's throne at the center, flanked on either side with twelve smaller thrones for the twenty-four elders. Above these flit golden and white and fiery angels against a blue sky. Arranged around the throne are four beasts in the images of a lion, an ox, a man, and an eagle; and before the throne stands the Lamb with marks of blood. This basic "up stage" set will be visible throughout the show, sometimes only in silhouette, sometimes briefly obscured by the violent lights projected in front of it on scrims. If you wish you can imagine a large concert band in the pit just below the footlights and jets for smoke effects.

The prologue begins when the house lights come down and the stage manager—not John of Patmos—comes out onto the small circular stage on our left and announces: "This is the revelation of Jesus Christ which God gave him so that he might show his servants what must soon take place. He made it known by sending his angel to his servant John. . . ." Within another verse or so the manager withdraws and is replaced by John himself, who tells about his vision of the risen Lord as that vision actually appears in front of the darkened heavens. It is a good test of the readers' affinity for Near Eastern poetics—and perhaps their patience.

> *one like a man,* robed down to his feet, with a *golden girdle round his breast. The hair of his head was white as snow-white wool, and his eyes flamed like fire; his feet gleamed like burnished brass* refined in a furnace, and his voice was *like the sound of a rushing waters.* In his right hand he held seven stars, and from his mouth came a sharp, two-edged sword; his face shone like the sun in full strength. (Rev. 1:13–16)

You will note that not every element in such a description is meant to appeal to the sense of sight in the manner of a two-dimensional painted image. To prove this you need only look into the cheapest illustrated Bible you can get your hands on. The sword in the mouth is a particular stumbling block for the inexpert draftsman, as are the flaming eyes and white woolly hair of the

Ancient of Days. But try imagining the same thing rendered dynamically through film—perhaps the tongue rapidly moving in and out, and so on.

Such images are not unique to John; on the contrary, they are firmly grounded in Middle Eastern art. Though you may be put off by them in Revelation, when similar imagery is used by a greater poet on a more attractive subject you may find it moving and even "sensible."

> How beautiful you are, my dearest,
>   how beautiful!
> Your eyes behind your veil are like doves,
> your hair like a flock of goats
>   streaming down from Mount Gilead.
> Your teeth are like a flock of ewes
>   just shorn
>
> . . . .
>
> Your lips are like a scarlet thread,
>   and your words are delightful;
> your parted lips behind your veil
>   are like a pomegranate cut open.
> Your neck is like David's tower,
>   which is built with winding courses;
> a thousand bucklers hang from it
>
> . . . .
>
> Your two breasts are like two fawns. (Song of Songs 4:1–5)

As the first projected imagery now recedes, we may imagine the spotlight coming up on John, who now declaims his "cover letter" to the seven churches, telling them that while he was in a trance an angel instructed him to write the book they are reading—a conventional device of apocalyptic writing. He then announces the imminent coming of the Lord in the fashion we have seen (from the book of Daniel), followed by a series of remarks which John insists are the words of the Lord himself, including attacks on various Christian sectaries. In the course of these, several individuals are mentioned by name or pseudonym. The condemnation of the "false Jews" of Smyrna (2:9ff.) is particularly interesting. Presumably these were Christians who had falsely declared themselves to be Jews in order to avoid emperor worship; for members of the legal, monotheistic religion of Judaism were excused from this ritual. This situation is not only interesting in itself—and dreadfully ironic in terms of later Christian-Jewish relations—it also suggests the complexity of life in the early church and how little we really know about it. The cover letter concludes with the condemnation of the lukewarm people of Laodicea, whom the risen Lord spits out of his mouth; and there is preparation for the first series of visions (4:1).

The back of the stage is now illuminated as John describes the courts of heaven, again in conventional Eastern imagery taken from Ezekiel 1:10 and Isaiah 6.

> *In the center, round the throne itself,* were *four living creatures, covered with eyes* in front and behind. The *first* creature was like *a lion, the second* like *an ox,* the third had a *human face,* and *the fourth* was like an *eagle* in flight. The four living creatures, each of them with *six wings, had eyes all over,* inside and out; and by day and night without a pause they sing: "*Holy, holy, holy is God the sovereign Lord of all,* who was, and is, and is to come. (Rev. 4:6–8)

Note how the names of beasts are used to suggest power and how *eye* and *wing* function as symbols of intelligence but with no anatomical feeling whatever. Note also the presence of the ancient doxology.

The figure on the throne is now seen to have a seven-sealed scroll which no one is worthy to break open except the "Lamb with the marks of sacrifice on him." As the Lamb breaks each scroll in turn, we will be given seven visions arranged in a repeated, climactic, and interlocking pattern: visions 1-6, followed by an "interlude," then vision 7. We can imagine these as successive projections with music that appear before the throne of God as a kind of after-dinner magic lantern show. From the first four seals come the horses (from Zechariah) symbolizing disasters: white, red, black, pale (or *green* in *koinē* Greek)—perhaps galloping straight out at us in three dimensions. The fifth seal reveals the Christian martyrs under the throne of God. The sixth gives us an earthquake at the end of the world, "the day of wrath." In the interlude, John sees 144,000 saints from the tribes of Israel who are marked on the forehead so they won't suffer, and an uncounted crowd of Gentile saints all robed in white. Finally, the seventh seal brings—are you ready for this?—a half hour of silence.

As is often the case in books of visions (and in music) we now have a varied repetition of the same material. Seven trumpets are blown by seven angels, perhaps to be imagined entering singly from the rear and ranging themselves across the stage; with every new solo occurs a new projection. The fifth trumpet brings a wonderful plague of locusts almost as frightening as in their source, the prophet Joel. The sixth brings destroying angels who are to eliminate a third of humanity. There are 200 million of them, a number the author—God bless him—thinks of as impossibly large. In this interlude, the angels bring a small scroll to John, which he eats; it contains the second half of Revelation. Before this small scroll can be opened, however, we have a series of half-developed motifs: John measuring the Temple in Jerusalem, for instance, and the prediction (much scrutinized by later millenarians) that the Temple will be subjected to evil for forty-two months after which a "beast will ascend from the bottomless pit" and the martyrs will be called up to heaven. Finally, the seventh trumpet is blown to signal God's sovereign rule over the world. By imagining the director quick cutting among several projectors, it is possible to recreate all this as a kind of Michael Jackson show—but perhaps the reader needs no further production hints.

In any case, there follow visions more closely related to Rome. A woman appears in the heavens along with a fiery red dragon with seven heads and ten horns. The woman (Israel) then bears a child (Jesus) destined to rule the world. The dragon (Rome) tries to devour the child but fails, and in heaven the archangel Michael (cf. Daniel) defeats the dragon, which, falling to earth, is revealed as Satan. Once on earth, the dragon seems also to metamorphose into *the beast* with ten horns and seven heads which rises out of the sea and enjoys a hegemony for forty-two months as he wars against God's saints together with a second beast, who implements his orders.

But now the author fears he has become too complex and adds the following parenthesis, Revelation 13:18.

(This calls for skill; let anyone who has intelligence work out the number of the beast, for the number represents a man's name, and the numerical value of its letters is six hundred and sixty-six.)

Though the matter is much debated, the numerological value of this number in the Hebrew alphabet yields the consonants for *Neron* (the emperor's name in Greek). That this is what the author intends seems clear from the fact that some manuscripts have 616, lowering the number by fifty, or exactly the value of the final consonant *n*, giving the familiar Latin version: *Nero*. Behind all this fiddle-faddle there probably lies a myth that the dead emperor would return sometime in the 90s.

In any case, we soon see the Lamb standing on Mount Zion with his 144,000 saints singing praise. Angels sail about saying things like "Worship God," and "Fallen is Babylon," and crying vengeance on anyone who worshiped the beast. It is now that the "one like a son of man" appears in the clouds and "reaps" (judges?) the earth.

Chapter 15 opens with another group of seven angels, this time with seven bowls from which they pour out God's wrath, destroying Babylon (Rome), which is imagined alternately as a city and a woman mounted on a scarlet beast. Fearing that his code has again become too complex—though he has described Rome as still having its seven heads and the ten horns—the author adds:

But here is the clue for those who can interpret it. The seven heads are seven hills on which the woman sits. They represent also seven kings, of whom five have already fallen, one is now reigning, and the other has yet to come. When he does come he is only to last a little while. . . . *The ten horns* you saw *are ten kings* who have not yet begun to reign, but who for one hour are to share with the beast the exercise of royal authority; for they have but a single purpose among them and will confer their power and authority on the beast. They will wage war on the Lamb, but the Lamb will defeat them, for he is *Lord of lords* and *King of kings,* and his victory will be shared by his followers, called and chosen and faithful. (Rev. 17:9–14)

Now Babylon or Rome falls like a stone cast into the sea along with all the kings and merchants and ship captains that catered to her—all the successful people; and chapter 19 opens with a great heavenly Hallelujah. Victory in heaven is one thing, but the popular mind craves to know earthly matters. How will it all end, Lord? Revelation 19:11–22:9 is dedicated to answering that perennial question. Christ, as Word of God, wearing a blood-soaked robe and riding a white horse, defeats the Beast, his allied kings, and his false prophet. He then chains these evildoers into the "lake of fire," along with Satan (the Dragon), who is to remain there a thousand years, during which Christ will reign over the universe accompanied by his martyrs. At the end, Satan "must be let loose for a little while" to fight a final battle attended by "Gog and Magog." Defeated a second time by Christ, Satan will be chained up with the beast and the false prophet forever in that lake of fire. Then the New Jerusalem shall descend to earth with the river of life flowing by the throne of God. Whereupon, as if coming awake from a bad dream, we are suddenly back on Patmos, and John is telling us that the angel (speaking for the Lord) says, "I am coming soon." He then adds a curse on anyone who tampers with his Revelation—"God will add to him the plagues described in this book," and the book ends. House lights up as orchestra hits its final chord.

Even as I summarize all this for you I can feel myself trying to reduce it to a consistent narrative. I should not do this. John's are broken visions in which the Roman Empire constantly changes from a man of evil to a woman, to a beast from above, to one from under the sea, and so on. The seven hills and the emperors and the tributary kings (the heads and horns) simply underline the same imperial enemy. In fact, all the horses and the locusts, the fires and abysses are really just one disaster directed at that evil city, the great beast on the Tiber. Yet in a sense all this contention is unnecessary, for *the Lord is coming soon.* That is all that matters.

Embarrassing? Of course. But as an image of the Messiah—and read in context—Revelation is not at all beside the point. You may recall that I complained of the *logos* theology that it seemed a grandiose theory applied to niggling, even *mean* events—eventually only a momentary feeling in the individual, human psyche. This theology required the Spirit through whom the universe was created to busy himself turning water into wine and having people born blind so that he could heal them. Well, Revelation restores a proper tone. Here is the *Lord!* This is the "Messiah of popular expectation," as Stephen Harris calls him, "a conquering warrior-king who slays his enemies and proves beyond all doubt his right to rule" [and] "to inflict a wrathful punishment upon his opponents" (*New Testament,* 319). Unlike later Christian writers, the author of Revelation still hates the world and has no interest in an *aggiornamento* with it. Like General Booth of the Salvation Army, his home is over Jordan, and he is marching, marching ever upward to that new, sweet land.

> (Bass drum beaten loudly)

> Booth led boldly with his big bass drum—
> (Are you washed in the blood of the Lamb?)
> The Saints smiled gravely and they said: "He's come."
> (Are you washed in the Blood of the Lamb?)
> . . . .
> Bull-necked convicts with that land make free.
> Loons with trumpets blowed a blare, blare, blare
> On, on upward thro' the golden air!
> (Are you washed in the blood of the Lamb?)
> . . . .
> (Sweet flute music.)

> Jesu came from out the courthouse door,
> Stretched his hands above the passing poor.
> Booth saw not, but led his queer ones there
> Round and round the mighty courthouse square.
> Yet in an instant all that bleak review
> Marched on spotless, clad in raiment new,
> The lame were straightened, withered limbs uncurled
> And blind eyes opened on a new, sweet world.

> (Bass drum louder)

> —"General William Booth Enters Heaven," by Vachel Lindsay

Our third and final "backward-looking text" is what is called in most Bibles, "A Letter to Hebrews." It is often grouped with the letters of Paul, but even the ancients knew that it had not been written by Paul, and except for the closing paragraphs it makes no pretense to be a letter. Like us, however, the Fathers did not know who *had* written it or why it was so titled. Scholars have long assumed, therefore, that those closing letterlike paragraphs were added to an already existing sermon or essay in order to take advantage of a "fad" for Paul's correspondence in the 90s. Whether that is true or not, it is clear that this document is not directed at "Hebrews." It is in fact a Christian work, written, like Revelation and 2 Thessalonians, to strengthen the faithful in a time of persecution. Like those writings too, it has no interest in the developing institutional church or the details of church organization or the use of scripture or indeed any of the other "forward-looking" issues of the first quarter of the second century.

Unlike Revelation and 2 Thessalonians, however, Hebrews is not apocalyptic, though we can speak of a "revelation" or vision that underlies it and shapes its peculiar theology. The author believes that "in this final age," the truth of God's plan is made clear by a *typological* reading of the sacred Jewish writings. He believes, that is, that the Hebrew Scripture contains a series of forerunner *types* of Jesus Christ—Abraham, Melchizedek, Moses, and King David. His principal text for the last, for instance, is Psalm 110, which we have seen was cited also in the Gospels. King David is speaking:

> The LORD said to my lord:
> "Sit at my right hand,
> and I shall make your enemies your footstool."

The writer understands this poem to mean that Yahweh, or God, has said to Jesus Christ (David's "Lord"), "Sit at my right hand," and so on. Like the patriarchs, therefore, David is not only a forerunner of Jesus, but *inferior* to him—in fact, his servant. The author believes that the meaning of such prophetic material was not recognized by the Jews because God spoke to "our forefathers" in a fragmentary fashion. "But in this final age he has spoken to us in the Son whom he has made heir to the whole universe, and through whom he created all orders of existence" (Heb. 1:1-2).

Another ancient personage who functions in this typological way is the mysterious Melchizedek. Conveniently, Psalm 110 also supports this view, which makes Jesus the *heir* of David, and, by calling him a priest and a "Melchizedek," gathers to Jesus the roles of both a Judaic and a pagan religious leader.

> The LORD extends the sway of your [Jesus'] powerful sceptre,
>   saying,
> "From Zion reign over your enemies."
> You gain the homage of your people on the day of your power.

> Arrayed in holy garments, a child of the dawn,
>   you have the dew of your youth.
> The LORD has sworn and will not change his purpose:
> "You are a priest forever, a Melchizedek in my service."

All anyone knows of Melchizedek is that he once ruled the hill country that later became Jerusalem and that when Abram was coming back south after defeating the Syrian kings around Damascus, this king-priest came out to meet him with "food (bread?) and wine." Yet by New Testament times, Melchizedek had come to be thought of as the almost angelic being who announced the plan of God to humans, and was represented this way in the literature of Late Judaism. It is apparently this later "literary" and mysterious being, rather than the scriptural Melchizedek, whom the author invokes in his effort to prove that Jesus—who also offered bread and wine—was long ago prefigured. By the time of the composition of Hebrews, it also probably helped that Melchizedek was a Gentile.

In any case, Jesus is now seen to have been foreshadowed not only in the royal diadem of David but in the priestly mantle of this ancient pagan priest. Whatever happened to either of these ancient heroes was a hint, so to speak, of something to be fulfilled by the Lord. It is also clear, however, that the author sees these ancient figures as still existent in some perfect world, perhaps through the haze of Plato's cave. In Hebrews, as in *2 Esdras,* as in the *Republic,* there are two correlated realms, the *real* one above and this other (less real) on earth below. The sanctuary the Jewish high priests entered on earth was "only a shadowy symbol of the heavenly one." Christ and his types have now entered the "real" sanctuary in heaven.

> For Christ did not enter a sanctuary made by human hands, a mere copy of the true one, but he entered into heaven itself, now to appear in the presence of God on our behalf. Nor was it to offer himself again and again, as the high priest enters the Holy Place year after year with blood that is not his own; for then he would have had to suffer again and again since the foundation of the world. But as it is, he has appeared once for all at the end of the age to remove sin by the sacrifice of himself. And just as it is appointed for mortals to die once, and after that the judgment, so Christ, having been offered once to bear the sins of many, will appear a second time, not to deal with sin, but to save those who are eagerly waiting for him. (Heb. 9:24-28)

This is powerful stuff. I remember being scared to death by a sermon Father Sullivan preached on this text in a darkened Holy Thursday church one spring in the early 1940s. I can still hear the awkward, not quite English of the Douay translation, which for "climax of history" has "end of the ages" and "it is appointed unto men to die once and after this comes the judgment." Like the Logos Hymn, this was also serious and intellectual theology, I thought, *and* Platonic. But the upper-world correspondences are observed, of course, only by those who "have had the good news preached" to them. Converted Christians are like Plato's prisoners newly released from the cave, who "are able to see the sun, and not mere reflections of him ... [and] will then proceed to argue that this is he who gives the season and the years, and is the guardian of all that is in the visible world, and in a certain way the cause of all things. . . ." To the unconverted, however, Abraham and Melchizedek and Moses and David remain only ancient figures with no connection to Jesus of Nazareth. Indeed, one might argue that without some prior faith, Jesus himself looks rather ordinary.

> In Jesus, however, we do see one who for a short while was made lower than angels ... so that by God's gracious will, in tasting death he should stand for us all. . . . And therefore he had to be made like these brothers of his in every way, so that he might be merciful and faithful as their high priest before God, to expiate the sins of the people. For since he himself has passed through the test of suffering, he is able to help those who are meeting the test now. (Heb. 2:9, 17–18)

The fact that the conceptions of Jesus as man and Jesus as God are both found in Hebrews suggests that its well-educated author sat down deliberately to fuse the theologies of the Synoptic Gospels with that of Paul and John. Hebrews is in fact a synthesis of *all* that has gone before. As in Mark and perhaps Q, Jesus' life is a drama that had to be played out in order for the kingdom to come. As in Matthew and Luke, this drama is foretold in the Hebrew Scripture. As in Paul, since Jesus was truly human his death is somehow a sacrifice for our sins. As in John, he rose and remains the eternal *logos* in heaven. Hebrews fuses low and high Christologies: Jesus is the Christ who is both perfectly human and perfectly divine—dynamically becoming the one and ascending *back* to the other. I do not think all this is an accident.

Having established this "synthetic" theology, the author now extends and elaborates his theory of types, beginning with the correspondence between Moses and Jesus. What Moses was on earth, Jesus is in heaven—but more so. Both were appointed to rule God's house, but Jesus is more "honorable" because as *logos* he *created* that house. Both were appointed to lead human beings to a Sabbath rest: Moses to Canaan, but Jesus to the heavenly realm from where he will mercifully judge mankind—though some people will always be found unworthy. Jesus was therefore foreshadowed by Moses but is superior to him; the same is true of Abraham: "Before Abraham was born, I am" (John 8:58).

The author now returns to Jesus' typological relation to Melchizedek, a parallelism that he tells us represents *mature* (Gentile?) belief. This churchly distinction of a higher understanding and a lower is missing from earlier New Testament documents; for it is the hallmark of *established* religion. "Let us stop discussing the rudiments of Christianity" (Heb. 6:1), says the author of Hebrews, citing as "rudimentary" ideas of repentance, cleansing rites, laying on of hands, resurrection of the dead, and eternal judgment. But if these are the beginnings of Christianity, what is the mature faith? Apparently it hinges on an exalted notion of Jesus. Melchizedek is again the symbol, he whose name

> means "king of righteousness"; next he is king of Salem, that is, king of peace." He has no father, no mother, no ancestors; his life has no beginning and no end. Bearing the likeness of the Son of God, he remains a priest for all time. (Heb. 7:2–3)

Like this ancient priest of Jerusalem, Jesus was beyond or apart from the law, "For the Law contains but a shadow and no true image of the good things which were to come; it provides for the same sacrifices year after year, and with these it can never bring the worshipers to perfection for all time" (Heb. 10.1–2). Like Melchizedek also, Jesus sacrificed (offered) bread and wine rather than the blood of the animals; and importantly, he surpassed the Jewish priesthood because he had no need to offer *daily* sacrifice. As we have seen, the sanctuary in which the Jewish high priests sacrificed was "only a shadowy symbol of the heavenly one . . . only a pointer to the reality." Jesus, on the other hand, having "taken his seat at the right hand of the throne of Majesty in heaven," became once and for all "a minister in the *real* sanctuary." In taking on this priestly function, Jesus has also fulfilled the words of Jeremiah: "The time is coming says the Lord when I shall conclude a new covenant with the house of Israel and the house of Judah . . . to bring liberation from sins committed under the former covenant; its purpose is to enable those whom God has called to receive the eternal inheritance he has promised them." The relationship between the two covenants and between what are now two separate faiths is powerfully stated.

> Remember where you stand: not before the palpable, blazing fire of Sinai with the darkness, gloom, and whirlwind, the trumpet-blast and the oracular voice, which they heard, and begged to hear no more. . . . No, you stand before Mount Zion, the city of the living God, heavenly Jerusalem, before myriads of angels, the full concourse and assembly of the first-born citizens of heaven, and God the judge of all, and the spirits of good men made perfect, and Jesus the mediator of a new covenant whose sprinkled blood has better things to tell than the blood of Abel. (Heb. 12:18–25)

Hebrews ends with a parenetic section in imitation of the Pauline letters. Its readers are told that they have not yet resisted to the point of death and must be ready for that eventuality and that they are not to be "swept off their feet" by "all sorts of outlandish teachings" concerned with "rules about food." The complimentary close is significant for a doctrine apparently drawn from the notion that Jesus entered the sanctuary once, and once only. The author here repeats that, in a similar fashion, the grace of salvation comes only once:

> Look to it that there is no one among you who forfeits the grace of God, no bitter, noxious weed growing up to poison the whole, no immoral person, no one worldly-minded like Esau. He sold his birthright for a single meal, and you know that although he wanted afterwards to claim the blessing, he was rejected; though he begged for it to the point of tears, he found no way open for a second thought. (Heb. 12:15–17)

The church will not, thank goodness, follow this chilling dictum, though Father Sullivan seemed to think it had; but in a very remarkable way it *will* accept the theological synthesis and even to some degree the imagery of Hebrews. Put another way, Hebrews is an expression of the church's desire to "rationalize" a two-book, two-covenant religion and to synthesize the various theologies implied in the Synoptics and made explicit in Paul and John. The author does all this with great aplomb in an excellent, learned Greek comparable to that of its contemporary, Plutarch.

Looking Forward

The remaining canonical material is generally thought to reflect "Early Catholicism." For better or worse, these last epistles look forward to the Great Church which will eventually triumph in the time of Constantine. The concerns of these authors are those of the first-century community which is "maturing" (as Hebrews says) in its theology, its institutional organization, its liturgy, its notion of its *own* sacred documents, and its attitude toward the "world." Apparently these early members of the church first began to develop an orthodox theology in defending themselves against the more extreme Gnostics. In particular, they came to terms with the delay of the *parousia,* abandoning all operatic, apocalyptic notions in favor of a long "waiting time." This adjustment tremendously elevated the value of the visible church and forever changed its nature; for in the time now envisaged, it would be the church that would mediate between the individual and God—a role Paul had assumed was unnecessary and John thought would be performed by the Paraclete. Whereas in both of these earlier writers faith was a kind of charismatic rapture, it now becomes something close to "public assent to specific beliefs" and a studied loyalty to the organization that proclaims them. An unexpected problem, which becomes acute with the "heresies" of the second century, is the necessity of *shutting off* such beliefs; for it becomes clear that it is impossible to maintain an orthodoxy if the saints continue to receive new illuminations.

I use the term "visible church" to describe an institution that pretty much has to be inferred from the late epistles themselves. We don't have much external evidence until 110 C.E., and even then it is skimpy. But a few things are fairly certain. As is apparent in Acts, a reverence for the "apostles" came to be a central tenet; and as successors to the apostles, the bishops were soon considered the direct representatives of the risen Jesus. They ruled their city flocks like monarchs. Below them, elders, deacons, deaconesses, official widows, and others ranged in a hierarchy, while the prophets and speakers in tongues and interpreters of tongues and so on of Paul's house-churches simply disappeared, perhaps because they threatened both orthodoxy and authority.

A form of worship had existed even before Paul's time, but the only evidence we have is the material embedded in his letters. From a later date there survives a description of church order called the *Didache*, or "The Teaching of the Twelve Apostles." Discovered in 1875, it has sections that may date to the first century. From these, together with one letter of Pliny the Younger, it is possible to form an idea of what the earliest liturgy was like: a sacred meal and a number of sacraments—although it will be a long time before these are made completely regular.

In all these late writings there are two very clear and contradictory attitudes toward the "world." On the one hand, early "catholics" felt themselves superior to the culture and success of the empire; on the other, they desperately admired and envied it. They wanted to be thought well of and to *arrive*; at the same time they longed for heaven. The problem was not confined to our forefathers, of course; in fact, the reader acquainted with the history of the Christian church will recognize that nearly all of the issues I have enumerated as peculiar to the second century are in fact perennial: What shall be our theology, our churchly structure, our liturgy, our Bible, our way of life?

In these letters we also find a few hints toward defining what would become *Christian* scripture. This begins with a sense that revelation really *was* complete and that no more sacred books were to be expected. The books that had already been written then tended to be revered, and "approved" authorial names were attached to them. Old pieces of earlier Christian writings were now pasted together, named, and considered precious; and, as we have seen, new pseudonymous epistles were produced in the name of Paul or John or Peter or a relative of the Lord like James or Jude. There was no canon or official list of approved works. The earliest attempt was made about 150 C.E. by a man named Marcion, who wished to rid the religion of all Jewishness. His list itself has not survived, but from Christian attacks on it, it can be reconstructed: an edited version of Luke and some letters of Paul. A second roster of approved works dates from 170; it is difficult to read but seems to contain four Gospels and some letters of Paul, along with materials that would later be rejected. Our precise canon of twenty-seven documents would not appear in any surviving document until in 367 C.E. in a letter of Athanasius.

The epistles we are now to read may be conveniently grouped as the "Legacy of John," the "Legacy of Paul," and the general or "Catholic Letters." The first of these is made up of three short documents commonly assigned to the author of John's Gospel. But their differences are marked enough so that most scholars believe that, together with the Gospel, they are the products not of a single author but of the "Johannine community." They contain some of the basic Johannine ideas but are directly concerned with matters occurring in the time of their writing—somewhere between the 70s and the 90s. All three warn against false teachers and admonish the brotherhood and their sister churches to maintain communal love.

1 John is the most significant, and the only one of these letters much read outside the academy. First referred to in 117 C.E., it was assigned by some to the Gnostic Cerinthus but was eventually and "authoritatively" attributed to John by Irenaeus. Irenaeus came to this conclusion, perhaps, because this text begins with what seems a deliberate evocation of the Logos Hymn of the Fourth Gospel, which in turn, as we have seen, was a deliberate evocation of Genesis.

> It was there from the beginning: we have heard it; we have seen it with our own eyes; we looked upon it, and felt it with our own eyes; we looked upon it, and felt it with our own hands; and it is of this we tell. Our theme is the word of life. This life was made visible; we have seen it and bear our testimony; we declare to you the eternal life which dwelt with the Father and was made visible to us. What we have seen and heard we declare to you, so that you and we together may share in a common life, that life which we share with the Father and his Son Jesus Christ. And we write this in order that the joy of us all may be complete. (1 John 1:1–4)

Clearly we have here not only the vocabulary of John's Gospel but its theology: the *logos* become flesh. We also have the same confusing pronouns coupled with a similarly straightforward declaration of the reason this tract (it obviously is not a letter) has been composed; there is even the same symbolic blood and water. Such similarities to John's Gospel will continue throughout: "God is light," the "world is darkness"; we share the life of both Father and Son who dwell in us; the single positive commandment is love. But unlike John's Gospel, which was at least partially written so that the community might believe or continue to believe, this author writes only to true believers of the community, warning them against "sin," against the "world," and especially against their own defectors, the Antichrists (cf. 1 John 1:4; 2:1, 15–17, 18ff.). These last are apparently former community members who did not "keep hold of what you heard at the beginning" and went on to deny that the human being, Jesus of Nazareth, was the Christ. The Antichrists seem to have taken up a radical Gnosticism. In fact, the Antichrists of 1 John sound remarkably like those "docetists" of later centuries, who would maintain that the *logos* only "seemed" (*dokeō*) to be human.

It is interesting that the enemies now are "in-house" heretics. They "went out from our company," says our author, "but never really belonged to us; if they had, they would have stayed with us" (1 John 2:19). His logic is the logic of election, determinism, and vertical eschatology: "No man therefore who dwells in him [Jesus] is a sinner; the sinner has not seen him and does not know him. . . . A child of God does not commit sin, because the divine seed remains in him; he cannot be a sinner, because he is God's child" (1 John 3:6, 9). The defection from a grace once possessed, an unforgivable sin in Hebrews, is viewed here as *impossible*. Yet it is difficult to assess how seriously this idea was taken, for at the end of this letter, we discover that there are sins and *sins*:

> If a man sees his brother committing a sin which is not a deadly sin, he should pray for him, and he will grant him life—that is, when men are not guilty of deadly sin. There is such a thing as deadly sin, and I do not suggest that he should pray about that; but although all wrongdoing is sin, not all sin is deadly sin. (1 John 5:16–17)

Which is to say that the saints *can* sin after all. But since this piece of writing is quite disorganized, perhaps pieced together from fragments, we may have here only an accidental contradiction. We may also be looking at another fusion of time: the original, austere position of this community *and* its later rueful adaptation to human frailty.

1 John also contains the following warning about itinerant preachers, a warning that will appear throughout the early church:

> But do not trust any and every spirit, my friends; test the spirits, to see whether they are from God, for among those who have gone out into the world are many prophets falsely inspired. This is how we may recognize the Spirit of God: every spirit which acknowledges that Jesus Christ has come in the flesh is from God, and every spirit which does not acknowledge Jesus is not from God. (1 John 4:1–3)

I suppose this problem is reached fairly early in the history of every religion—in every religious person—and a certain melancholy always attaches to it. Clearly the Johannine community (one wonders what sort of "monasticism" is assumed by the words "have gone out into the world") has been burned by frauds. No wonder. The cultic religious world painted by the late New Testament authors is a kind of Southern California of the second century in which people routinely utter the sort of ecstatic expression we found in the Jesus discourses of John's Gospel. It must have been hard to choose which prophet to listen to; one can imagine conversations like the following:

"But how do we tell if this holy man speaks the truth? Is what he says true prophecy? Does it come from the Holy One?"

"Ask him if he believes in Jesus Christ. [It has now become a two-part name.]

Pause.

"He says yes!

Pause.

"Ask him if he believes that Christ became *a man!*"

In some such way does orthodoxy begin. In such simple questioning are born the highest flights of religious creeds.

There are nevertheless *new* elements in the theology of 1 John. It contains, for instance, two references to the *sacrificial* death of the Lord (see 2:2; 4:10), a concept foreign to John's Gospel and only touched on in Mark, but which would become orthodox. Apparently the doctrine that Jesus "atoned" for human sins by offering himself as some sort of sacrifice "floated" about in the documents of the early church. But what has seemed to some the most important "new" element in 1 John is what is sometimes called "separatism." As Wayne Meeks puts it: "The confrontation with the other Jews has disappeared from the view of the letters; 'the other world' that the writer of I John views with such suspicion is no longer a Jewish world. It now looks more amorphous, and more unrelievedly evil, though formally the more hopeful side of the Johannine ambivalence occasionally shines through" (*Origins,* 60). The community members reflected in John believe that because the world is evil they should *separate* from it, an idea that contrasts remarkably with that beloved sentiment in John's Gospel, "God so loved the world that he gave his only son . . . ." For the author of 1 John, the world is the "godless world," and the brothers should not to be surprised that it "hates you."

> Do not set your hearts on the godless world or anything in it. Anyone who loves the world is a stranger to the Father's love. Everything the world affords, all that panders to the appetites or entices the eyes, all the glamour of its life, springs not from the Father but from the godless world. And that world is passing away with all its allurements, but he who does God's will stands for evermore. (2:15–17)

Separatism will have a long subsequent history. Both the *Didache* and the writings of the African theologian Tertullian witness to it; and through the first three centuries many Christians believed that the "world" was the province of the Prince of Darkness, all of whose works and pomps were to be avoided. Accordingly, it was thought that good Christians could not become good soldiers or doctors or philosophers or politicians or artists or actors or athletes. Tertullian memorably summed up this attitude in saying "What indeed has Athens to do with Jerusalem?" The same notion will be defined and defended by Augustine in terms of the City of God and City of Man, and it will, of course, underwrite the later monastic movement.

Yet the spiritual value of separatism, what H. Richard Niebuhr called "Christ Against Culture," will continue to be debated right down to our own day. Separatism is at the heart of the "Deer Spring" community of Hutterite Brethren near my home. Their *Brüderhof* lies on forty acres in Norfolk, Connecticut, a community of poor folk set down in a countryside where million-dollar homes are the rule rather than the exception. Founded shortly before the close of World War I by a man named Eberhard Arnold, this group was meant to be a re-creation in the Germany of the twenties of the kind of primitive Christian community that lies behind 1 John, a "separated" discipleship of "full community." Their way of life is undeniably attractive. The brothers own everything in common, take their main meals together, make their decisions by consensus, and educate their own children through the first eight grades. They wear very plain, very modest clothing, work diligently, and pray together frequently. I like these people a lot; I cherish the notion of men and women who think they are an embassy of heaven and *actually act as if they were.* I like the idea that an honest-to-God New Testament community exists not an hour from my house. After I have visited the *Brüderhof* I come home with the realization that I have been *somewhere else* for the weekend, somewhere outside the *world*.

But as you might imagine, such people are also genuinely puzzled by the world. If the separated community is God's embassy in a foreign and fallen land, what should be its "witness" about emperor worship or gladiatorial combat or United Nations peace plans or capital punishment? Should the group's opposition to the death penalty go beyond comforting prisoners and extend to civil disobedience? Should the community oppose nuclear weapons in the militant fashion of the Berrigans? Should it picket abortion clinics—even after the recent murders? These are difficult questions. Like the Good Samaritan, the Brothers want to rush to the side of the man fallen among robbers. But today the Jericho road is crowded with wounded travelers—they are coming down by the busload—and robbers are legion. If you ran out every ten minutes with bandages and oil, you could not slow the ghastly parade.

Like a good many early Christians—like the Johannine community in all probability—the Hutterite brothers want both to correct the evils of the world and remain "uncorrupted" by it. But if your ethical mode is based on fleeing evil, you are in a poor position to deal with mammon. Unhappily, also, you enter these frays at your peril. Given half a chance, the world will simply kill you. The same problem exists elsewhere in the New Testament. You may recall that in Luke's Gospel, near the end of his life Jesus remembers that he once sent out the disciples without purses or even sandals. He then reverses himself, "If you have no sword, sell your cloak and buy one."

Unlike the sermonic 1 John, 2 *and 3 John* are real letters, both written by someone calling himself "the Elder." In 2 John, he conceives of the church he is writing to as "the Lady." So male-oriented and "working-class" is the world of Christian scripture that when I first looked at this letter in Greek I could not believe the text. An epistle could *not* have been written to a *lady!* (The word *kyria* is simply the feminine of *lord*.) In fact, it was with a kind of relief that I discovered the author was simply personifying a neighboring church, so quickly do we adapt to the literary and social conventions of what we read. The theology of this letter, what there is of it, seems consonant with 1 John and uses some of the same phrasing: "he commanded" and "we had from the beginning." It also issues warnings about people who deny the incarnation. 3 John, on the other hand, is a carping complaint against one Diotrephes, a member of a neighboring church. Apparently Diotrephes is stuck-up and full of himself and tries to "expel people from the congregation." It is a trivial piece of papyrus and should never have been made canonical. What's worse, it isn't very convincing: the reader inevitably sides with Diotrephes.

Compared to this Legacy of John, as I have called it, the epistolary continuation of the Pauline tradition is more complex and extended. As we have seen, Christians in the 90s began to compose pieces of writing in imitation of the authentic Pauline letters, which were then perhaps first beginning to circulate. In addition to 2 Thessalonians, already discussed, there survive from that period a Letter to the Colossians and, dependent on it, a Letter to the Ephesians. (The author of all three letters is often called the "Paulinist," a name intended to represent not a single writer, but rather a "school" or a tendency.) Unfortunately, things are never that simple.

Colossians may be a genuine letter of Paul to which later material has been added. That is in fact how it reads even in English—as if passages by Paul were interspersed with sections by someone else—though this effect can also be the result of an imitator's inconstant skill. In any case, Colossians is directed to Christians in the town of Colossae to the east of Ephesus who, we are told, had been originally evangelized by a certain Epaphras. Its author thinks of himself as "Paul" writing from prison, but we are not told where or why he is imprisoned. Perhaps he is imagined as being under the Roman house arrest described at the end of Acts. In its opening salutation, thanksgiving, and so on, Colossians sounds thoroughly genuine, but then in 1:13–20 we suddenly find ourselves in a world very much like that of the Johannine school. Christ is said to have *already* rescued us from the realm of darkness and we are now in his kingdom. The Christology is similarly high: "He is the image of the invisible God; his is the primacy over all creation. In him everything in heaven and on earth was created, not only things visible but also thrones, sovereignties, authorities, and powers: the whole universe has been created through him and for him. And he exists before all things and all things are held together in him" (Col. 1:15–17). The reader is warned against false teachers who may:

> capture your minds with hollow and delusive speculations, based on the traditions of human teaching and centered on the elemental spirits of the universe and not on Christ. . . . Allow no one therefore to take you to task about what you eat or drink, or over the observance of festival, new moon, or Sabbath. . . . You are not to be disqualified by the decision of people who go in for self-mortification and angel-worship, and try to enter into some vision of their own. (Col. 2:8, 16, 18)

No one knows precisely what cult the author has in mind, but such warnings appear in the genuine Pauline letters only in a few passages that are themselves thought to be interpolations. In any case, Christ is said to have "disarmed the cosmic powers and authorities," meaning perhaps that he has in some way eliminated those spirits thought to inhabit the air between earth and heaven who prevent our rising; but the idea is unclear, even perhaps to the writer. Unlike the authentic Paul, this author cannot leave his readers alone to invent their manner of worship. On the contrary, they are admonished to stay away from undefined pagan celebrations and to reject some sort of contemporary mysticism—tantalizing, half-open windows into the religious life of the day. Colossians also assumes that the *parousia* is delayed into the distant future, or at least for the period of the spread of the Gospel, which is "coming to men the whole world over; everywhere it is growing and bearing fruit as it does among you, and has done since the day when you heard of the graciousness of God and recognized it for what in truth it is" (1:6–7). The writer here recognizes that the church is no longer only a local group of converts, but the people of God whose head is Christ—a metaphor to become famous. "He is its origin, the first to return from the dead, to become in all things supreme. . . . It is now my happiness to suffer for you . . . for the sake of his body, which is the church" (1:18, 24). As usual, the last sections of the letter are given over to *parenesis*, in this case simply a list of vices not very distinguishable from pagan lists of the same period. As I have said, Christians of later periods right down to today will consult these passages as guides for living, only to find that women should be subject to their husbands and slaves obedient to their masters, and other helpful advice. The close of the letter is, like the opening, either Paul's or a careful imitation.

Whatever may be the truth about the authorship of Colossians—authentic Paul, partially authentic, wholly made-up at a later time—around 100 C.E. someone incorporated it into a document that was intended to make even more explicit the themes that collectively mark the emergence of Early Catholicism. The *Letter to the Ephesians* (the earliest and best manuscripts are addressed simply to the "faithful") incorporates about half of the verses of Colossians, either quoted directly or alluded to. In repeating this material, the author eliminated what appeared to be any local concerns regarding Colossae apparently in order to universalize the "new" conception of a visible church. In fact, he now uses the Greek word *ekklēsia* to mean something like our present "Christian *church*," rather than simply a local assembly. This is to say that Ephesians is not a letter but a tract designed to explain that the church is one body in Christ, its constitution laid down by God before "the foundation of the world." The author believes that the plan of world history "was hidden for long ages in God the Creator of the universe, in order that now through the church, the wisdom of God in his varied forms might be made known to the rulers and authorities in the realms of heaven" (Eph. 3:9–10). The Christian saints have likewise been "predestined" to be God's adopted children, both Jew and Gentile, and they have been forgiven their sins through the shedding of Christ's blood. Christ himself is now in heaven enthroned above all "government and authority, all power and dominion, and any title of sovereignty that commands allegiance, not only in this age but also in the age to come." God has "put everything in subjection beneath his feet, and appointed him as supreme head to the church which is his body, and as such holds within it the fullness of him who himself receives the entire fullness of God" (Eph. 1:21, 22–23).

Several things are striking about this view. Note that there are rulers and authorities even in heaven! Note also that the saints are *already* saved—as in John's Gospel. The author writes, "And he raised us up in union with Christ Jesus and enthroned us with him in the heavenly realms." We are also simultaneously on earth, of course, where in the church we find not only unity but secure knowledge, love, and growth. Here is the first declaration that the members of the church make up the mystical body of Christ, though in fact this is a reworking of an old Roman idea that expressed a similar relationship between the city and its ruler. The consequence is that members of the church must now be orderly, ethical, even respectable; therefore contrary to the dim view Paul takes of marriage, this author celebrates it—properly regulated of course. "Wives, be subject to your husbands, as though to the Lord. . . . Husbands love your wives, as Christ loved the church. . . .

"This is why" (in the words of scripture) "a man shall leave his father and mother and be united to his wife, and the two shall become one flesh." There is hidden here a great truth, which I take to refer to Christ and to the Church. (Eph. 5:1, 31–32)

In the same suburban vein, children are to be obedient; fathers are not to be too harsh; slaves should cheerfully do what they are told; masters are to be kind. Finally, in that very famous concluding passage, everyone is to put on the armor of the Christian "against cosmic powers, against the authorities and potentates of this dark age, against superhuman forces of evil in the heavens" (Eph. 6:12–13).

In Colossians and Ephesians, we see the Great Church beginning to define itself. A later stage is observable in three additional letters also written in the name of Paul, the so-called Pastoral epistles: *I and II Timothy* and *Titus*. These letters are pseudonymous both in author and addressees: Timothy and Titus are said to be in Ephesus and Crete respectively, and the letters date from sometime in the first half of the second century. Written in a style and vocabulary quite unlike that of the authentic letters—they do not appear in the earliest collections—these letters assume a more formalized, visible church in which the Pauline doctrines of justification by faith and redemption by the cross have disappeared. The argument with the Jews is past; 1 Timothy in fact contains a *defense* of the law! So clearly do these letters reveal a later tradition that they have been recognized as non-Pauline since the late eighteenth century. Yet even here some passages still have a Pauline ring and may contain authentic fragments. More probably, this verisimilitude comes from the fact that, unlike Acts, these letters display a familiarity with Paul's actual writing.

The author of 1 Timothy, the "Pastor," as scholars call him, imagines himself as Paul in Macedonia writing instructions to Timothy at Ephesus (cf. Acts 16:1; 1 Cor. 4:17; 2 Cor. 1:19). As befits the middle of the second century, when faith was no longer a trust in the spirit but the assertion of a certain body of propositions, these instructions are overwhelmingly concerned with preserving right belief. The author introduces his dogmas with the formula, "Here is a saying you may trust," and he sometimes presents them in poetic paragraphs that will become models for the later Christian creeds.

> He who was manifested in the body,
> > vindicated in spirit,
> > > seen by angels;
> who was proclaimed among the nations,
> > believed in throughout the world,
> > > glorified in heaven. (1 Tim. 3:16)

Like the earlier pseudo-Pauline letters, the Pastorals are interested in protecting orthodox belief from Gnosticism. Timothy, for instance, rejects "doctrines inspired by devils" which forbid marriage and "inculcate abstinence from certain foods, though God created them" (1 Tim. 4:2–3). But their more significant concern is "church order," a kind of orthodoxy of clerical organization to go along with an orthodoxy of behavior and belief. Readers are admonished that the religion is to be practiced with dignity by those on whom the elders have laid hands and that Christians should not be "overhasty" in selecting these people. The chief officer of the community is the overseer, or bishop—priests will appear only much later—and various tests are laid down for the bishop's selection. (I'm afraid Paul would have failed many of them.) The bishop must be temperate regarding drink, not avaricious, gentle, and so on. The bishop also must conform to some contemporary marriage code, the details of which are unclear except that polygamy and concubinage are forbidden; perhaps he may not marry again after the death of his wife. Most significantly, the bishop must "have a good reputation with the outside world, so that he may not be exposed to scandal and be caught in the devil's snare." If he maintains a good reputation, he deserves a double stipend (see 1 Tim. 3:1–7).

How much sad experience and recognition of the fact that the church is a human institution lie in such remarks! Mockery of this sort of "job description" is easy—and I have done my share—but the ideal, if not the practice, will have a very long life. Concealed within it, however, is a problem the church will *never* solve: that "relation to the world" I discussed in regard to 1 John. Let me briefly repeat myself. This early on, one can see the double-think at work: on the one hand, these Christians want the world's good opinion; on the other, they want to despise the world. In the institutional church, it is the first that wins out, producing what Niebuhr described as "the Christ *of* Culture," rather than the separatists' "Christ *against* culture." Implicit in almost every line of the Pastorals, therefore, is the *rejection* of separatism. Religion and the world are seen as symbiotic; there is no insurmountable chasm between faith and empire. Christians are thought to make *excellent* soldiers and judges and artists and so on—all the better, in fact, for their Christianity.

All well and good, perhaps, for those who belong to the culture and participate in the enjoyment of its goals. But what about those who have no stake in society? When the author of the Pastorals comes to describe *this* kind of Christian, he invokes a different image of the religion. Though the men of the congregation are instructed to pray with uplifted hands, the women are not to participate. They are to keep quiet and learn. Wasn't Adam created first? In a like manner, slaves should be obedient to their masters, and slaves of Christian masters—in particular—should not get uppity just because they are "brothers." Having no status in *this* world, slaves and women should live for the next. They brought nothing into this world, they are told, and they can take nothing out; if they have food and clothing let them rest content. Women should dress modestly, in any case, eschewing fancy hairstyles, jewelry, and expensive clothes. Besides, the rich fall into the temptations and snares of many foolish and harmful desires which plunge people into ruin and destruction. That the love of money is the root of all evil—*radix malorum est cupiditas*, as it will become—is well known. Oddly enough, this view, which is tailored for the under class, is paradoxically close to the "separatism" John's Gospel recommends for us all.

The result of such double-think is the church's acceptance of a class society at odds with the radical democracy of the original gospel. Consider, for instance, the position of the "official widows" who are regularly enrolled on the church charity list. These are restricted to Christian women who are (a) above reproach, (b) over sixty, (c) married only once, (d) had not only lost their husbands but had no immediate family who could support them, and (e) showed evidence of good deeds: child care, washing people's feet—you know the sort of thing. Here for the first, but not the last, time we hear of the *respectable* poor, a class of sufferers who deserve charity. What would Jesus say about this? And what would he say, finally, of the notion that parishioners who misbehave are to be rebuked in public "to put fear into others" (see 1 Tim. 5:3–16, 20)? The Pastorals are not nice.

II Timothy assumes that Paul is in prison in Rome and Timothy still in Ephesus. It condemns the same idea that caused the composition of 2 Thessalonians: "that our resurrection has already occurred" (2 Tim. 2:18). The idea that Christians are already saved occurs in Ephesians (2:5–10); but that letter was probably written in the 90s. Now we are long past the time when such optimism was thinkable, and we have a long way to go. The grand apocalyptic destruction that was to accompany Jesus' return has been exchanged for the following *moral* destruction:

> You must face the fact: the final age of this world is to be a time of troubles. Men will love nothing but money and self; they will be arrogant, boastful, and abusive; with no respect for parents, no gratitude, no piety, no natural affections. (2 Tim. 3:1–3)

With the end of belief in Jesus' immediate return and in the face of this realistic portrait of humanity, a stoic, diurnal attempt "to reform" replaces Paul's characteristic joy. The guide for this reformation is the tradition found in "scripture."

> . . . remember that from early childhood you have been familiar with the sacred writings which have power to make you wise and lead you to salvation through faith in Christ Jesus. All inspired scripture has its use for teaching the truth and refuting error, or for reformation of manners and discipline and in right living, so that the man of God may be capable and equipped for good work of every kind. (2 Tim. 3:15–17)

This passage may represent a watershed in the New Testament, for though the word *scripture* almost certainly refers here to the now codified Jewish Bible; it may just possibly also embrace some of the "sacred writings" peculiar to the new faith. At the time of the composition of this epistle that could only mean Paul's letters—including the work of the imitator you are reading! (Some would say I go too far here, and I will settle for the same point regarding 2 Peter, which was written a generation later.)

Finally, in the brief letter to *Titus,* who is supposedly in a Christian community on Crete, we have a reaffirmation of the same institutional themes. The writer is again concerned with the qualifications for office in the church; and as for theology, he is upset that converts, particularly Jewish converts, are "undisciplined in their speculations." They must be sharply rebuked. In addition to this concern for the internal workings of the group, there is here the same code of outward-looking respectability we find in the other Pastorals:

> Remind them [the Cretan Christians] to be subject to rulers and authorities, to be obedient, to be ready for every good work, to speak evil of no one, to avoid quarreling, to be gentle, and to show every courtesy to everyone. . . . After a first and second admonition, have nothing more to do with anyone who causes divisions. (Titus 3:1–2, 10)

In assuming the stance of emergent Catholicism, all the Pastorals reveal that a *religion* has now replaced the *faith* of the Pauline house-church. There is an inevitable sadness in this desire for respectability and good public relations, as mystical rapture gives way to bishop and deacon and deaconess, to the collection plate and the bingo game; and the letters end as one feels they must with the un-Christian practice of *shunning.* The Great Church is in place.

The remaining documents in the New Testament are called the *Catholic Epistles,* because they were directed at the church in general (catholic) or at least large segments of it, rather than to specific recipients. They are so heterogeneous that it is not possible to group them very intelligently. Nor can we simply put them in historical order; though all clearly assume a social setting far later than that of the Gospels. *2 Peter* is very late, perhaps the latest work in the New Testament, but otherwise we have no real clues. Moreover, these documents are all pseudonymously written in the names of apostles or relatives of the Lord despite the fact that none betrays the slightest personal knowledge of Jesus. Generally speaking, they are concerned with *parenesis* rather than dogma; and when they *are* discussing dogma, they try to bring orthodoxy out of multiplicity of belief.

The *Letter of James,* undated and so far undatable, is enigmatically directed to "the twelve tribes dispersed throughout the world." The author calls himself "James, a servant of God and the Lord Jesus Christ," but we know nothing about him. Traditionally he was assumed to be James the brother of the Lord, who took over the church in Jerusalem and was killed there just before the outbreak of hostilities with Rome; but the historical circumstances assumed by the writer make that attribution unlikely. It is more probable that the anonymous writer chose the name James (*Jacob* in the original) to go with the "twelve tribes." Nor is this work a letter—it has a salutation but no closing. Nor is it concerned with matters Jewish. What we have here is simply advice. In no particular order, "James" recommends that we not be doubters, that we eschew wealth, endure trials, guard our tongues, not be envious, and so on—all virtues prized by early catholicism and by many Hellenistic cults. He also has this odd notion:

> Above all things, my friends, do not use oaths, whether "by heaven" or "by earth" or by anything else. When you say "Yes" or "No," let it be plain Yes or No, for fear you draw down judgment on yourselves. (Jas. 5:12)

What on earth did James have in mind? The prohibitions in the Torah are against *false* oaths; and the passage in Matthew (5:33–37) from which this idea is bodily lifted is surely a primitive fence around the Torah intended to make sure the believer never swears falsely. Many a baffled Christian will come to think this injunction means simply to tell the truth, but it doesn't. Like those 153 fish caught in John or the conundrum about the five loaves and the seven loaves in Matthew, this verse will, I suppose, remain opaque forever. Only the Quakers ever took it seriously, and then only for a time.

James also contains what will be considered the foundation statements for the Catholic sacraments of Extreme Unction (today's Sacrament of the Sick) and Penance (today's Sacrament of Reconciliation).

> Are any among you sick? They should call for the elders of the church and have them pray over them, anointing them with oil in the name of the Lord. The prayer of faith will save the sick, and the Lord will raise them up; and anyone who has committed sins will be forgiven. Therefore confess your sins to one another, and pray for one another, so that you may be healed. (Jas. 5:14–16)

But by far the most interesting aspect of this epistle is its quarrel with Paul (Jas. 2:14–26). James believes that religion is in the doing, rather than the believing: "A pure and faultless religion in the sight of God the father is this: to look after orphans and widows in trouble and to keep oneself untarnished by the world." The author is aware that not all Christians agree.

What good is it, my brothers and sisters, if you say you have faith but do not have works? Can faith save you? If a brother or sister is naked and lacks daily food, and one of you says to them, "Go in peace; keep warm and eat your fill," and yet you do not supply their bodily needs, what is the good of that? . . .

Show me your faith apart from your works, and I by my works will show you my faith. You believe that God is one; you do well. Even the demons believe—and shudder. (Jas. 2:14-16, 18-19)

It was because of this argument that Martin Luther called James "an epistle of straw" and considered it on a lesser level of inspiration. Clearly it contradicted his own view of the matter. More importantly, it contradicted *Paul's* theology. Though critics have always disagreed over whether or not this is a *conscious* contradiction, it seems clear to me that "James" is perfectly aware of his opponent. Note the illustration he chooses: "Was not our ancestor Abraham justified by works when he offered his son Isaac on the altar? You see that faith was active along with his works, and faith was brought to completion by the works. . . . You see that a person is justified by works and not by faith alone." This is precisely the same story Paul chose to prove the opposite view. In the Letter to James we see illustrated a fundamental notion that arises from a sensible reading of the New Testament: there is no single theology in this book.

Like the letter attributed to James, *1 Peter* is written in an elegant Greek and assumes a much later social milieu than would be appropriate to its putative author. Since one of its aims is to strengthen Christians in a period of persecution, a date in the 90s seems probable. (It is not quoted, however, until 135 C.E.) 1 Peter accepts the delay of the *parousia,* but insists that, since salvation will be "revealed at the end of time," readers should rejoice even though they are now suffering—"even gold passes through the assayer's fire" (1 Pet. 1:7). Like the author of Hebrews, the writer of 1 Peter is also interested in synthesizing the beliefs of his time. In his first chapter alone he has a sacrificial death ("You were set free by Christ's precious blood"), God's dispensational and deterministic plan ("He was predestined before the foundation of the world"), a resurrected Lord ("Through him you have come to trust God who raised him from the dead and gave him glory"), a vertical eschatology ("You have been born again, not of mortal but immortal parentage, through the living and enduring word of God"), and a touch of the *logos* ("And this *word* is the gospel which was preached to you").

Chapter 2 begins the *parenesis.* Playing with that same Christian image of Christ as the stone rejected by the builders, the author extends its meaning to his readers, whom he calls "a chosen race" and "a royal priesthood." He can then insist that they should live respectably, submitting to every authority, reverencing God and honoring the emperor. As in Colossians 3:18 and Ephesians 5:32, we have "Wives, be subject to your husbands"; and, as elsewhere, Christian women are warned away from fancy hairdos and jewelry, and Christian men are called upon to love their wives. As I have said too often perhaps, these and other such household prescriptions are not peculiar to Christianity; they are simply the ethical assumptions of the Hellenistic age. We might remember this when, in controversy over our own twentieth-century assumptions, we begin labeling certain moral dicta as "Christian" or "pagan" or even as the "word of God."

In chapter 3, the author announces a doctrine we have so far only had hints of: that after his death and before his resurrection, Jesus *descended into hell*:

> In the body he was put to death; in the spirit he was brought to life. And in the spirit he went and made his proclamation to the imprisoned spirits, those who had refused to obey in the past, while God waited patiently in the days when Noah was building the ark. (1 Pet. 3:19–20)

The meaning of "imprisoned spirits" is opaque, though one might suppose that a logical problem of justice may have been involved. The writer may have asked himself, What is the condition of the souls of those who lived and died *before* the word was revealed? A possible solution was that the "the gospel was preached to the dead in order that, although in the body they were condemned to die as everyone dies, yet in the spirit they might live as God lives." This notion will become traditional, even finding its way into the Apostles' Creed; and it becomes very popular in the Middle Ages as the "Harrowing of Hell." The same idea may also underlie that otherwise enigmatic verse (1 Cor. 15:29) in which Paul mentions people—apparently not in his group—who had been baptized "on behalf of the dead." In nineteenth-century America, *this* version of the idea will be revived by the Church of the Latter-Day Saints.

But the mention of Noah also brings to the author's mind ideas of salvation and water, and he therefore proceeds to the "definition" of the sacrament:

> in it a few people, eight in all, were brought to safety through the water. This water symbolized baptism, through which you are now brought to safety. Baptism is not the washing away of bodily impurities but the appeal made to God from a good conscience; and it brings salvation through the resurrection of Jesus Christ, who is now at the right hand of God, having entered heaven

and received the submission of angels, authorities, and powers. (1 Pet. 3:19–22)

In the latter third of 1 Peter, the sufferings of the people addressed suddenly seem much more immediate and actual: "do not be taken aback by the fiery ordeal which has come over you" (1 Pet. 4:12ff.). Indeed, this suffering is now understood as signaling the last days: "The end of all things is upon us. . . . The time has come for the judgment to begin: it is beginning with God's own household. And if it is starting with us, how will it end for those who refuse to obey the gospel of God?" This is perhaps a reference to the persecution under Domitian, but the change in tone also suggests that the letter may be composed of originally separate fragments, a kind of sermon used for Christian baptism and a letter written to encourage persecuted Christians.

In his conclusion, the author appeals to his readers as a "witness to Christ's sufferings"; and aware, perhaps, of the incongruity of a Galilean fisherman writing excellent Greek, he points out that he, Peter, is writing through someone named Silvanus. He then greets everyone "with a loving kiss from his 'sister church' in *Babylon*" (still a code word for Rome). By this time the kiss may be liturgical.

Before leaving 1 Peter, we should note something both peculiar and inevitable in these later writings: the appearance of *self-conscious* theology. The author writes, "Hold blessed the Lord Christ in your hearts and be prepared always with an explanation for anyone who demands an account of the hope that is in you" [my translation]. The French theologian Claude Geffré calls this verse a "charter" for apologetics, and I think he is quite right (*New Age*, 12). Though our tendency is to identify theology with the institutional church and especially with the definitions of doctrine that emerged from later great controversies, we should be aware that the interpretation of scripture begins in the New Testament itself. Just as the Gospels are a commentary on and an exegesis of the "Old Testament," so now James and 1 Peter are commentaries on the New.

The *Letter of Jude* is a very brief document promoting orthodoxy and attacking false belief. It has salutation and blessing, but no thanksgiving section and no traditional close, which is replaced by a doxology. The author claims to be "servant of Christ and brother of James," by which he apparently means that he is that Judas or Jude who is one of Jesus' brothers (Mark 6:3). As such he addresses himself to "those whom God has called," warning them against others who have "wormed their way in" among the faithful and "pervert the free favor of our God into licentiousness." Alluding perhaps to Acts 20:29–30, he reminds his readers of a statement by the "apostles" that predicted this trouble: "In the final age there will be those who mock at religion and follow their own ungodly lusts" (Jude 18). As Burton Mack points out, this sort of contemporary allusion rather spoils the author's pretense of being a sibling of Jesus (*Who Wrote the New Testament*, 211).

Exactly what these bad people preach, however, is never clear; the closest we come to an explanation is the remark that they disown Jesus, defile their own bodies, and flout authority; they carouse at "love feasts," apparently those *agapai* or communal meals of early Christianity that have not survived as a ritual. Mysteriously, Jude's opponents are also said to "insult celestial beings." The writer doesn't debate these accusations; he simply condemns his innovating opponents, insisting—in a fashion that will become habitual in the next century—that God has revealed his plan "once and for all."

The most interesting aspect of Jude is its use of mythological materials. The author paraphrases or quotes sentences from uncanonical apocalyptic Jewish works as if they were scriptural. To illustrate how God punishes unbelievers, for instance, he cites the rebellious angels "who were not content to maintain the dominion assigned to them, but abandoned their proper dwelling-place; God is holding them, *bound in darkness with everlasting chains for judgment on the great day*" (Jude 6). The italicized material is drawn from the pseudepigraphic book of *Enoch*. In the same way, the author's reference to the Archangel Michael disputing with the devil over Moses' body is taken from another intertestamental Jewish work, the *Assumption of Moses*. Finally, in vv. 14–15, he *directly* quotes the book of *Enoch*. The clear inference is that this letter was written sometime before the closing of the canon of Hebrew Scripture about 90 C.E. at Jamnia on the Palestinian coast.

This argument seems confirmed by the fact that at a later date (perhaps 150 C.E.) some other author rewrote and expanded Jude in the guise of a second letter by Peter. But the author of *2 Peter* eliminates all its dependencies on what were by his time nonauthoritative books. The theology of this letter, as might be expected, is synthetic: one must add virtue to faith and knowledge to virtue, and self-control to knowledge and fortitude to self-control, and so on. Nevertheless, humanity is predetermined to be saved or not, though the author puts the matter in a way that pleased our Calvinistic forefathers: "exert yourselves to clinch God's choice and calling of you" (2 Pet. 1:10). Peculiarly, there is no concern here with church organization, but a very sophisticated view of Christian writings. Referring to the delay of the *parousia*, the author of 2 Peter says:

> Bear in mind that our Lord's patience is an opportunity for salvation, as Paul, our dear friend and brother, said when he wrote you with the wisdom God gave him. He does the same in all his other letters, wherever he speaks about this, which the ignorant and unlearned misinterpret to their own ruin, as they do the other scriptures. (2 Pet. 3:15–16)

This is that awareness of being *itself* sacred scripture to which I earlier referred. Here at the very end of the canonical writings we have a recognition that at least Paul's letters have now come to be regarded as "holy scripture" and that people are already misinterpreting them. They must realize that scripture is not subject to private understanding, pleads the author: "But first note this: no one can interpret any prophecy of Scripture by himself" (2 Pet. 1:20). It is clear, of course, that that is exactly what is going on. The author is also aware that people are restive because of the delay of the *parousia*:

> in the last days there will come scoffers who live self-indulgent lives; they will mock you and say, "What has happened to his promised coming? Our fathers have been laid to rest, but still everything goes on exactly as it always has since the world began." [But we are not to forget that] . . . in the Lord's sight one day is like a thousand years and a thousand years like one day. It is not that the Lord is slow in keeping his promise, as some suppose, but that he is patient with you. (2 Pet. 3:3–9)

Time has passed and "everything goes on exactly as it always has since the world began"; as in Jude, the writer forgets that he is supposed to be a contemporary of the Lord. Nevertheless, this sentence is hauntingly prophetic. One of the last meditations Dietrich Bonhoeffer smuggled out of the Nazis' Tegel prison begins: "It is becoming evident that everything gets along without God—and, in fact, just as well as before." This sort of despair—if that's what it was—annihilates nearly two millennia.

The author closes by carefully reminding the reader that he is reading Peter's "second letter"—Peter who once saw the Lord with his "own eyes" and was present at the transfiguration. "Yet I think it right to keep refreshing your memory so long as I still lodge in this body. I know that very soon I must leave it; indeed our Lord Jesus Christ has told me so. But I will see to it that after I am gone you will have means of remembering these things at all times" (2 Pet. 1:13-15).

With this last unsettling paragraph, our reading of the New Testament comes to an end.

Conclusion

That then is how I think you read the New Testament today—if you set out to read it sensibly. Not that I insist very firmly on any specific detail of this commentary. As I said at the beginning, all I can hope for in these matters is something close to the "state of the art." But the question I raised in the introduction remains: Is the New Testament a better or a worse book for this kind of reading? Each person will have his or her own answer. Personally, I think it is a much better book when read sensibly: more complex, more interesting, more moving, more honest. If I am no longer frightened or deluded by it, I am left with a greater reverence for it—though, to be sure, an "awkward reverence."

I think that phrase and the poem from which it comes, "Church Going" by the late British poet Philip Larkin, well describe the state of mind of today's informed Christian when confronted with the New Testament—a sort of unwieldy admiration. The informed reader is like the speaker in Larkin's poem, who enters an ancient English church and tries to imagine what will become of these buildings when even "disbelief is gone"; that is, when we are so far removed from "faith" that there is no cachet in its opposite. Larkin takes faith to mean an assertion of particular doctrines, which—as we have seen—is a late development in the history of the gospel. As we have seen, the New Testament Greek word we translate as "faith" meant *trust*—often a very vague trust—in life itself, in the possibility of goodness, and in speculation about these. This trust is still alive in Larkin's speaker—though perhaps only dimly—and he reaches the same conclusion about his ancient church building that I have reached regarding to the New Testament.

> A serious house on serious earth it is,
> In whose blent air all our compulsions meet,

> Are recognized, and robed as destinies.
> And that much never can be obsolete. . . .

Whether or not you agree with these sentiments, I hope I have convinced you that it is no longer possible to ignore two hundred years of scholarship. Even those who believe that this Hellenistic anthology contains the word of God must today—if they are informed—make their leap of faith from this *same sort of reading*. They must assume, that is, that God made use of Mark and the Q source and saw to it that Matthew and Luke combined and rewrote these documents in different ways and so on. Difficult as such an assumption may be, I have no quarrel with it. Indeed, one can argue *sensibly* that in order to put value into our world we *all* make such leaps to an absolute—whether from this particular set of religious writing or from some other intellectual platform is a matter of choice. This being the case, it seems to me that such believers should know what sort of book it is that holds their divine revelation. Even religious people—perhaps especially religious people—should read the New Testament *sensibly*.

This situation is one of the new facts about the Christian religion in our time; and yet few Christians are aware of it. There is a kind of conspiracy of silence among the preachers, many of whom nowadays receive good academic training and understand these matters. For what they often describe as pastoral reasons, these men and women continue to behave toward scripture as if they and their flocks lived in a previous century, regularly palming off on their parishioners as "Bible Study" what is only a kind of therapy. Members of their study groups generally end in using these texts like Rorschach blots, as a means to evoke free association.

That religious leaders consciously dissemble is therefore another new fact about the Christian religion today. Back in the 1930s, most ordinary English-speaking Christians were innocent fundamentalists, clergy and laity alike, Catholics by osmosis from their Protestant neighbors. Except for the well-educated, whom we hardly ever met (and non-Christians, of course) most of us believed in what people still call a "literal interpretation of the Bible." This did not mean that we all drew the same meanings from these God-given documents—not at all; it only meant we believed that the texts were the exact words of God. The logical and linguistic problems posed by this odd view never seemed to bother us. Moreover, we never believed that the *whole* Bible was normative. We had no thought of obeying the Jewish holiness code in Leviticus, for instance, and we took our moral views— "divorce" was an obvious example—not from these contradictory texts but from the traditions of our separate denominations. In saying that scripture was the word of God, therefore, we only meant that we accepted a few passages as a kind of odd canon within the canon and that even then they meant only whatever Father Sullivan or Reverend Moeller or the Vicar said they meant. Such mini-canons differed from denomination to denomination. Catholics rarely talked about what we all called the "Old Testament" and still more rarely read it; though oddly enough our priests made their way through the 150 Psalms once a week and in Latin! Many Protestants seemed to read nothing but Paul's letters, in order—it seemed—to ignore Peter, the first pope. Seventh-Day Adventists were big on Hebrews; Lutherans on Romans; and evangelicals cited John.

In a sort of guilty way, we understood the theological comic opera we lived in. But maintaining the truth of the "whole Bible," often when we hadn't read it, became a mark of lower-middle-class respectability. When our intellectual horizons broadened somewhat, this attitude came to be a problem. I remember discovering as an adolescent that hardly any of our first-rate novelists or poets or thinkers were Bible believers and silently asking myself, How come *my* family is? Yet as early as 1900, a good many of us had been made aware that among the educated the "Bible was under attack." And this was not the first time such a thing had happened. In America, a skepticism about scripture—almost always associated with the name of Jefferson—who had edited his own version of the New Testament—had been popular during the Revolution; and the New England Transcendentalism which followed was even more cavalier about this source of divine revelation. But by the 1930s several waves of revivalism had created a nationwide bibliolatry. In our family we simply ignored such historical paganism and talked of Jefferson and Emerson—when we *did* talk of them—as if they had been good Christians like us; not Catholics, of course, but perhaps Methodists like the Vilbergs down the block. The rest of the country did somewhat the same thing, even naming high schools after these old reprobates; they even pretended that Walt Whitman was a Christian and named schools after *him*.

Yet by 1900, almost all the foundational works of scientific biblical studies had been written and translated: Strauss's *Life of Jesus* (1835), which concluded that the evangelists had mythically embroidered the life of Jesus; Weisse's *Gospel History*, which proposed the primacy of Mark theory; and Harnack's seven-volume *History of Dogma* (1900), which illustrated how our beliefs had developed over time. Moreover, with the exception of Princeton University, which would remain a bastion of literalism for another two decades, these works and their viewpoint had been assimilated by nearly all our major departments of theology. On the surface at least, this academic revolution of the nineteenth century had had little effect on

Christian churches of the twentieth, though with hindsight one can see that secularism was already eroding Western Christianity even among the unlettered. This was apparent in the casual way people had come to talk about their various beliefs or *stopped* talking about them. By the late 1930s many English-speaking Protestants had begun to view New Testament theology—heaven, hell, the judgment, the resurrection, and so on—as somehow incidental to their Sunday worship, though they persisted in that worship. Bible reading declined. Finding the sacred text problematical and irrelevant, even some mainline preachers increasingly ignored it in favor of psychology.

It was during the 1940s, therefore, that such courses as I now teach today—spring semester, "The Bible As Literature: New Testament"—first began to appear in publicly funded American colleges and even in some high schools. They represented no triumph of rationality. These "nondenominational" courses in scripture were created for the same reasons we create everything in our culture, as a response to what the educationists call "a felt need." The makers of our school and college curricula had discovered that students, though then still solidly "religious," were increasingly unfamiliar with the most important book of their culture. The answer was, "Give them a course in it."

These courses came to be housed in departments of literature for reasons that are also peculiar to the United States. Religion departments were then nonexistent in most public colleges and would have only compounded the problem. The department of philosophy wouldn't do—its professors would take biblical ideas all too seriously and want to argue about them. The English department, on the other hand, peopled with harmless, myopic drudges who made a living out of explaining Shakespeare and correcting the comma splice, was just the place. Weren't there *stories* in the Bible? Presented as studies in "literature," then, these courses represented the very secularism they were meant to ameliorate; their existence was a sure sign of the waning of the supernatural—at least among the kinds of people who routinely shared in the nation's success and sent their children to the local state college. For those who had never shared in our national expansion, however—religious people who lived far from the centers of American intellectual life—farmers, Southerners still nursing their wounds, small entrepreneurs with chips on their shoulders—such courses were either unknown or anathema. For these people, the Bible remained what it had always been, a magical ensign to which they owed allegiance, a symbol of their modest but respected place in society and of whatever morals went with it. Historians often suggest that when the Scopes trial of 1925 had subjected the literalist biblical beliefs of these people to national ridicule, they retreated into the hinterlands. Defeated in Dayton by a smart lawyer and the sophisticated Eastern press, the story goes, the fundamentalists retired to lick their wounds and wait. I don't think this happened. They (we) didn't go anywhere. We were right where we had always been in Gary, Indiana, or Dubuque, Iowa, or Pittsburgh. Though beginning to hear of what was taught in the colleges, we barely listened to it. Some of us were *afraid* to listen to it because Sister Emily had warned: "When you go on to college, watch out for godless professors." In those years, liberal views on any subject, let alone the Bible, became mixed up in our minds with "atheistic communism."

It is also part of American popular history that during the Depression these religious folk began to make a comeback. Again I think this is an exaggeration of what was a kind of steady, widespread religious state. Yet undoubtedly radio ministries of the 1930s reminded the country that it still had a backbone of old-time religion; and television, when it came along, capitalized on it. To some, this phenomenon has seemed like a renascence of ignorance—the way today's talk radio seems to reveal the abject failure of our educational system. But ignorant or not, with the coming of television this same Bible-believing Christianity went on to enjoy a spectacular, if brief, notoriety. Oral and Pat and Rex and Jimmy became nearly unavoidable North *or* South; television dragged us all into their tent sooner or later, even though we may not have knelt down in the ethereal sawdust. Though they always exaggerated their audiences, for a time these men conducted a very big business indeed. Perhaps as many as twenty million once watched their nationally syndicated programs, and they are not yet quite defunct. But scandals of one sort or another and mixed feelings about the politics of conservative religion have hurt. Jerry Falwell's Moral Majority turned out to be an ecclesiastical and financial mistake—as well as a political one. Swaggert and Bakker fell to all-too-human sinfulness. Roberts went too far. But no matter how crass their motives, no matter how many professionals with blow-dried hair masqueraded on their programs as simple Christian tenors or sopranos, these men demonstrated that there was still something called America's religion and that it was based on the Bible.

The pervasiveness of this indigenous American religion used to be disguised by our denominations. Yet most of these were the result of European immigration patterns—overlaid with class distinctions—rather than serious theological differences. Moreover, since the late nineteenth century our mainline churches have not only preached a single, homogenized creed; they have exported it to England and the continent. This religion is still best represented by the incomparable Billy Graham. His is the hard-core thing in itself, complete with vague certitudes and universal appeal. Listen to his altar call:

> I'm going to ask you to come now. Up here—down there. You may be way up in those last rows, you may be in the choir. But I want you to come. Start now. We'll wait on you. You may be a church member, you may not. But you've never had that encounter with God. You may never have another chance. Do it now. This is the harvest time. Come quietly now and say, "Billy, tonight I accept Christ."

A thing like that doesn't happen by itself—or overnight. Where in the world did America's religion come from? Well, its remote source was England and George Whitefield, a stumpy little divine who first went up and down our land in 1739, the best preacher any American colonist had ever heard. The great eighteenth-century actor David Garrick said that Whitefield could send an audience into a paroxysm by merely pronouncing the word *Mesopotamia*. Though it was always preached as "biblical," this revivalist religion never had a very close relation to the text we have just read. On the contrary, evangelical religion has been from the beginning direct, personal, emotional, as democratic as hamburger, unmediated by traditional liturgy or ritual or theology. Like our high schools, our religion doesn't require much reading. So deeply ingrained are we in this anti-intellectual tradition that we automatically assume an opposition between learning and piety. If your local minister is said to be "pious" or "devout" or "spiritual," you know—if you're an American—that he is not smart. The consequence has been that in each generation, the mantle of Whitefield has descended upon a *naïf*. Our National Religious Service is always conducted by unabashed amateurs: Finney, Moody, Billy Sunday, Billy Graham—not one of them with serious theological training. Once asked to consult the book of Daniel, Dwight Moody confessed he did not know whether to look in the Old or New Testament. And Billy Sunday, an ex-baseball player, was just the sort of man American Christians always want in their pulpit. He used to announce:

> I am not a mountebank, I am not an aper or reprint of someone else. I am and always have been plain Billy Sunday trying to do God's will in preaching Jesus and Him crucified and arisen from the dead for our sins.

All these men had in common a belief in the "literal truth of the Bible," which by World War I had turned into "inerrancy." Generally, it was the King James Version of 1611 that was without flaw, though the more learned talked mysteriously of the inerrancy of the "originals." Yet for most of us, as I've said, this belief has been almost purely symbolic. As a people we have never made much dogmatic use of the New Testament, though a few smaller groups have always read and reread particular works (Hebrews and Revelation, for instance) often for odd, magical reasons. But in this racier form, bibliolatry functions only in local churches and on late-night television. Pre-, as opposed to Post-, millenarianism, the Great White Throne, speaking in tongues—the Kabala, so to speak, of our national religion—are not for everyone. Such extremes remain available, however, for those who want them. What *is* for everyone is that conventional, not quite serious allegiance to an "inerrant" Bible. Why? Why should a survey taken in New York City in December 1981 show that fully one-third of those interviewed believed that "the Bible is the actual word of God and is to be taken literally, and word for word"?

Writing about the South in 1879, the poet Sydney Lanier said:

> Our people have failed to perceive the deeper movements under-running the time, they lie wholly off, out of the stream of thought, and whirl their poor old dead leaves of recollection round and round in a piteous eddy that has all the wear and tear of motion without any of its rewards of progress.

Sydney Ahlstrom, whose monumental *Religious History of the American People* provides me with this quotation, suggests that the "major religious corollary of this memory-laden view would be a firm attachment to the evangelicalism of antebellum days and a refusal to admit the relevance of issues raised by modern thought" (p. 682). This is in fact what happened, both North and South. Yet in their turning away from biblical and philosophical study Americans of the post–Civil War period were only repeating a national anti-intellectual pattern. Their remote ancestors had first taken up evangelical religion from itinerant preachers like Whitefield, who denounced the learned, bookish, settled New England clergymen as hopelessly mired in vain inquiries. In the same way, the children of Lanier's Southerners rejected biblical criticism—when they heard about it—and *their* grandchildren rejected the evolution of species. Such a national fondness for nostalgic opinion has nothing fundamentally to do with New Testament scholarship, any more than opposition to Darwinian evolution has anything to do with a serious interest in zoology. It is purely defensive, an attitude assumed by people who feel threatened by change.

Paradoxically, it was serious Christian New Testament scholarship itself which was initiating that change. Beginning in the last decades of the nineteenth century, there was introduced to England and America a body of scholarship which for the first time dealt comprehensively and critically with the sources of Christian faith. Lutheran clergymen who held chairs in

German universities had used the same tools, techniques, and presuppositions as secular historians to read the sacred texts sensibly. Today, the knowledge of the Bible and church history they gained remains solidly in place, the stuff of any introductory course in scripture. The Hebrew Bible is now recognized as a repeatedly rewritten compendium of ancient literature, some literary, some historical, some ecclesiastical. The New Testament stands as twenty-seven disparate pieces of Hellenistic Greek prose which express five or six different ways of understanding a new religious cult and are either ambiguous about the most familiar doctrines of later Christianity or lack them all together. The Trinity, the divinity of Jesus, and the efficacy of sacraments—all these were later defined and declared true by narrow majority vote of legislative bodies every bit as meretricious as the United States Congress.

The nineteenth-century scholars who participated in these discoveries were the first to agonize over them. In England, F. J. A. Hort, who with B. F. Westcott put together the first truly modern Greek text of the New Testament, wrote the following to his colleague in 1860:

> I do most fully recognize the special "Providence" which controlled the formation of the canonical books. . . . But I am not able to go as far as you in asserting the absolute infallibility of a canonical writing. . . . I shall rejoice on fuller investigation to find that imperfect knowledge is a sufficient explanation of all apparent errors, but I do not expect to be so fortunate. (see Mark A. Noll's *Between Faith and Criticism,* 196)

For some educated Christians, this new awareness of biblical error simply meant less emphasis on the supernatural (without an outright denial of traditional views) and more emphasis on what came to be called the "social gospel." In America two particular divines, Walter Rauschenbush and Washington Gladden, made concern for *this* world the mainstay of American Protestantism into the twentieth century. But for others, the new findings spelled an end to institutional Christianity. Its beliefs disappeared into myth and poetry to be replaced by philosophy—or nothing. For some few educated conservatives and for the mass of unlettered believers, however, a kind of intellectual and emotional siege ensued. On the same page, Mark Noll quotes an 1881 remark of Princeton's B. B. Warfield, which in its rhetorical contortion suggests the intellectual burden believers now carried:

> No organism can be stronger than its weakest part . . . if error be found in any one element, or in any class of [biblical] statements, certainty as to any portion could arise no higher than belongs to that exercise of human reason to which it will be left to discriminate the infallible from the fallible.

In other words, once you begin to question, *you* become the test of truth, you yourself have to be infallible.

That was more than many people could bear, and in the following decades, conservative religionists, like prelates at the Council of Trent, turned their backs on biblical scholarship to take refuge in some form of "inerrancy," not only repeating, as I've said, a national anti-intellectual pattern, but exporting it to England, Scotland, and Wales. They were also obeying a very basic impulse. In the cyclic histories of most primitive peoples there come times when the day-to-day behavior and experience of the natives begin to deviate from their traditional beliefs. Parents find themselves no longer able to guide their children; shaman and elder quarrel over what is acceptable tribal conduct; the people grow restive under leaders who openly profess different, novel moralities. Crime increases, mental illness becomes common, people turn violent and run amok. Husbands and wives begin to hate. Throughout much of primitive America this was now about to happen. The tenets of the Protestant Ethic, which persisted into the 1950s throughout our society, despite declining belief in the supernatural, finally began to crumble. Confidence in the value of self-reliance, honesty, hard work, the family, and so on—which lasted well into the Eisenhower years—began to go. Even the notion of free will came into question. Anyone who has seen a film of the interior of an American prison and noted who is there—and who isn't—must wonder whether free will or individual responsibility exists—or, if they do, whether they are operative among us.

People know this. They know that sin is now in the racial and cultural aggregate and characterized by the inevitabilities that accompany gender, age, and fortune. As a result, many no longer believe much in the future, either secular or spiritual; they believe in quick pleasure and luck. American youngsters are fond of saying, "Do your own thing," or "whatever turns you on," phrases that conceal a deep-seated dissatisfaction with what is left of middle-class morality *and* the facile hedonism that has replaced it. But the mood is not limited to the young and feckless. Even some of the professional people I know have abandoned their ideals for "instant" gratification.

Against all of this stands the religious right, people who continue to hold to "old-time" religion. Remarkably, these people also continue to hold to biblical inerrancy. Deliberately turning away from what they perceive as the "world," these so-called fundamentalists have embraced a new but limited "separatism." They do not oppose automobiles or central heating. They have not moved to isolated dwellings like the Hutterites. They haven't *gone* anywhere. They simply reject what they call "godless" liberalism, including the serious study of sacred texts. But it is nostalgia for the past that continues to support biblical religion, not the other way around.

If you paid close attention to those right-wing television preachers with accents, they would have told you that it was the American past they yearned for, not Greek and Hebrew theology. If you listened carefully to Jerry Falwell, you discovered that he had only one sermon, which he varied no more than Billy Graham varies his Altar Call. It is the nostalgic tale of his own conversion: How on Sundays before she left for church, his mother always turned the radio to Charles E. Fuller's Old Fashioned Revival Hour. How Jerry would lie there abed, only half listening, while the preacher's subliminal message reached his soul. Then one summer's evening he and his friend Jim Moon wandered into the little Park Avenue Baptist Church in Lynchburg, Virginia, and made their decision for Christ. Over and over again this middle-aged, respectable-looking preacher, indistinguishable from a small town bank president or high school principal, quietly speaks his piece from the pulpit. It is a tale redolent of summer evenings, porch swings, the security of the past. The Blue Ridge Mountains stand off to the west of the little Southern town. And there on the locust-lined streets of Lynchburg the Second Blessing descends and Jerry walks out into the twilight streets—saved. It is the way we were.

I do not mean to sit in judgment on this broad, now international movement which appeals to so many. No stranger to a sentimental love of the past, I have a good deal of sympathy for these conservatives. I too am old enough to remember better times—times when cities were rather clean in both senses of the word and rather safe. I remember when sex was still romantic—even sinful, if you were lucky—a time when people "did right," in Flannery O'Connor's phrase. Caught in nostalgia, none of us is able to think clearly, especially about something as complex as the New Testament. But we must not remain out of "the stream of thought," like Lanier's defeated Southerners, whirling *our* "poor old dead leaves of recollection round and round in a piteous eddy." We can no longer read Sacred Scripture as we once read it, whatever our personal or community demons might be. We must give up the pretense that there is one portrait of Jesus in these documents: one gospel. Each of our writers presents his own "historical Jesus," a portrait consonant with that interiorized Christ of faith he believes in. And since these writers speak not only for themselves but for their individual communities, their portraits of Jesus and his preaching are largely the products of the early church. Even as these Gospels were being set down, however, they had entered into a process of selective interpretation that still endures. Christian faith has always been a faith in the *developing* beliefs of the church. Christians have always founded their faith not on a set of marvelous occurrences in the first century but on a group of varied and sometimes contradictory interpretations of those events written down between 50 and 150 C.E.—interpretations that have continued to evolve into the present. Though in every age reformers have said they were going back to the Christ of the first two centuries, a brief comparison of the beliefs they recommend compared with those of Justin Martyr or Irenaeus or Origen will quickly show this to be untrue.

Christians cannot help this. Any preaching necessarily addresses its contemporary world—both in doctrine and morals—and necessarily sponsors the notion of the risen Christ elicited by that world. The clearest examples of this sort of thing come from those fringes of Christianity, the apocalyptic sects, which periodically thrust upon their Bibles—and their adherents—not only a particular Christ but a detailed and conclusive theory of history. But even among the orthodox, interpretations of the New Testament have never stopped. Once the canon was established toward the end of the fourth century, each age in succession settled on a concept of Christ, and then—through omission and emphasis—adjusted that image to the traditional text.

The same process has gone on within the individual, each of us being a little theology department, a little seer, a little interpreter of texts; for all people inherit their religious texts. Jesus found his already to hand; so did the evangelists. So do we. Like Paul, we are powerless to rid ourselves of them. All we can do, as I have said too often in these pages, is try to read and interpret them sensibly. It is very difficult to live with the open mind this requires: so difficult, in fact that some contemporary Christian theologians have come to consider the New Testament irrelevant to religious instruction. Indeed, one can make the case that mainline Christianity has been moving toward a scripture-less state for some time now: overtly in certain denominations, by default in others. Ask yourself what supernatural beliefs are necessary for Christian identity? Heaven? Hell? Purgatory? (Catholics have only recently given up limbo.) Put it another way. What moral or ethical question would most major churches settle by turning to scripture? Capital punishment? Divorce? The limits of the welfare state? Abortion?

Outside the conservative right, one finds at best a vague, mystical will to do good in the "manner of Jesus." This feeling has a long history, tracing a parallel but subdued developmental line beneath that of conservative biblical evangelism. It produced the Quaker meeting and the Unitarian fellowship, forms of religion that emphasize inner experience *as proof of the Bible*—standing the text on its head, as I have called it. This same sort of sentimentality has also produced "high church" Catholics and Anglicans who have fought free of the Bible in favor of a sacramental tradition. Among the educated, this general movement away from biblical theology was inevitable. Sooner or later each informed pewholder realizes that these documents cannot demonstrate anything about the universe, that they have the logical status of imaginative literature only. The truth content of the New Testament is in no way to be despised, but—as I said at the beginning—it is of the same kind as the truth of *Hamlet* or *The Brothers Karamazov*. And even that is misleading, for Shakespeare's play and Dostoyevsky's novel are each the product of a single intelligence and therefore those texts have a certain minimal unity. The documents of the New Testament, on the other hand, do not harmonize, nor are they stable. The texts themselves are fluid, changing as new manuscripts are discovered or old ones are better understood; and even if we should all agree on the meaning of an unchanging text, it would still—modern moral philosophy assures us—have only subjective, phenomenal value.

The struggle over this situation is the stuff of contemporary theology. Hans Urs von Balthasar, for instance, would rest content with the faith of those who believe in the risen Christ *on other grounds* and therefore have no essential need for the tragic tale of the historical Jesus. This is the notion I have already mentioned, the belief that we have gained the important "facts" of Christianity from experience and only find them "illustrated" in scripture. He is not alone in this view. The next time you're in a suburban Christian Church listen for this theology of condescension. Often the only way the preacher can "bring in" the Gospel for his educated parishioners is to use one of its anecdotes as an example of a moral truth they already agree on. Dietrich Bonhoeffer was well aware of this development in modern Christianity. In the 1930s, before the Nazis put him in jail, before the famous theology of his later letters, before he himself had doubts about the meaning of religion, Bonhoeffer contrasted this new paganism with what was for him, then, the true Christian message:

> It is not in our life that God's help and presence must be proved, but rather God's presence and help have been demonstrated for us in the life of Jesus Christ. It is in fact more important for us to know what God did to Israel, to his Son Jesus Christ, than to seek what God intends for us today. The fact that Jesus Christ died is more important than the fact that I shall die, and the fact that Jesus Christ rose from the dead is the sole ground of my hope that I, too, shall be raised on the Last Day. (*Life Together*, 54)

Other theologians think that the sensible interpretation of the New Testament reaches at least to a few moral ideals. In our day these pretty much reduce to the virtue of "hope," either for personal wellness or political improvement. Such a theology has the attraction of being a "liberation" in both a political and a personal sense, but it tends to convert ordinary ministers into inept psychologists and political theorists, experts on the sexual drive and the Bill of Rights. A Hispanic friend of mind who used to have a parish in the South Bronx says that he left the priesthood when he discovered that people were coming to him with *real* problems—problems for which he had no remedies.

As might be expected, a recognition that evil is intractable often leads to more rarefied theologies. Between the wars, the mysticism of the Word, promulgated by Karl Barth, was popular: the Truth is not *in* the scripture, but somehow *arises* between the word and the individual who "hears" it. After the war, this "neo-orthodoxy," as it was called, was largely replaced by a Christian existentialism which accepts the "mythology" of the New Testament as a kind of code for the perennial human situation. Influenced by the writings of Paul Tillich, for instance, theologians both Protestant and Catholic have come up with a mystical "minimalism." From this point-of-view the stories of the Gospel reduce to a few defensible axioms which one accepts without qualification. On such a foundation, the Catholic theologian Karl Rahner produced three creeds which are printed at the end of his monumental *Foundations of Christian Faith.* Here is the briefest: "Christianity is the religion which keeps open the question about the absolute future which wills to give itself in its own reality by self-communication, and which has established this will as eschatologically irreversible in Jesus Christ, and this future is called God." One is tempted to compare Rahner's effort with that famous eighteenth-century creed which claimed the existence of "an omnipresent, intelligent, benevolent divinity that foresees and provides; the life to come; the happiness of the just; the punishment of sinners; the sanctity of the social contract and the law." Would anyone deny that Rousseau is here more "Catholic" than Rahner? Or that in his last statement he is more pertinent and contemporary?

These various attempts to translate the New Testament into meaningful religious doctrine suggest, therefore, that Christian thinkers have not yet found a way of reading scripture in the light of *both* the scholarship *and* their traditional theological positions. It may well be that in our present state of the art this simply is not possible. If that is so, it seems to me that it would be better for church leaders simply to teach the texts historically and critically without pulling any punches. Indeed, it is scandalous that they don't do so already. Have Christians themselves no confidence in the Truth? Even if they don't, one would think that fear of embarrassment would lead them to honesty. Contemporary ministers of the word must surely recognize that the people in the pews have probably at least read the Christmas issues of *Time* or the *New Republic* or their British counterparts and therefore now know more truth about the scripture than they have ever heard from a pulpit.

Yet telling the truth about scripture is not as devastating as it might seem. It largely affects a set of mythological beliefs congregations are no longer much interested in anyway; and in the words of Claude Geffré, it "more radically affects dogmatic theology than the church itself and the current forms of Christian service among men" (*New Age,* 32). According to Geffré, the general process of secularization in our society has already so eroded belief in the supernatural as to reduce "Christian faith to a human ethos which is general enough for Christians and non-Christians who believe in the future of man to be at ease with one another." Many of today's practicing Christians—perhaps most—have therefore silently abandoned a theology that no longer makes any sense. Unfortunately, they have also often abandoned the great and beautiful first-century anthology that recorded these rejected beliefs. About the only people who still read this text seriously are those godless professors Sister Emily warned me about, who read it for the same reasons the speaker of Larkin's poem visited old churches.

> ... For, though I've no idea
> What this accoutred frowsty barn is worth,
> It pleases me to stand in silence here;
>
> A serious house on serious earth it is,
> In whose blent air all our compulsions meet,
> Are recognized, and robed as destinies.
> And that much never can be obsolete,
> Since someone will forever be surprising
> A hunger in himself to be more serious,
> And gravitating with it to this ground,
> Which, he once heard, was proper to grow wise in,
> If only that so many dead lie round.

Further Reading

Achtemeier, Paul J. *Mark.* Philadelphia: Fortress, 1975.

Ahlstrom, Sydney. *A Religious History of the American People.* New Haven, Conn.: Yale University Press, 1972.

Beker, J. Christiaan. *Heirs of Paul.* Minneapolis: Fortress, 1991.

Bonhoeffer, D. *Letters and Papers from Prison.* London: SCM Press, 1967.

——. *Life Together.* New York: Harper, 1954.

Borg, Marcus. *Meeting Jesus Again for the First Time.* New York: Harper, 1994.

Bornkmann, Günther. *Paul.* New York: Harper, 1971. A starting place.

Branick, Vincent. *The House Church in the Writings of Paul.* Wilmington, Del.: Michael Glazier, 1989.

Brown, Raymond E. *The Churches the Apostles Left Behind.* New York: Paulist Press, 1984. A good introduction to the various ways of being a Christian during the first years of the faith.

——. *The Gospel According to John.* 2 vols. Anchor Bible 29, 29A. Garden City, N.Y.: Doubleday, 1966, 1977. May be this great scholar's major work.

——. *New Testament Essays.* New York: Paulist Press, 1965.

——, ed. *Peter in the New Testament.* Philadelphia: Fortress, 1973.

Bultmann, Rudolf. *Primitive Christianity.* New York: New American Library, 1956.

Chadwick, Henry. *The Early Church.* Baltimore: Penguin, 1967.

Collins, John J. *The Apocalyptic Imagination.* New York: Crossroad, 1984.

Conzelmann, Hans. *Theology of St. Luke.* New York: Harper, 1960. An important theological work.

Crossan, John Dominic. *The Cross That Spoke.* New York: Harper, 1988. The Gospel of Peter as source of all the passion stories.

——. *Jesus: A Revolutionary Biography.* New York: Harper, 1994.

Davies, Stevan L. *The New Testament: A Contemporary Introduction.* San Francisco: Harper, 1988.

Dix, Gregory. *The Shape of the Liturgy.* 2nd ed. Glasgow: The University Press, 1949.

Dodd, C. H. *The Founder of Christianity.* New York: Macmillan, 1970.

Drane, John. *Introducing the New Testament.* New York: Harper, 1986. A recent textbook by a believer intent on holding as close to traditional thought as possible—not scientific, but very well done.

Eusebius. *The History of the Church.* Grand Rapids: Baker, 1987. The source for nearly all early information; once you get past the opening pages of piety, riveting.

Fiori, Gabriella. *Simone Weil: An Intellectual Biography.* Athens, Ga.: University of Georgia Press, 1989.

Fox, R. L. *Pagans and Christians.* New York: Knopf, 1987. A much-praised account of the church during the second to fourth century, but quirky and tiring.

Frazier, Sir James. *The Golden Bough.* Abridged edition. New York: Macmillan, 1922.

Funk, Robert W., et al. *The Five Gospels: The Search for the Authentic Words of Jesus.* New York: Macmillan, 1993. Controversial and illuminating; Jesus' sayings color-coded as to authenticity; worth the money for the racy new "Scholars" translation.

Geffré, Claude. *A New Age in Theology.* New York: Paulist, 1972.

Grant, Frederick, *Hellenistic Religions.* Indianapolis: Liberal Arts Press, 1953.

Grant, Michael. *Jesus: An Historian's Review of the Gospels.* New York: Scribner's, 1977.

Harris, Stephen L. *The New Testament: A Student's Introduction.* 2nd ed. Mountain View, Calif.: Mayfield, 1995. The best introductory college text.

Hengel, Martin. *Studies in the Gospel of Mark.* Philadelphia: Fortress, 1985.

Horsley, Richard A., and John S. Hanson. *Bandits, Prophets, and Messiahs.* New York: Harper, 1985.

Johnson, Paul. *A History of Christianity.* New York: Simon & Schuster, 1976.

Johnson, Sherman. *Jesus and His Towns.* Wilmington, Del.: Michael Glazier, 1989.

——. *Paul and His Cities.* Wilmington, Del.: Michael Glazier, 1987.

Josephus, Flavius. *The Works of Josephus, Complete and Unabridged.* Peabody, Mass.: Hendrickson, 1991.

Kee, H. C. *Community of the New Age: Studies in Mark's Gospel.* Philadelphia: Westminster, 1977.

——. *Jesus in History: An Approach to the Study of the Gospels.* 2nd ed. New York: Harcourt, 1977. Good introduction to the subject.

———. *The New Testament in Context: Sources and Documents*. Englewood Cliffs, N.J.: Prentice Hall, 1984. There are many such collections.

Kelber, W. H. *The Kingdom in Mark*. Philadelphia: Fortress, 1974.

———. *Mark's Story of Jesus*. Philadelphia: Fortress, 1979. One of many good attempts to make sense of this puzzling and most important Gospel.

Kingsbury, J. D. *Matthew: Structure, Christology, Kingdom*. Philadelphia: Fortress, 1975.

Kloppenborg, John S. *The Formation of Q: Trajectories in Ancient Wisdom Collections*. Philadelphia: Fortress, 1987. Perhaps a major breakthrough in the historical "layering" of Q. Kloppenborg's work should be read in connection with Burton Mack's.

Koester, Helmut. *Introduction to the New Testament*. 2 vols. Philadelphia: Fortress, 1982. A middle-of-the-road, important scholarly work which at times is tedious.

Kümmel, Werner. *Introduction to the New Testament*. Nashville: Abingdon, 1973. A standard and encyclopedic German work in its 17th edition.

———. *The New Testament: The History of the Investigation of its Problems*. Nashville: Abingdon, 1972.

Laws, Sophie. *In the Light of the Lamb: Imagery, Parody, and Theology in the Apocalypse of John*. Wilmington, Del.: Michael Glazier, 1988.

Mack, Burton. *The Lost Gospel: The Book of Q and Christian Origins*. New York: Harper, 1993.

———. *Who Wrote the New Testament?* New York: Harper, 1995.

MacMullen, Ramsey. *Christianizing the Roman Empire*. New Haven, Conn.: Yale University Press, 1984.

Markus, Robert. *The End of Ancient Christianity*. Cambridge: Cambridge University Press, 1990.

Marxsen, Willi. *Mark the Evangelist: Studies on the Redaction History of the Gospel*. Nashville: Abingdon, 1969.

McBrien, Richard. *Catholicism: New Edition*. New York: HarperCollins, 1994.

Meeks, Wayne. *The First Urban Christians: The Social World of the Apostle Paul*. New Haven, Conn.: Yale University Press, 1983.

———. *The Origins of Christian Morality: The First Two Centuries*. New Haven, Conn.: Yale University Press, 1993.

Meier, John P. *A Marginal Jew: Rethinking the Historical Jesus*. 2 vols. New York: Doubleday, 1991, 1994. An attempt to review *all* the data; may not have been worth it.

Metzger, Bruce M. *A Textual Commentary on the Greek New Testament*. London: United Bible Societies, 1975.

———. *The Canon of the New Testament*. New York: Oxford University Press,

1989. An authoritative work by a member of the committee that produces our New Testament.

Noll, Mark. *Between Faith and Criticism: Evangelicals, Scholarship, and the Bible in America.* San Francisco: Harper, 1986.

Pagels, Elaine. *The Gnostic Gospels.* New York: Random House, 1979. Brought these discoveries to general attention; the author's work often has a feminist theme.

Pelikan, Jaroslav. *Jesus Through the Centuries.* New Haven, Conn.: Yale University Press, 1985.

Perrin, Norman, and Dennis Duling. *The New Testament: An Introduction.* New York: Harcourt, 1982. Very good work, but maddeningly disorganized.

———. *Rediscovering the Teaching of Jesus.* New York: Harper, 1967. Pioneering work on "authentic" Jesus sayings.

Rahner, Karl. *Foundations of Christian Faith.* New York: Crossroad, 1987.

Reimarus, Hermann S. *Fragments.* Philadelphia: Fortress, 1978.

Robinson, James M., ed. *The Nag Hammadi Library.* 3rd ed. New York: Harper, 1988.

Romer, John. *Testament: The Bible and History.* New York: Holt, 1988.

Sandmel, Samuel. *Judaism and Christian Beginnings.* New York: Oxford University Press, 1978. A scholarly work from a Jewish authority.

Schweitzer, Albert. *Out of My Life and Thought: An Autobiography.* New York: The New American Library, 1953.

———. *The Quest of the Historical Jesus.* New York: Macmillan, 1961. First published in 1906. After Reimarus's "Fragments," it is the second great work in the field.

Senior, D. P. *What Are They Saying About Matthew?* New York: Paulist, 1983. A careful Roman Catholic scholar surveys the literature. Don't let the corny running title of this series put you off; some of these small pamphlets are quite good.

Sheehan, Thomas. *The First Coming: How the Kingdom of God Became Christianity.* New York: Random House, 1986.

Smith, Morton. *Jesus the Magician.* New York: Harper, 1978.

Vermes, Geza. *Jesus the Jew: A Historian's Reading of the Gospels.* Philadelphia: Fortress, 1973.

———. *The Dead Sea Scrolls: Qumran in Perspective.* London: Collins, 1977. Still the best introduction to the subject.

von Wahlde, Urban. *The Earliest Version of John's Gospel.* Wilmington, Del.: Michael Glazier, 1989. Good account of the "evolving" text of John's Gospel.

Wilson, A. N. *Jesus: A Life.* New York: Norton, 1992.

Index